RORKE'S DRIFT AND ISANDLWANA

The Battle of Isandlwana on 22 January 1879, the first major encounter in the Anglo–Zulu War, witnessed the worst single day's loss of British troops between the Battle of Waterloo in 1815 and the opening campaigns of the First World War in August 1914. Moreover, decisive defeat at the hands of the Zulu came as an immense shock to a Victorian public that had become used to easy victories over less technologically advanced indigenous foes in an expanding empire.

The successful defence of Rorke's Drift, which immediately followed the encounter at Isandlwana (and for which eleven Victoria Crosses were awarded), averted military disaster and went some way to restore wounded British pride, but the sobering memory of defeat at Isandlwana lingered for many years, while the legendary tale of the defence of Rorke's Drift was re-awakened for a new generation in the epic 1964 film *Zulu*, starring Michael Caine.

In this new volume in the Great Battles series, Ian F. W. Beckett tells the story of both battles, investigating not only their immediate military significance but also providing the first over-arching account of their continuing cultural impact and legacy in the years since 1879, not just in Britain but also from the once largely inaccessible and overlooked Zulu perspective.

Ian F. W. Beckett retired as Professor of Military History at the University of Kent in 2015. A Fellow of the Royal Historical Society, he is internationally known for his work on the history of the British army in the nineteenth and twentieth centuries, and on the First World War, and he has held chairs in both the US and the UK, including as Major General Matthew C Horner Distinguished Professor of Military Theory at the US Marine Corps University, Quantico, Virginia. From 2001 to 2014 he was Chairman of the Council of the UK Army Records Society.

T0201134

Praise for *Rorke's Drift and Isandlwana*

'A thorough, authoritative and perceptive account . . . Beckett's coverage of the cultural legacy of the war is excellent.'

Lawrence James, *The Times*

'Professor Beckett's concise account of these twin actions is a model of readable military history.'

Allan Mallinson, *The Spectator*

'[A] meticulously researched book.'

Jules Stewart, *Military History Matters*

'A very balanced book in its re-evaluation of the battles . . . quite thought-provoking and very readable . . . highly recommended.'

Chris May, *Battlefield*

'a comprehensive account of the battle and its legacy.'

Brian Murphy, *Times Literary Supplement*

'Overall, this work offers historians and students alike a valuable and meaningful resource to understand the many nuances of well-documented and commemorated battles in South African history . . . [His] . . . thought provoking work . . . will allow for more interest and discussion among everyone from the classroom to the political arena.'

Jodie Mader, *Journal of Military History*

'Ian Beckett displays remarkable scholarship in placing the battles within the context of Victorian imperial expansion . . . Any reader will benefit from the prodigious scholarship of Ian Beckett and his many insights on the impact of these battles.'

Edward Spiers, *Journal of the Society for Army Historical Research*

'Professor Beckett's book brings alive the many aspects of the Zulu War and its consequences.'

Rodney Atwood, *Soldiers of the Queen*

'In his splendid new study of Isandlwana and Rorke's Drift, historian Ian Beckett . . . succeeds in placing these battles that took place at the outset of the Anglo-Zulu War of 1879 into their broader imperial context, references the misinformation associated with each conflict, and examines the role of popular culture in broadening the public's interest in these intercultural encounters.'

James Gump, *Small Wars & Insurgencies*

GREAT BATTLES

RORKE'S DRIFT AND ISANDLWANA

IAN F. W. BECKETT

OXFORD
UNIVERSITY PRESS

OXFORD
UNIVERSITY PRESS

Great Clarendon Street, Oxford, OX2 6DP,
United Kingdom

Oxford University Press is a department of the University of Oxford.
It furthers the University's objective of excellence in research, scholarship,
and education by publishing worldwide. Oxford is a registered trade mark of
Oxford University Press in the UK and in certain other countries

First published 2019
First published in paperback 2021

Impression: 1

Published in the United States of America by Oxford University Press
198 Madison Avenue, New York, NY 10016, United States of America

British Library Cataloguing in Publication Data
Data available

Library of Congress Cataloging in Publication Data
Data available

ISBN 978–0–19–879412–7 (Hbk.)
ISBN 978–0–19–879413–4 (Pbk.)

Printed and bound by
CPI Group (UK) Ltd, Croydon, CR0 4YY

For
Major General (Ret'd) Don Gardner and the students
of the Victorian Small Wars Electives,
USMC University, 2002–4

FOREWORD

For those who practise war in the twenty-first century the idea of a 'great battle' can seem no more than the echo of a remote past. The names on regimental colours or the events commemorated at mess dinners bear little relationship to patrolling in dusty villages or waging 'wars amongst the people'. Contemporary military doctrine downplays the idea of victory, arguing that wars end by negotiation not by the smashing of an enemy army or navy. Indeed it erodes the very division between war and peace, and with it the aspiration to fight a culminating 'great battle'.

And yet to take battle out of war is to redefine war, possibly to the point where some would argue that it ceases to be war. Carl von Clausewitz, who experienced two 'great battles' at first hand—Jena in 1806 and Borodino in 1812—wrote in *On War* that major battle is 'concentrated war', and 'the centre of gravity of the entire campaign'. Clausewitz's remarks related to the theory of strategy. He recognized that in practice armies might avoid battles, but even then the efficacy of their actions relied on the latent threat of fighting. Winston Churchill saw the importance of battles in different terms, not for their place within war but for their impact on historical and national narratives. His forebear, the Duke of Marlborough, commanded in four major battles and named his palace after the most famous of them, Blenheim, fought in 1704. Battles, Churchill wrote in his biography of Marlborough, are 'the principal milestones in secular history'. For him 'Great battles, won or lost, change the entire course of events, create new standards of values, new moods, new atmospheres, in armies and nations, to which all must conform'.

Clausewitz's experience of war was shaped by Napoleon. Like Marlborough, the French emperor sought to bring his enemies to battle. However, each lived within a century of the other, and they fought their wars in the same continent and even on occasion on adjacent ground. Winston Churchill's own experience of war, which spanned the late nineteenth-century colonial conflicts of the British Empire as well as two world wars, became increasingly distanced from the sorts of battle he and Clausewitz described. In 1898 Churchill rode in a cavalry charge in a battle which crushed the Madhist forces of the Sudan in a single day. Four years later the British commander at Omdurman, Lord Kitchener, brought the South African War to a conclusion after a two-year guerrilla conflict in which no climactic battle occurred. Both Churchill and Kitchener served as British cabinet ministers in the First World War, a conflict in which battles lasted weeks, and even months, and which, despite their scale and duration, did not produce clear-cut outcomes. The 'Battle' of Verdun ran for all but one month of 1916 and that of the Somme for five months. The potentially decisive naval action at Jutland spanned a more traditional twenty-four-hour timetable but was not conclusive and was not replicated during the war. In the Second World War, the major struggle in waters adjacent to Europe, the 'Battle' of the Atlantic, was fought from 1940 to early 1944.

Clausewitz would have called these twentieth-century 'battles' campaigns, or even seen them as wars in their own right. The determination to seek battle and to venerate its effects may therefore be culturally determined, the product of time and place, rather than an inherent attribute of war. The ancient historian Victor Davis Hanson has argued that seeking battle is a 'western way of war' derived from classical Greece. Seemingly supportive of his argument are the writings of Sun Tzu, who flourished in warring states in China between two and five centuries before the birth of Christ, and who pointed out that the most effective way of waging war was to avoid the risks and dangers of actual fighting. Hanson has provoked strong criticism: those who argue that wars can be won without battles are not only to be found in Asia. Eighteenth-century European commanders, deploying armies in close-order formations in order to deliver concentrated fires, realized that the destructive consequences of battle for their own troops could be self-defeating. After the First World War, Basil Liddell Hart developed a theory of strategy which he called 'the indirect approach', and suggested that manoeuvre might substitute for hard fighting, even if its success still relied on the inherent threat of battle.

The winners of battles have been celebrated as heroes, and nations have used their triumphs to establish their founding myths. It is precisely for these reasons that their legacies have outlived their direct political consequences. Commemorated in painting, verse, and music, marked by monumental memorials, and used as the way points for the periodization of history, they have enjoyed cultural afterlives. These are evident in many capitals, in place names and statues, not least in Paris and London. The French tourist who finds himself in a London taxi travelling from Trafalgar Square to Waterloo Station should reflect on his or her own domestic peregrinations from the Rue de Rivoli to the Gare d'Austerlitz. Today's Mongolia venerates the memory of Genghis Khan while Greece and Macedonia scrap over the rights to Alexander the Great.

This series of books on 'great battles' tips its hat to both Clausewitz and Churchill. Each of its volumes situates the battle which it discusses in the context of the war in which it occurred, but each then goes on to discuss its legacy, its historical interpretation and reinterpretation, its place in national memory and commemoration, and its manifestations in art and culture. These are not easy books to write. The victors were more often celebrated than the defeated; the effect of loss on the battlefield could be cultural oblivion. However, that point is not universally true: the British have done more over time to mark their defeats at Gallipoli in 1915 and Dunkirk in 1940 than their conquerors on both occasions. For the history of war to thrive and be productive it needs to embrace the view from 'the other side of the hill', to use the Duke of Wellington's words. The battle the British call Omdurman is for the Sudanese the battle of Kerreri; the Germans called Waterloo 'la Belle Alliance' and Jutland Skagerrak. Indeed the naming of battles could itself be a sign not only of geographical precision or imprecision (Kerreri is more accurate but as a hill rather than a town is harder to find on a small-scale map), but also of cultural choice. In 1914 the German general staff opted to name their defeat of the Russians in East Prussia not Allenstein (as geography suggested) but Tannenberg, in order to claim revenge for the defeat of the Teutonic Knights in 1410.

Military history, more than many other forms of history, is bound up with national stories. All too frequently it fails to be comparative, to recognize that war is a 'clash of wills' (to quote Clausewitz once more), and so omits to address both parties to the fight. Cultural difference and, even more, linguistic ignorance can prevent the historian considering a battle in the round; so too can the availability of sources. Levels of literacy matter here, but so does cultural survival. Often these pressures can be congruent but they can also be divergent. Britain enjoys much higher levels of literacy than Afghanistan, but in 2002 the memory of the two countries' three wars flourished in the latter, thanks to an oral tradition, much more robustly than in the former, for whom literacy had created distance. And the historian who addresses cultural legacy is likely to face a much more challenging task the further in the past the battle occurred. The opportunity for invention and reinvention is simply greater the longer the lapse of time since the key event.

All historians of war must, nonetheless, never forget that, however rich and splendid the cultural legacy of a great battle, it was won and lost by fighting, by killing and being killed. The battle of Waterloo has left as abundant a footprint as any, but the general who harvested most of its glory reflected on it in terms which have general applicability, and carry across time in their capacity to capture a universal truth. Wellington wrote to Lady Shelley in its immediate aftermath: 'I hope to God I have fought my last battle. It is a bad thing to be always fighting. While in the thick of it I am much too occupied to feel anything; but it is wretched just after. It is quite impossible to think of glory. Both mind and feelings are exhausted. I am wretched even at the moment of victory, and I always say that, next to a battle lost, the greatest misery is a battle gained.' Readers of this series should never forget the immediate suffering caused by battle, as well as the courage required to engage in it: the physical courage of the soldier, sailor, or warrior, and the moral courage of the commander, ready to hazard all on its uncertain outcomes.

HEW STRACHAN

ACKNOWLEDGEMENTS

Quotations from the Royal Archives appear by gracious permission of Her Majesty the Queen. Quotations from Crown Copyright material in the National Archives appear by permission of Her Majesty's Stationery Office. Thanks are due to the following for permission to consult and/or quote from archives in their possession and/or copyright: the Bodleian Library; the Campbell Collections of the University of KwaZulu-Natal; the KwaZulu-Natal Archives; the National Army Museum, the Royal Engineers Museum; the Royal Pavilion Libraries and Museum (Hove Public Library); the Royal Welsh Regimental Museum, and the University of Kent.

I was made most welcome by Richard Davies at the Regimental Museum of The Royal Welsh (Brecon), and have benefited greatly from the assistance of Dr Adrian Greaves, Pat Rundgren, Pam McFadden of Talana Museum, and Peter Harrington of the Anne S. K. Brown Military Collection at Providence, Rhode Island.

On past trips to the KwaZulu-Natal battlefields I have mined the knowledge of the late Fred Duke, the late Ray Steel, the late Rob Gerrard, Evan Jones, and Sean Friend. I was fortunate to have the insights of Major-General Don Gardner and my students from the Command and Staff College, USMC on battlefield tours to KwaZulu-Natal in 2003 and 2004 while privileged to hold the Major-General Matthew C. Horner Chair in Military Theory at Quantico. The work of members of the Victorian Military Society and the Anglo-Zulu War Historical Society has eased the path of all who research the war. I am also particularly grateful to Professors John Laband and Sir Hew Strachan for their sound advice. None of the foregoing is responsible for my errors of interpretation.

IFWB

CONTENTS

LIST OF FIGURES

LIST OF MAPS

ABBREVIATIONS

ASKBMC	Anne S. K. Brown Military Collection
BOD	Bodleian Library
CC	Campbell Collections
HCCP	House of Commons Command Papers
HPL	Hove Public Library
ILN	*Illustrated London News*
JAH	*Journal of African History*
JAZWHS	*Journal of the Anglo-Zulu War Historical Society*
JICH	*Journal of Imperial and Commonwealth History*
JMH	*Journal of Military History*
JNZH	*Journal of Natal and Zulu History*
JRUSI	*Journal of the Royal United Services Institute*
JSAHR	*Journal of the Society for Army Historical Research*
KZNA	KwaZulu-Natal Archives
NAM	National Army Museum
Parl. Debs.	Parliamentary Debates (Hansard)
RA	Royal Archives
REM	Royal Engineers Museum
RWM	Royal Welsh Museum
SAHJ	*South African Historical Journal*
SAHR	Society for Army Historical Research
SOTQ	*Soldiers of the Queen*

TNA	The National Archives
UKC	University of Kent Collection
VS	*Victorian Studies*
WH	*War in History*
W&S	*War and Society*

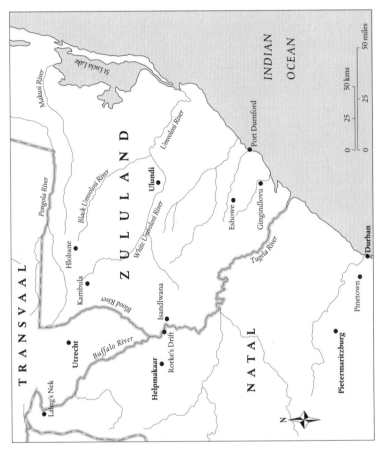

Map 1. Zululand.

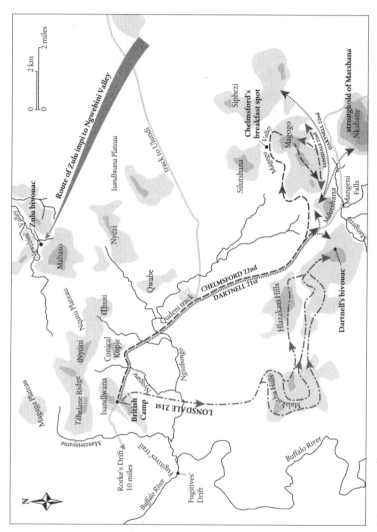

Map 2. Isandlwana, 21–22 January.

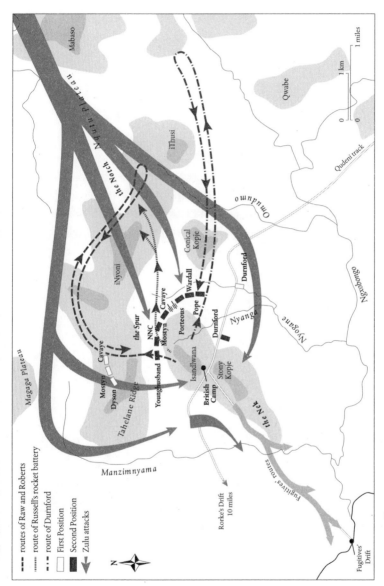

Map 3. Isandlwana, 22 January.

routes of Raw and Roberts
route of Russell's rocket battery
route of Durnford
First Position
Second Position
Zulu attacks

N

Magaga Plateau

Mabaso

Nyutu Plateau

the Notch

iNyoni

iThusi

Qwabe

Qudeni track

Omdunno

Conical Kopje

Mostyn
Dyson
Cavaye

Cavaye

the Spur

NNC
Mostyn
Cavaye
Wardall
Porteous
Pope

Tahelane Ridge

Youngbusband

Durnford

Durnford

Nyanga

Isandlwana

Stony Kopje

British Camp

Ngobongo

Nyogane

Manzimnyama

the Nek

Fugitives' routes

Rorke's Drift
10 miles

Fugitives'
Drift

1 miles
1 km
0 0

1 miles

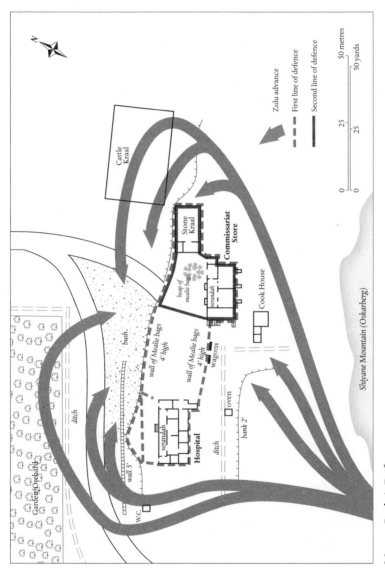

Map 4. Rorke's Drift.

N

Cattle Kraal

Stone Kraal

Commissariat Store

heap of mealie bags

verandah

Cook House

bush

wall of Mealie bags 4' high

wall of Mealie bags 4' high

wagons

wall 5'

ditch

Garden/Orchard

Hospital

verandah

ditch

oven

bank 2'

W.C.

Shiyane Mountain (Oskarberg)

Zulu advance

First line of defence

Second line of defence

50 metres

50 yards

0   25   50 metres

0   25   50 yards

1

Introduction

The Anglo-Zulu War was one of the shortest Victorian colonial campaigns, yet it has become the best known. In 1964 the commercial success of the film *Zulu*, starring Stanley Baker and a young Michal Caine, and depicting the defence of Rorke's Drift on 22–3 January 1879, unleashed an extraordinary interest in a war largely forgotten for over eighty years. It spawned a veritable industry in terms of popular titles and, eventually, a substantial increase in tourism to the battlefields of KwaZulu Natal. It also created or revived many myths. Some of these have persisted despite the rigorous academic scholarship applied to the conduct of the Anglo-Zulu War over the last twenty-five years or so. The juxtaposition on 22 January 1879 of disastrous defeat at Isandlwana with the successful defence of Rorke's Drift—for which eleven Victoria Crosses (VCs) were awarded—on 22–3 January provided instant redress for a British public and press used to easy victories over indigenous foes in an expanding empire. The war marked a striking example of a cross-cultural encounter.

Donald Morris's *The Washing of the Spears*, published in 1965 and coinciding fortuitously with *Zulu*, also played a significant part in the revival of interest. An American, Morris characterized Rorke's Drift as 'a more satisfactory battle than such better-known events as the Alamo or the Little Big Horn'.[1] Far more lives were lost at Isandlwana than at either of these two American battles, but the comparison extends to the wider legacies and popular cultural memories of Western imperial campaigns. Explicit comparison has been made between the subjugation of the Sioux (Lakota) and the Zulu, and thereby between George Custer's defeat at the Little Big Horn on 25 June 1876 and Isandlwana.[2]

The contemporary and later cultural responses to the Alamo, which fell to the Mexicans during the Texas War of Independence on 6 March 1836, and to the Little Big Horn are remarkably similar to

Figure 1. The iconic shape of Isandlwana framed by whitewashed burial cairns.

those to Isandlwana.[3] Despite Isandlwana, Victor Davis Hanson chose Rorke's Drift as one of his case studies in his controversial *Carnage and Culture: Landmark Battles in the Rise of Western Power* in 2002, which posited the historical inevitability of the triumph of Western arms over non-Western opponents from antiquity onwards. It was a case of 'Zulu bravery pitted against British discipline'.[4]

It has been claimed that, from the moment of the defeat at Isandlwana, the Zulu 'were Britain's favourite Africans' to the exclusion of other indigenous opponents.[5] Certainly, the political impact of Isandlwana lingered in Britain in terms of the attribution of blame for the defeat. The cultural legacy of Isandlwana and Rorke's Drift was of even longer duration. More recently, the Zulu perspective, once largely inaccessible and overlooked, has become more developed as part of a cultural (and political) reawakening in South Africa.

While there have been many accounts of Isandlwana and Rorke's Drift, there has been no overarching analysis of their continuing impact since 1879. This study is intended to fill that gap. It places events in the context of imperial expansion and its ramifications, before examining the battles themselves. It then outlines the contemporary search for scapegoats for defeat before exploring the contemporary impact of events. Following an analysis of the historiography, it examines the Zulu perspective.

2

Contexts

I sandlwana was an immense shock to a Victorian public accustomed to easy victories over indigenous opponents in the previous decade as in Abyssinia (1867–8), Asante (1873–4), and in the opening phase of the Second Anglo-Afghan War (1878–81). There had been no such reverse to British arms since the opening of the Indian Mutiny (1857–8), with which the press specifically drew comparison.[1] A total of 858 Europeans from Lieutenant-General Lord Chelmsford's Nos. 2 and 3 Columns died at Isandlwana, including 710 British regular soldiers, the majority from the 1st and 2nd Battalions, 24th Foot.[2] It was the worst single day's loss of British troops between Waterloo in June 1815 and the opening campaigns of the Great War in August 1914. Some 1,372 British and King's German Legion officers and men were killed at Waterloo.[3] The number of British troops killed, died of wounds, and died in August 1914 was 1,382.[4] Including colonial and native forces, more officers—fifty-two—died at Isandlwana than in the 1815 campaign. Just twenty-five officers, together with 362 other ranks, had been killed at the Alma in the Crimea on 20 September 1854, and thirty-nine officers and 597 other ranks at Inkerman on 5 November 1854.[5]

With the addition of those native auxiliaries killed—usually estimated at 471—at least 1,329 men were killed from a strength in the camp at Isandlwana of 1,774 (74 per cent). The only other occasion on which over 100 British troops were killed on a single day between 1857 and 1899 was at Maiwand in Afghanistan on 27 July 1880, when 969 British and Indian troops were killed, 305 of them British regulars.[6]

Figure 2. Lord Chelmsford and his staff, 1879. Back Row (left to right): Major Matthew Gosset; Lieutenant Berkeley Milne. Front Row (left to right): Commander Fletcher Campbell RN; Lieutenant-General Lord Chelmsford; Lieutenant Colonel John North Crealock.

By way of comparison, the number of Alamo defenders killed is now reckoned at 250 rather than the traditional 185.[7] A total of 263 members of the US 7th Cavalry died at the Little Big Horn, 225 with Custer himself in the 'Last Stand'.[8] The worst disaster befalling any European imperial force was at Adwa in Abyssinia on 1 March 1896, where the Italians lost at least 5,600 dead (1,000 of them native *askaris*) with another 3,400 taken prisoner (including 1,500 *askaris*).[9]

The Cultural Clash

Because European imperial defeats were few, the impact of atypical events was the greater. After Isandlwana, there was an immediate sense of emotional shock for those who returned to the battlefield on the evening of 22 January 1879. In the early hours of the same day some 560 men—mostly from the 2/24th Foot—had left under Chelmsford's command to join advanced parties of colonial volunteers and the Natal Native Contingent, together totalling about another 1,900 men. They had experienced only desultory action.

The camp was thoroughly looted by the Zulu and anything useful carried away, including at least 800 Martini-Henry rifles and 40,000 cartridges. Many oxen were killed in the frenzy of bloodlust. A few horses were taken but most were killed as the Zulu believed them 'the feet of the white men'.[10] Pets, too, were killed. Dogs that survived formed packs that subsequently ravaged the corpses. A Zulu boy, Muziwento, who visited the battlefield shortly after the action, recalled in 1884, 'Dead was the horse, dead, too, the mule, dead was the dog, dead was the monkey, dead were the wagons, dead were the tents, dead were the boxes, dead was everything, even to the very metals.'[11] Some plundering had dire consequences: the Zulu were so thirsty that they consumed any liquid they found, including ink and paraffin.

Some of the carnage had been apparent in the fading twilight and from the light cast by burning tents and wagons, as well as to those who searched by candles or other means. In the early dawn light of 23 January Chelmsford's men well knew they had slept among the dead. The overpowering stench was described as like 'a sweet potato that has been cooked when it is just beginning to go bad'.[12] The most horrifying aspect was the ritual disembowelling (*qaqa*) of erstwhile comrades. Zulu believed it necessary to slit open a slain enemy's stomach to allow the spirit to escape, lest the victim haunt his slayer. Further mutilation was inflicted in many cases, with some body parts used for the preparation of ritual medicines (*intelezi*). Facial hair was specially prized and a number of bearded jawbones disarticulated. Another part of Zulu ritual was to stab a corpse to denote participation in the kill (*ukuhlomula*), this 'washing of the spears' extending to those who shared in it by their presence. It was a mark of honour: post-mortem stabbing was reserved for the most dangerous prey such as lions. Stripping the dead was also common since wearing an enemy's clothes was beneficial to the slayer's subsequent purification.[13]

Sergeant Warren of N Battery, 5th Brigade Royal Artillery 'could not help crying to see how the poor fellows were massacred. They were first shot and then assegaied... the Zulus mutilated them and stuck them with the assegai all over the body.' A Natal Mounted Policeman, Joseph Carter, reported, 'Every man had been mutilated and round the ambulance wagon they were lying in heaps piled up as they were left by the Zulus who had dragged the poor fellows out wounded as they were and ripped them open.' Similarly, James Cook of the 2/24th wrote, 'The sight at the camp was horrible. Every white man that was killed or wounded was ripped up, and their bowels torn out; so there was no chance of anyone being left alive on the field.'[14] Charles 'Noggs' Norris-Newman of *The Standard* remembered the night spent on the field:[15]

> But oh! How dreadful to all were those weary hours that followed! while all had to watch and wait, through the darkness, with what patience we could muster, for the dawn of day; with the knowledge that we were standing and lying amid and surrounded by the corpses of our late comrades—though in what fearful numbers we then but little knew. Many a vow of vengeance was breathed in the stillness of the night; and many and deep were the sobs that came from the breasts of men who, perhaps, had never sobbed before, at discovering, even by that dim light, the bodies of dear friends, brutally massacred, stripped of all clothing, disembowelled, mutilated, and in some cases decapitated. How that terrible night passed with us I fancy few would care to tell, even if they could recall it.

A persistent story was that two drummer boys had been hung up on butcher's hooks and disembowelled alive. This was unlikely although they would certainly have been disembowelled along with the other dead. In any case, 'boy' was a misnomer since it applied to anyone enlisted under the age of 18 as musicians, tailors, or shoemakers. The official lowest age of enlistment was 15: of the drummers killed at Isandlwana, the youngest was probably 16.[16]

Chelmsford chose not to stay to bury the dead but to move off early to the depot and hospital established at the Revd Otto Witt's Swedish Mission Society station at Rorke's Drift, where No. 3 Column had crossed the Buffalo River (Mzinyathi) into Zululand twelve days before. The store—established by James Rorke in 1849 and known to the Zulu as KwaJimu—was purchased by the Surtees family after Rorke's death in 1875 and sold to Witt in 1878.[17] Firing had been heard in the direction of Rorke's Drift the previous night and the shape of the distinctive hill near the drift, the Oskarberg (Shiyane), had been illuminated by the red glare of flames. Chelmsford excused not lingering at Isandlwana by claiming burials could not have been carried out properly. To do so partially 'could only have the effect of bringing home to the troops the full extent of the disaster, of which they were to a certain extent kept in ignorance owing to the darkness'.[18] In reality, there was sufficient light to view the horrors, especially in the case of the rearguard, which did not quit the camp until after dawn.[19]

When burial parties finally returned to Isandlwana, the scene remained grim. The first foray on 21 May to recover serviceable wagons resulted in the burial of the bodies of artillerymen and colonial volunteers. In a larger operation on 20, 23, 25, and 26 June, the bodies of the 24th were buried. In June Archibald Forbes of the *Daily News* observed artillery horses dead in their traces, and the remains of the defenders lying where they fell. It was a sobering sight:[20]

Some were almost wholly dismembered, heaps of yellow clammy bones. I forbear to describe the faces, with their blackened features and beards bleached by rain and sun. Every man had been disembowelled. Some were scalped and others subjected to yet ghastlier mutilations. The clothes had lasted better than the poor bodies they covered, and helped to keep the skeletons together. All the way up the slope I traced by the ghastly token of dead men, the fitful line of flight . . . It was like a long string with knots in it, the string formed of single corpses, the knots of clusters of dead.

There was general detritus including 'brushes, toilet bags, pickle bottles, and unbroken tins of preserved meats and milk' in the grass and the crops, which had now sprouted from mealie bags torn open at the time. For Melton Prior of the *Illustrated London News*, it was far worse than any other battlefield he had witnessed over seven campaigns:[21]

> Here I saw not the bodies, but the skeletons of men whom I had known in life and health, some of whom I had known well, mixed up with the skeletons of oxen and horses, and with wagons thrown on their side, all in the greatest confusion, showing how furious had been the onslaught of the enemy. Amidst the various articles belonging to them which were scattered over the field of carnage, were letters from wives at home to their husbands, from English fathers and mothers to their sons, portraits of those dear to them, and other homely little things, remembrances of the dearest associations.

Significantly, Patrick Farrell of the 2/24th wrote of the immediate aftermath, 'It was enough to make your blood run cold to see the white men cut open, worst than ever was done in the Indian Mutiny.'[22]

Figure 3. The first burial party visiting Isandlwana, 21 May 1879.

The allusion to 1857 is apposite, for the mutiny had presented a significant challenge to the rationality and tolerance of Victorian liberal sensitivities.[23] European casualties at its outbreak were not numerous but the mutineers' butchering of women and children had a disproportionate and traumatic impact because India had been seen as 'a key site for the realisation of the British ideal of progress, improvement, and civilisation'.[24] The centrality of the marked admiration for 'progress' in Victorian society had an equally destabilizing influence when scientific and technological innovation itself posed a threat to domestic security in the 1850s through the fears of steam power 'bridging' the Channel and rendering a French invasion possible.[25]

Retribution

It has been argued that, with increasing domestic stability and order between 1780 and 1850, the English 'ceased to be one of the most aggressive, brutal, rowdy, outspoken, riotous, cruel and bloodthirsty nations in the world, and became one of the most inhibited, polite, orderly, tender-minded, prudish and hypocritical'.[26] This hardly applied to the colonies, retaliatory savagery in most Victorian campaigns being rationalized by the perception of barbarism among the uncivilized. Zulu treatment of the dead was a result of cultural practices wholly alien to the British, but British treatment of the Zulu rested on baser instincts. Cultures of violence that flouted the other sides' military norms led easily to the justification of excessive force.[27]

Reprisal was common after Isandlwana. All but three of the Zulu wounded were finished off at Rorke's Drift on the morning of its relief on 23 January, the precise number being unknown. Those who relieved the garrison had seen the field at Isandlwana. As Commandant George Hamilton-Browne of the 1/3rd Natal Native Contingent, later recorded, 'War is war and savage war is the worst of the lot. Moreover our men were worked up to a pitch of fury by the sights they had seen in the morning and the mutilated bodies of our poor fellows lying in front of the hospital building.'[28]

Commonly, killing of the wounded was ascribed to the Natal Native Contingent, who were generally despised by British officers as cowardly compared to the Zulu, but they were not alone. Captain Henry Hallam-Parr refuted allegations of misconduct by British soldiers after Rorke's Drift, suggesting 'it was impossible to prevent the Natal natives, who were slipping away to their homes, killing, according to their custom, any wounded they came across on their way'. British officers were determined to preserve the army's 'high reputation . . . of forbearance to an enemy who asks or who will receive quarter'. Yet, Hallam-Parr qualified his denials: wounded Zulu were dangerous and the rules of 'civilised warfare' could not always be observed. In any case, he argued, the Russians in Central Asia and the French in Algeria had behaved much worse.[29]

In the days following, mounted units moved out from Rorke's Drift to raid into Zululand. Hamilton-Browne commented, 'No decent kraal could retire at rest and be sure they would awake in the morning to find themselves alive in their huts and [their] cattle intact.'[30] Some Zulu captives were lynched although Chelmsford had issued strict orders that officers must 'exert their influence with all ranks to prevent there being in any way molestation or oppression'.[31] Chelmsford likewise complained that renaming Rorke's Drift as Fort Revenge was wrong because it was 'unwise to give public vent' to such feelings.[32]

In spite of Chelmsford's words, revenge was most certainly a motive in the pursuit of the Zulu after their repulse at Kambula on 29 March 1879, the day after No. 4 Column's reverse at Hlobane, when British casualties had again been heavy.[33] The pursuit was ruthless, stopped only by fading light. Captain Cecil D'Arcy of the Frontier Light Horse encouraged his men, 'No quarter, boys, and remember yesterday!' They responded by 'butchering the brutes all over the place'.[34] Another officer reported, 'We were no longer men but demons, screaming the same refrain "Remember yesterday".'[35] That any wounded or cornered Zulu survived was due to the column commander, Brevet Colonel Evelyn Wood VC, promising the Natal Native

Contingent a stick of tobacco for any prisoner they brought in.[36] Zulu wounded were also killed after the action by Colonel Charles Pearson's No. 1 Column at Gingindlovu on 2 April.[37]

The 'exultant' British pursuit after the final victory over the Zulu at Ulundi (oNdini) on 4 July 1879 was, as John Laband has expressed it, 'the ugliest face of colonial war'. The 17th Lancers 'proudly showed off their lance-pennons, all caked with blood, and negligently passed off their deadly work as being "just like tent-pegging at Aldershot"'.[38] There were only two prisoners for, as Lieutenant Charles Commeline remarked, 'few prisoners are made in these sorts of wars'.[39] Less reticent than most, Commeline wrote that the Pedi, in Sir Garnet Wolseley's subsequent campaign against their chief, Sekhukhune, in November 1879, were blown out of caves with guncotton charges. Nonetheless, some were taken captive, to the astonishment of the Swazi allies of the British, 'who spare neither sex nor age and laughed at us for protecting men who had been firing on us all day'.[40]

British soldiers were appalled by indigenous cultures in other Victorian campaigns. Evidence of human sacrifices and fetishism by the Asante horrified Wolseley and his officers when they advanced towards the Asante capital at Kumasi (Kumase) in 1874.[41] The object of the reconquest of the Sudan between 1896 and 1898, as Lord Salisbury expressed it, was to 'extirpate from the earth one of the vilest despotisms...ever seen...compared with which the worst performances of the worst minion of the Palace at Constantinople are bright and saintly deeds'.[42]

On the North-West Frontier and in Afghanistan, it was accepted there would be no quarter. Sir Charles Gough wrote of the Afghans in March 1880,[43]

> They *never* spare, and reprisal becomes absolutely necessary among such brutes so as to strike terror into them—it is a *mercy* in the end and leads to less bloodshed. They are the most bloodthirsty villains going, such is the case with *all* Orientals. War with them means Death and Destruction to their enemy.

Recalling the 1888 Black Mountain expedition, George MacMunn wrote that Wahabi fanatics 'lay blowing froth bubbles from lungs that were perforated, hacking fiercely at anyone who would tend them. The end of such can only be the bayonet, but pity may go out for human folks so possessed.'[44] Familiar with frontier realities from his experience in the Malakand in 1897, young Winston Churchill recognized there were disadvantages in the demonization of an enemy. When 'an army in the field becomes imbued with the idea that the enemy are vermin who cumber the earth, instances of barbarity may very easily be the outcome'.[45] But, given the assumption of fanaticism, extreme measures were invariably employed.[46]

Pseudoscience, curiosity, or trophy collecting akin to big game hunting, justified the collection of indigenous heads or other body parts. The body of the amaXhosa chief, Hintsa, killed during the Sixth Cape Frontier War (1834–6), was mutilated while Xhosa heads were routinely taken in the Seventh Cape Frontier War (1846–7). Frederick Carrington acquired the purported skull of the Xhosa chief, Sandile, in 1878: in fact, Sandile was not decapitated.[47] The Royal United Service Institution displayed the skull of a mutinous Indian sepoy until at least 1911 while another skull brought back from the mutiny was discovered in a Kent public house in 1963.[48] Following the capture of Omdurman in 1898, Herbert Kitchener toyed with the idea of sending the Mahdi's skull to the Royal College of Surgeons.[49]

There were cases in Zululand. Visiting Isandlwana in July 1879, Hugh McCalmont was sketching the scene when he heard a 'queer sort of rattling noise'. It was his civilian groom collecting teeth: 'It was his inexorable method of handling the skulls of defunct Zulus that was making the drumming, and he carried off some forty of these ghoulish treasures in his pocket with the intention of sending them home as keepsakes to his many inamoratas.' McCalmont himself had a skull and a hardened sole from the foot of a dead Zulu in his study.[50] Lieutenant Henry Harford, attached to the Natal Native Contingent, recorded that Surgeon James Reynolds of Rorke's Drift fame 'brought away one or two bones of scientific interest, and the soles of the feet which had become detached and were just solid pieces of horn'. Harford, an amateur entomologist, took a collarbone for a Durban museum.[51]

The Dutch trader Cornelius Vijn, detained by the Zulu during the war, was asked why the British cut off Zulu heads: 'What did they do with these heads? Or was it to let the Queen see how they had fought?'[52] Zulu heads were received by the Royal College of Surgeons and appeared for sale in Rowland Ward's taxidermist shop in Piccadilly.[53] The practice continued long after: Bhambatha, the leader of the Zulu rebellion against the Natal authorities in 1906, was decapitated but it was increasingly less accepted.

Killing the wounded and other perceived brutalities raised objections. The extreme British reaction to the Indian Mutiny had not gone unchallenged.[54] Parliamentary criticism surfaced over the hanging at Kabul in October and November 1879 of (officially) eighty-seven Afghans who were supposedly implicated in the massacre of Sir Louis Cavagnari and his escort in the city back in September.[55] Similar controversy dogged the pacification campaign in Burma in 1885–6.[56]

In his 'Midlothian' campaign leading up to the 1880 general election, William Gladstone condemned those who violated the 'rights of the savage' by invading Zululand and Afghanistan. At Glasgow on 5 December 1879 Gladstone intoned that 10,000 Zulu had died 'for no other offence than their attempt to defend against your artillery, with their naked bodies, their hearths and homes, their wives and families'.[57] When the *North Devon Herald* published a letter on 3 April 1879 written by a soldier present at Kambula, Private John Snook of the 13th Foot, the Aborigines' Protection Society protested to the War Office. It forced Evelyn Wood into a disingenuous official denial of post-battle atrocities.[58] A similar soldier's letter then appeared in the *Hereford Times*, its editor questioning the veracity of Wood's 'cleverly written' account. While Wood said no white men had killed the wounded, the editor suggested this was because that 'pleasant office has been entrusted to the black men, whom we arm and turn loose upon vanquished and wounded men; and to whose tender mercies we consign villages full of women and children'.[59] After the publication of further unconsciously incriminating soldiers' letters, an Irish MP asked questions in Parliament, while the Aborigines' Protection Society continued to collect evidence of more widespread abuse.[60]

Respect

Paradoxically, the depiction of indigenous savagery justifying retribution was juxtaposed with respect afforded those considered worthy military opponents. While assumptions of racial hierarchies based on evolutionary theories remained, attitudes were far more variable than often suggested. Those expressed towards the Zulu changed dramatically after Isandlwana. Queen Victoria proclaimed that the Zulu were 'the finest and bravest race in South Africa'.[61] *The Times*, which had assumed an easy victory like much of the press, asserted on 21 February 1879, 'We have often before encountered barbarian enemies, but seldom enemies who united ferocity of barbarism with the discipline and unity which have been supposed to be characteristics of civilisation.'[62] In August *The Graphic* proclaimed that the Zulu 'have proved themselves a brave and capable race and we have to some extent incurred a moral obligation to help them to a higher stage of civilisation'.[63] Referring also to the pro-Zulu views of the Bishop of Natal, John Colenso, and to the death of the Prince Imperial of France in Zululand on 1 June 1879, Prime Minister Benjamin Disraeli, now Lord Beaconsfield, famously remarked, 'A very remarkable people: they defeat our generals; they convert our bishops; they have settled the fate of a great European dynasty.'[64]

The general theory of 'martial classes', which informed the recruitment of native soldiers in India and elsewhere, perhaps partly explains the admiration for the Zulu.[65] Though all non-whites were considered inferior, indigenous African cultures were ranked according to a mixture of pseudoscientific racism and assumptions regarding environmental factors. Those inhabiting forests, deserts, and highlands were deemed manlier than those inhabiting coastal areas and lowlands.[66]

The Zulu represented the 'highest type' of barbarism. To an extent, too, contrasts drawn between the impressive physique of many Zulu and the poorer specimens recruited from urban Britain presaged later fears of imperial physical degeneration.[67]

Major Waller Ashe wrote of Gingindlovu that the Zulu had 'magnificently fought and drenched [the battlefield] with their blood'. Similarly, of an action near Ulundi on 3 July, 'it was impossible not to admire...the magnificent manner in which they charged right down to the river's edge, amidst a storm of grape and shrapnel'.[68] Shortly after Ulundi, Henry Harford came across a Zulu who asked if anyone had been at Isandlwana. The Zulu warmly shook Harford's hand, showed him his wounds, and re-enacted the fight, saying how well both sides had fought:[69]

> Could anything more clearly show the splendid spirit in which the Zulus fought us? No animosity, or revengeful feeling, but just the sheer love of a good fight in which the courage of both sides could be tested, and it was evident that the courage of our soldiers was as much appreciated as their own.

Such respect accorded the opponent served to heighten the gallantry of the British in overcoming them.[70]

The 'Last Stand' became a motif of British character. Demonstrable qualities of heroism were more important than success, although it has been argued that 'heroic failure' was also an indulgence that 'only the world's dominant military, naval and imperial power could afford'. Such episodes 'made it possible for Britons to see their empire in a positive and moral light, particularly at moments when the reality was different'.[71] At Isandlwana there were many 'last stands' to equal that of the 44th Foot at Gandamak in January 1842 during the First Anglo-Afghan War, the 'last eleven' of the 66th Foot at Maiwand, or Allan Wilson's Shangani Patrol in December 1893 during the Matabele (Ndebele) Revolt.

Praise of Maori heroism and chivalry during the three New Zealand Wars (1846–7, 1860–1, and 1863–6), while often genuine, served similarly to obscure the degree of Maori success. British failures were attributed instead to British deficiencies, the terrain, or even Maori imitation of British methods, particularly the engineering skills required in constructing formidable *pa* fortifications.[72] The supposed deficiencies of the Bombay army rather than Afghan skill accounted for the disaster at Maiwand.[73] Contemporary explanations for Zulu success at Isandlwana on 22 January 1879 dwelled on British failures including the performance of the Natal Native Contingent rather than Zulu success. Chelmsford suggested on 23 January 1879 that the 'desperate bravery of the Zulu has been the subject of much astonishment'. He further qualified defeat by suggesting the Zulu had 'succeeded by force of recklessness and numbers'.[74]

Contemporary reaction to other Western colonial defeats bears similar markers. Characterized by one contemporary commentator as a 'clap of thunder from a cloudless sky', Custer's defeat was attributed to the weak Indian policy of President Grant's administration and to reductions in military expenditure.[75] It also echoes the rationalization of defeat associated with the 'Lost Cause' of the Confederacy in the American Civil War (1861–5).[76] More accurately, George Pickett once reputedly remarked, when asked why his 'Charge' had failed at Gettysburg in July 1863, 'I always thought the Yankees had something to do with it.'[77]

Expectations and Assumptions

Complacency was a common factor in imperial defeats. Archaeological investigation has revealed that the Sioux and Cheyenne outgunned Custer's command on the Little Big Horn. The cavalry had single-shot breech-loaders but the Indians possessed between 300 and 400 firearms, of which at least 200 were repeating rifles.[78] Resembling Chelmsford, Custer's only concern was that the Indians would flee before they could be brought to battle.[79] Like Chelmsford, Custer also divided his command.

Although the British were experiencing difficulties in the ongoing campaign against the Pedi, there had been expectations of easy victory over the Zulu. The Zulu had numbers but the British had firepower. Chelmsford was aware of the Zulu military system and of Zulu methods. He issued a pamphlet, *The Zulu Army*, compiled by the border agent Frederick Fynney, in November 1878 although details of the composition of the Zulu army were not always accurate. The War Office Intelligence Branch published a separate guide, *Précis of Information Concerning the Zulu Country with a Map*. Chelmsford also issued field regulations and detailed tactical instructions to his column commanders. Yet, he seemed unable to believe what he read or was told as to Zulu fighting capacity.[80]

Chelmsford expected the Zulu to fight much like the Xhosa, who had been shattered by British firepower at Centane on 7 February 1878 in the Ninth Cape Frontier War (1877–8). Chelmsford had originally been sent out to South Africa after early British setbacks in this last of the conflicts fought against the Xhosa tribes on the frontier of the Cape Colony in South Africa since the late eighteenth century, first by the Dutch and then by the British. Centane ended Xhosa resistance.[81]

By advancing directly to the centre of the authority of the Zulu king, Cetshwayo kaMpande, at his main homestead at Ulundi along well-established access routes, Chelmsford hoped to entice the Zulu into attacking in the open. So anxious was he to induce attack that the artillery was not to open fire until the Zulu were at 600 yards' range lest it deter them from advancing.[82] Superior firepower would more than compensate for the small numbers of troops deployed. Chelmsford wrote to Evelyn Wood in November 1878, 'I am induced to think that the first experience of the power of the Martini-Henrys will be such a surprise to the Zulus that they will not be formidable after the first effort.'[83]

Chelmsford's initial strategy recognized Zulu vulnerabilities. Three columns—Nos. 1, 3, and 4—entering Zululand would divide the Zulu army (*impi*) as well as destroying as many military homesteads (*amakhanda*) as possible, systematically reducing Zulu capacity to resist by destroying crops and livestock. In 1879 there were twenty-seven *amakhanda* in Zululand, thirteen of them close to Ulundi. The three columns would converge on Ulundi, assuming they could be effectively coordinated over the largely uncharted distances involved. Two further columns—Nos. 2 and 5—were in reserve to prevent any Zulu counter-incursion into Natal. Additionally, Colonel Hugh Rowlands's No. 5 Column would keep a wary eye on the Swazi and any dissident Boers. The columns would also be operating along those axes considered most vulnerable to Zulu incursions into Natal.[84]

In its timing the British invasion was well judged. Delay in military operations until the next South African winter (June to August) would mean the grass in Zululand would be too dry and have little grazing value for the vast number of transport oxen needed to sustain any advance. It would be wet and uncomfortably hot, but the grass would be fresh and the Zulu inconvenienced by the need to gather their harvest. The rivers along Natal's frontiers would be high after the spring rains and impede Zulu incursions. By the time they subsided in March, the war would be over. Cetshwayo also faced the difficulty that he had called up his regiments (*amabutho*) in September 1878 in view of British military preparations when crops should have been planted. It was the end of an exceptionally dry season, leading to depletion of pasture and to the death of many cattle. Cetshwayo had little choice but to release the *amabutho* to their homesteads, but the harvest would inevitably be delayed. In the meantime, it would be difficult to feed a large number of men kept together for any length of time. Even if the war was not prolonged, any action must be followed by dispersion for ritual purification ceremonies, sharing of plunder, and recuperation.[85]

The British also anticipated exploiting Zulu internal divisions. In 1876 Cetshwayo had forced one younger female *amabutho* to marry the older men of two *amabutho* when they had promised themselves to a younger *amabutho*. This caused friction. Two *amabutho* came to blows in 1878. Although not reflecting Zulu opinion as a whole, several prominent Zulu clan chiefs and *izikhul* (elders) opposed war and counselled appeasement at any price. Among the members of the royal house opposed to war was Cetshwayo's full elder brother, Hamu kaNzibe, heir to his uncle rather than his father under the Zulu system. Hamu was to defect to the British in March 1879. The so-called white chief, John Dunn, who had settled in Zululand and adopted Zulu ways, crossed into Natal with his followers even before the war began. But it would take the imminent prospect of the dissolution of the kingdom after Zulu military defeat to accelerate the willingness of other chiefs to safeguard their positions by negotiating with the British.[86] One British miscalculation was that ordinary Zulu were so disaffected with Cetshwayo's rule that there might not be any fighting at all once they crossed the frontier.[87]

Outline knowledge of the Zulu system did not give Chelmsford precise information on the number of warriors at Cetshwayo's disposal. It was assumed Cetshwayo could call upon almost 42,000 warriors. The actual number who mustered at their *amakhanda* in January 1879 was probably around 29,000.[88] Some 20,000–24,000 warriors appear to have been committed against Chelmsford and No. 3 Column at Isandlwana. A much smaller force was sent to oppose Pearson's No. 1 Column crossing the Tugela at Lower Drift, and only limited reinforcements assisted the local clans facing Wood's No. 4 Column. A token force of elderly *amabutho* was retained at Ulundi as an emergency reserve. Cetshwayo discounted the risk of British use of Portuguese territory or any coastal landing, although the latter was briefly considered.[89]

The British assumed the capture of Ulundi as the administrative and economic focus of Zululand would end the war. They failed to recognize that the occupation of Ulundi would at best only diminish Cetshwayo's prestige since there were other royal homesteads. Ulundi had no special significance in the Zulu polity. Taking it would be more a signal of success to the British public than to the Zulu.[90] The British were correct in assuming that, since the *amabutho* could not be kept together for long, Cetshwayo must throw his army at the advancing columns to end the war quickly. Cetshwayo apparently hoped to fight a limited war, instructing his people not to attack unless attacked first. When, on entering Zululand, the British immediately attacked the stronghold of the chief of the Qungebe clan, Sihayo kaXongo— Sihayo and most of his warriors were at Ulundi—Cetshwayo ordered an offensive. He still made it clear that his warriors must not cross into Natal to enable him to continue to present himself as the injured party and to avoid further provocation. Aware that the British had enormous resources at their disposal, Cetshwayo appears to have hoped that a victory over the invading columns, especially that accompanied by Chelmsford, would enable him to threaten (but not invade) Natal and compel the British to negotiate. Zulu overtures to neighbouring tribal groups such as the Swazi to the north, the Basotho and Mpondo to the south, and the Mabhundu-Tsonga to the east were rebuffed. So was an approach to the Pedi despite the fact that Sekhukhune was also fighting the British.[91]

The Zulu Way of War

Ironically, in view of the British failure to entrench the camp at Isandlwana, Cetshwayo warned against attacking any entrenched position but, instead, to bypass it to force the British out into the open. The Zulu preference, in the absence of any actual experience of fighting European regulars, was for a pitched battle utilizing traditional Zulu tactics. These were the *impondo zankhomo* (bull's horn manoeuvre) and the ingrained Zulu desire for hand-to-hand combat. Essentially, the younger *amabutho* would form the left and right *izimpondo* (horns) of the *impi*, racing ahead of the main body or *isifuba* (chest) to encircle the opponents' flanks and draw them into the chest, itself supported by a reserve or *umuva* (loins). The Zulu did not advance in solid masses but in open skirmishing lines, though these could be ten to twelve ranks' deep.

The preference for such tactics marked the widely differing cultural approach to war between the two sides. The Zulu had firearms but did not rely upon them. Controlling Africans' acquisition of firearms formed part of the rationalization for the British policy of confederation in southern Africa. It remained a concern in Cape Colony and Natal from the arrest and trial of the amaHlubi chief, Langalibalele kaMthimkhulu, in 1873–4, through the Cape's Peace Preservation Act of 1878, to the Cape–Basotho 'Gun War' of 1880–1. The Xhosa and Mfengu had been effectively disarmed by the end of the Ninth Cape Frontier War.[92] Zululand lay outside the control of the colonial authorities, and firearms, which conveyed prestige on their owners, had been available to the Zulu for many years. The number of weapons imported into Natal rose sharply between 1872 and 1875. Many were re-exported to Mozambique before finding their way back to Natal. The Natal authorities made repeated efforts to prevent direct sales to Zululand and the Portuguese at Delagoa Bay were persuaded to impose a prohibition in 1878, but there was considerable illicit trade. Dunn was one of those involved.

Estimates of the firearms in circulation in Zululand in 1879 differ widely. Portuguese officials suggested 20,000 guns reached Zululand *annually* between 1875 and 1877. The majority of these firearms were percussion and even flintlock muzzle-loaders. Probably the Zulu only had about 500–1,000 modern breech-loaders. The Zulu were unaccustomed to maintaining firearms in reasonable condition. There were few spare parts available, the quality of powder was decidedly poor, and few Zulu knew how to use their firearms' sights.[93] But a far higher proportion of the Zulu than the Natal Native Contingent had firearms at Isandlwana.[94] The Zulu used firearms on occasion at Hlobane, Kambula, and Gingindlovu. Only five Martinis were recovered from dead Zulu at Gingindlovu, however, and the many taken at Isandlwana went largely unused.[95]

Firearms seemingly offered no real military advantage over traditional weapons, which the Zulu assumed would give them victory in any fight in the open. The Zulu had not fought Europeans since 1838 and had not engaged in any battle since Cetshwayo had defeated his brother in 1856. They had not adapted to military changes like the Pedi and the Basotho.[96] In any case, firearms did not fit the 'hegemonic masculinity' at the heart of Zulu culture. The warrior ethos demanded killing at close quarters as a matter of honour. While using a firearm at a distance did not result in ritual pollution, it was an inferior form of killing, unworthy of a warrior.[97] Each Zulu, therefore, carried a number of throwing spears (izijula), a knobkerrie club (iwisa), and a short stabbing spear (ikilwa) popularly known from the Arabic as an assegai.

Throughout the war the Zulu displayed the bankruptcy of their traditional hand-to-hand tactics. They were indignant at the continuing British refusal to fight them in the open. As one Zulu told Cornelius Vijn after Kambula, 'They are continually making holes in the ground and mounds left open with little holes to shoot through. The English burrow in the ground like pigs.'[98]

The heart of the Zulu military system was built upon the concept of grouping males according to age. The system appears to have derived from the Nguni practice of bringing boys together in circumcision groups. Between the ages of 14 and 18 youths would gather at amakhanda and serve for two or three years herding cattle, working the fields, and being trained for war. At 18 they would be brought before the King and formed into a new ibutho with instructions to build themselves a new ikhanda. Led by appointed commanders (izindunas), ibutho served as army, police, and labour force until marriage, when allegiance reverted to their clans. At that point a man established his own household (imizi). In some cases, an ibutho might be linked to a particular locality. In other cases, a new ibutho might be incorporated into an older one to maintain the latter's strength if the King wished to retain its identity.[99]

Marriage was not usually authorized until a unit reached 35 or 40 years in age, thus maximizing service to the King. This was a citizen rather than a standing army, whose members spent most of their time in a form of labour taxation.[100] Most amakhanda remained empty for much of the year unless the amabutho were mobilized, the Zulu dispersing to their own umuzi (homesteads). The amabutho reported for specific purposes such as the important and elaborate first fruits of harvest festival (*umKhosi*) held each December or January depending upon the waning of the full moon. Even when assembled at *amakhanda*, women supplied the warriors with food from their own homesteads. When the unit did marry, it was en masse, for women were also part of the system, providing most of the agricultural labour force and being formed into female *amabutho* for marriage. Upon marriage, the warrior had a head-ring of hemp coated with grease (*isicoco*) sewn into the hair—apparently a substitute for the former practice of circumcision. Married *amabutho* carried white cowhide shields rather than the coloured shields they carried as single men, although some of the conventions were breaking down by Cetshwayo's time. The shields were the property of the state.

The first fruits festival involved purification ceremonies and rituals to reduce the risks deriving from mystical dark forces (*umnyama*). It reaffirmed the unity and continuity of the Zulu nation but, in reality, there were divisions within the polity. The Zulu economy rested largely on cattle, theoretically distributed through royal patronage. In practice, the individual's control over cattle was such that the Zulu were not dependent upon the King for the functioning of individual homesteads. Clan ties remained strong and individual chiefs were granted a measure of autonomy, especially princes of the royal blood (*abantwana*) and hereditary chiefs (*amakhosi*). Chiefs with territory along the borders of Zululand, such as Sihayo, increased their autonomy through contacts with the whites, trade goods such as firearms enhancing their authority.

The British high commissioner appointed to South Africa in 1877, Sir Henry Bartle Frere, misunderstood the system in implying that Cetshwayo had a standing army of 40,000 warriors representing a 'frightfully efficient man-slaying machine'. To Frere, its maintenance was a burden on the Zulu polity and its existence depended upon 'a constant succession of conquests'.[101] Theophilus Shepstone, successively long-serving secretary of native affairs in Natal and administrator of the Transvaal, greatly influenced Frere. Shepstone wrote in January 1878 that, had the Zulu been converted into wage labourers,

Zululand would have been prosperous rather than 'a source of perpetual danger to itself and neighbours'.[102] Hallam-Parr echoed the general mood. Cetshwayo's army 'menaced with ruin the colonies whose border farms and homesteads were within a few hours' march of Cetywayo's capital'.[103] Assumptions regarding the nature of the Zulu polity played the major role in the determination to neutralize the supposed threat to Natal. Charles Callwell's classic *Small Wars: Their Principles and Practice*, first published in 1896, specified the Zulu War as an example of a campaign 'for the overthrow of a dangerous power'.[104]

The British Army

British military culture was very different. The army's problem was to meet its rapidly expanding commitments of home and imperial defence through a system of voluntary enlistment, which distanced the army from wider society. There was a lingering fear of a large standing army stretching back to the seventeenth century while the Royal Navy had a more obvious value to the Victorian mind. The domestic political context of recurring retrenchment in military expenditure and indifference to military requirements meant that there was a marked disparity between means and ends. As one secretary of state for war remarked, his task was 'to avoid heroics and keep the estimates down'.[105] Supposedly undertaken for organizational rationality, the army reforms of Secretary of State for War Edward Cardwell between 1868 and 1872 were driven primarily by the desire for savings.[106]

With voluntary enlistment, and uncompetitive pay, recruitment correlated closely with unemployment. Unskilled labourers were by far the largest single category of recruit, never dropping below 58.9 per cent of the total in any year between 1870 and 1900. Even then, most unemployed still shunned the army. Continually expanding trade meant civilian wages rose higher than the static pay for private soldiers. Overseas service; unsanitary barracks; harsh discipline; lack of recreational opportunities; the discouragement of marriage; the lack of training in trades; and a complete lack of provision for veterans and reservists in civilian life, all added to the unattractive features of military life and the soldier's unsavoury reputation. The country's male population aged between 15 and 24 doubled between 1859 and 1901 but the army's share of this age group remained static at around a pitiful 1 per cent. Excluding an increase in pay, which did not recommend itself to the taxpayer, the only alternative was conscription. That was regarded by politicians as tantamount to political suicide and was not compatible with the need to furnish foreign drafts for stations such as India.[107]

Prior to Cardwell's reforms, the majority of infantry and cavalry officers were appointed and promoted up to the rank of lieutenant colonel by purchase. Defenders of purchase claimed that men of wealth and position would not challenge the established political order and that it preserved the unique *esprit de corps* of the regimental system. Cardwell abolished purchase in November 1871, and endeavoured to complete earlier reforms by simplifying the army's administration and solving the recruitment problem. Abolition did little to change the composition of the officer corps. Those who had achieved seniority prior to 1870 still dominated, and the sections of society from which officers were drawn did not alter dramatically before 1914 although these included the sons of army officers and clergymen. Low financial rewards, the potentially high cost of mess living, and regimental tradition did much to ensure the continuing predominance of those with a public school education. Of the eighteen officers of the 24th killed at Isandlwana, eight were the sons of gentlemen, five of former army officers, and four of clergymen. Nine were educated at five public schools—Rugby (three), Marlborough (two), Haileybury (two), Eton (one), and Harrow (one).

The solution Cardwell envisaged to the recruiting problem in 1872 was one of linked battalions and short service to build up a reserve. Service for infantrymen would be reduced to six years with the Colours and a further six years with the reserve. Two regular battalions would share a home depot, with one battalion at home supplying drafts for its partner battalion abroad. Localization of the regulars and links with the auxiliary forces for home defence—militia and rifle volunteers—would aid recruiting by identifying regiments with a county. It would not only stimulate enlistment and reduce wastage, but also attract a better class of recruit and produce a viable reserve. Paradoxically, the army had to recruit more men than previously: whereas only 12,500 recruits annually had been needed between 1861 and 1865, 28,800 per annum were needed between 1876 and 1879. Between 1872 and 1879 an average of 659 men per 1,000 were lost before they had completed three years' service while, of the 30,889 desertions in the same period, almost three-fifths were men in their first year of service.[108]

Cardwell ignored the strain on linked battalions arising from imperial small wars, despite withdrawing imperial battalions from Canada, Australia, and New Zealand. Almost at once the balance of battalions was upset by the Asante War. By 1879 there were fifty-nine battalions at home and eighty-two abroad. The presence of both battalions of the 24th in South Africa illustrated the difficulties since one should have been at home sending reinforcing drafts to the other. Just over 10,400 officers and men were rushed to South Africa in February and March 1879. As a result, the balance of battalions by May 1879 was fifty-five at home with eighty-six abroad.[109] Under continuing economies, home battalions were reduced to 'squeezed lemons', with the reserve utilized to replace young and unfit soldiers in home units on the outbreak of hostilities. Home battalions mustered fewer and fewer men. Short service was not initially applied to cavalry and artillery but once it was, they too faced declining strengths at home.

War and Empire

If the British conduct of, and attitude to, the Zulu War conformed to the general pattern of colonial campaigning, the war also fitted within the wider context of British imperial expansion in Africa. The 1870s saw the subjugation not only of the Zulu but also of the Ngqika and

Gcaleka amaXhosa, Pedi, Griqua, Balthaping, Prieska amaXhosa, Korana, and Khoesan.[110]

The original British interest was the strategic importance of the Cape route to India. Cape Colony was seized from the Dutch in 1806. Disillusioned with British rule, not least the emancipation of slaves in British possessions in 1833, the sizeable population of Dutch Afrikaners or Boers began 'trekking' inland in 1835. They established themselves first in Natal. When the British annexed Natal in 1845 to secure the coast from Boer control, they trekked on again to the Transvaal (South African Republic) and the Orange Free State. British disinclination to continue expansion brought recognition for the Boer republics in 1852 and 1854 respectively.

The situation was transformed by the discovery of diamonds in 1867 in the loosely defined territory of Griqualand West, to which the Transvaal laid claim. The Griqua claimed British protection. An independent arbitrator found in favour of the Griqua and the Transvaal was excluded from the diamond fields, the British annexing them in 1871. Fearful of Boer designs on Basotho territory, the British also extended protection over what became known as Basutoland in 1868. It was absorbed into Cape Colony in 1870.

As Europeans drifted northwards into the interior from the late seventeenth century, so large-scale movements southwards by Bantu peoples occurred from the sixteenth century onwards, especially the Nguni tribes. One Nguni subdivision, the Xhosa, reached the North Eastern Cape, their power being broken by the Dutch and British in the nine Cape Frontier Wars between 1778 and 1878. The Xhosa were a more difficult, longer-standing opponent of the British than the Zulu since they invariably resorted to guerrilla tactics but their resistance has been largely forgotten. The British reaction to warfare on the Cape Frontier between 1834 and 1853 set the tone for racial stereotyping of 'treacherous savages and merciless barbarians', so justifying harsh measures.[111]

To the north of the Great Fish River, part of another Nguni subdivision was a small clan known as the amaZulu. A pastoral people, the

Zulu were transformed by their chief, Shaka kaSenzangakhona, into a formidable military force between about 1817 and his assassination by his half-brothers in 1828. The rise of the Zulu, so named after an early chief and meaning 'Celestial', coincided with the so-called *mfecane* ('the crushing'), which saw large-scale tribal movements over a large part of central, eastern, and southern Africa. There are varying interpretations of this upheaval. A period of prolonged drought and other environmental factors contributed greatly, as did competition for land amid overpopulation. While often exaggerated by early Natal traders anxious to justify British expansion, Shaka's success in crushing neighbouring clans played some part itself in the prolongation of conflict as people fled Shaka or attempted to emulate his success.[112]

The first European contact with Shaka came in 1824 through a small group of traders at Port Natal (later Durban) including Lieutenant Francis Farewell RN and Henry Francis Fynn, who were welcomed as a source of firearms and trade goods previously only available from the Portuguese at Delagoa Bay to the north-east. Europeans and Africans both focused on Natal because of its suitability for cattle: it was free of tsetse fly. The Zulu clashed with the Boers. Shaka's half-brother and successor, Dingane kaSenzangakhona, massacred a party led by Piet Retief in February 1838 and moved to destroy Boer settlements but was defeated by the Boers at Blood River (Ncome) in December 1838. Subsequently, the Boers allied themselves with Dingane's half-brother, Mpande kaSenzangakhona, who overthrew Dingane in 1840. As a consequence of their victory at Blood River and their support for Mpande, the Boers laid claim to large parts of Shaka's territorial inheritance between the Black Mfolozi and Tugela (Thukela) rivers. When Britain annexed Natal, an agreement on its frontiers was secured with the Zulu, fixing the boundaries on the Tugela and Buffalo rivers. The attraction of Natal's pastures, however, meant a constant flow of Africans into the colony, reaching a total of perhaps 305,000 by 1872 compared to barely 20,000 Europeans.

Land in Natal was in short supply and the wage rates available were too low to tempt Africans into employment, effectively limiting the colony's economic potential. Some colonists visualized a future in which Durban became a gateway for European goods into central Africa: the colony would be able to draw on cheap migrant labour from the north. In this scenario, while Zululand's economic potential was minimal, it stood in the way. The discovery of diamonds suggested that the vision of a thriving Natal feeding the exploitation of Africa was now possible, but it would require modern communications and an unhindered flow of cheap labour. Wage labour was seen as part of a civilizing process. Some historians have therefore interpreted the Anglo-Zulu War as brought on by colonial commercial interests, drawing Africans into the white economy on disadvantageous terms.[113]

Yet the strategic and political imperative of British imperialism also remained significant. Frere had previously served in India, where he was intimately involved in defence planning against the Russian threat. The neglect of Cape Town's defences fed fears of a Russian cruiser attack. War in Zululand cannot be divorced from the wider imperial crisis generated by the Russo-Turkish War of 1877–8 and the motivation for British intervention in Afghanistan. Settling affairs in South Africa was related to wider imperial security concerns.[114] The difficulty in maintaining paramountcy in southern Africa in strategic terms was not so much the rivalry of other European powers—although they must be excluded from southern Africa—but the politically fragmented nature of the region. In giving Frere his instructions in December 1876 the colonial secretary, Lord Carnarvon, wrote, 'To a considerable extent, if not entirely, we must be prepared to apply a sort of Munro [sic] doctrine to much of Africa.'[115] Contemporaries did not necessarily make a distinction between the demands of security and those of economic efficiency.

Attempting to advance colonial interests, Shepstone sought to intervene in the protracted struggle for succession to the Zulu throne, ongoing since the 1850s. In September 1873, Shepstone staged a 'coronation' of Cetshwayo, who had succeeded his father, Mpande, as the new king in October 1872. Cetshwayo had slaughtered the supporters of his rival half-brother Mbuyazi at Ndondakusuka in December 1856 and sought British support for his succession. Shepstone, an advocate of indirect rule through pliant chiefs, envisaged strengthening his potential influence over the Zulu kingdom. In return for British support, Cetshwayo assured Shepstone of his future good conduct including a promise to limit bloodletting, but Shepstone was unsuccessful in gaining concessions for missionaries. Mpande had been reasonably well disposed towards missionaries but they had found few converts, and Cetshwayo wanted to expel them. Dunn persuaded him to hold off in 1869 but he did so in April 1878. Thereafter rival Norwegian, German, and British missionaries set out to undermine Cetshwayo's reputation.[116]

The solution favoured by Benjamin Disraeli's new Conservative administration in Britain was a confederation to bring together the disparate elements in southern Africa, the economic benefits effectively making the concept self-financing. This might eventually enable Britain to withdraw its regular garrison. South Africa would follow Canada, Australia, and New Zealand in being responsible for its own internal defence. Successful federation of the white states depended upon resolving what was often termed the 'native question', the existence of independent black states like that of the Zulu. It was supposed that confederation would create a stable political structure and, by closing the frontiers, avoid costly conflict. Confederation had worked in Canada in 1867 and in the West Indies in 1871.

The first step towards confederation was the redrawing of the Natal constitution in 1875 to increase the power of the Crown. Sir Garnet Wolseley was sent out to achieve it. Soon to be celebrated as Gilbert and Sullivan's 'Model of a Modern Major-General', Wolseley had made his military reputation as an up-and-coming soldier, and earned considerable public and political cachet, as a result of his successful Asante campaign. Wolseley believed war against the Zulu, and the annexation of Zululand, to be both inevitable and necessary. While in Natal, therefore, he made detailed notes on Zululand in the expectation that he might soon be called upon to campaign there.[117]

The changes in Natal's constitution were followed by an attempted round table conference with the Boer republics. The latter failed but, two years later, in April 1877 when a bankrupt Transvaal could no longer prosecute a border war against Sekhukhune, Carnarvon approved the republic's annexation. The Transvaal leadership reluctantly accepted annexation largely because of Shepstone's manipulation of a supposedly imminent Zulu and Swazi threat.[118] Cetshwayo mustered his *impi* in April 1877 but Shepstone, increasingly hostile to the Zulu, ordered them to be dispersed. By annexing the Transvaal, the British earned the Boers' deep enmity, and doomed confederation. It was a reality soon grasped by Frere. Initially, the government was not necessarily opposed to removing the threat of the Zulu by war but its attitude changed through the course of 1878. Confrontation with Russia over the Balkans and the perceived Russian threat to India, the latter leading to the Second Anglo-Afghan War, combined with economic depression in Britain, precluded unnecessary expenditure on military adventures that could be postponed.

Frere's activities illustrated how determined individuals could hijack policy on the peripheries of empire. The same occurred in Afghanistan where the viceroy, Lord Lytton, engineered the outbreak of war in 1878 against the government's wishes. Frere considered that it was England's mission to spread Christian government and civilization. Drawing Africans into wage labour would enable them to acquire manufactured goods to their own benefit as well as that of the colonial economy. He needed little convincing by colonists and missionaries that the Zulu were behind the Xhosa disturbances that constituted the Ninth Cape Frontier War. The Zulu War was very much Frere's war, the only necessity being to find some legitimate grounds on which to act in what he saw as a pre-emptive strike to ward off some future Zulu onslaught on Natal. As Frere put it on 28 October 1878 in a despatch to Carnarvon's successor at the Colonial Office, Sir Michael Hicks Beach, peace depended 'simply on the caprice of an ignorant and blood-thirsty despot, with a most overweening idea of his own importance and prowess, and an organised force of at least 40,000 armed men at his absolute command, ready and eager at any moment to execute, in their ancient fashion of extermination, whatever the caprice or anger of the despot may dictate'.[119]

The legal grounds lay in the promises of good conduct Shepstone had supposedly extracted at Cetshwayo's coronation. The circumstances for exploiting them lay in the annexation of the Transvaal. By assuming its protection, the British inherited the existing frontier dispute between Boer and Zulu. Cetshwayo was surprised by the volte-face. Prior to annexation, the British supported Zulu claims over those of the Boers. However, by resolving the frontier dispute in their favour, Frere would demonstrate to the Boers the benefits of British rule, including security, whilst giving notice that nothing could be achieved by opposing British will. Unfortunately for Frere, the lieutenant governor of Natal, Sir Henry Bulwer, opposed war given the vulnerability of Natal's frontiers to Zulu incursion. In December 1877, Bulwer offered to establish an impartial commission to arbitrate the frontier dispute. To Frere's horror, the three-man commission found in favour of the Zulu in June 1878. Frere, who thought the commission far from impartial, took time to decide how to respond in view of the likely Boer reaction, fearing conflict with Boer and Zulu simultaneously. Bulwer, in turn, took time to respond to Frere's enquiries.[120]

In line with the new government policy, Hicks Beach instructed Frere to show a 'spirit of forbearance and reasonable compromise'.[121] He expressly ruled out war in November 1878. A number of border incidents gave Frere the excuse to act in such a way as to tie the boundary award to conditions that would weaken the Zulu and mollify the Boers. In July 1878, sons of Sihayo crossed into Natal to seize two of their father's errant wives and executed them. In September Zulu roughed up two Natal civil engineers who had crossed into Zululand while inspecting Wolseley's 'military' road—part of his preparations for a future war—down to the Middle Drift on the Tugela. In October Mbilini kaMswati, a Swazi who had settled in western Zululand with Cetshwayo's permission, having failed to wrest his father's throne for himself, launched a foray into disputed territory.

On 11 December 1878 Frere summoned Cetshwayo's representatives ostensibly to hear the decision of the border commission under the 'Ultimatum Tree' at the Lower Drift. In the morning the award was read out but, after lunch, an ultimatum was presented on the grounds that Cetshwayo had broken his coronation oath. Sihayo's sons and Mbilini must be surrendered, substantial reparations made in terms of cattle fines, and missionaries and a British Resident admitted to Zululand. Above all, the entire military system must be dissolved. Cetshwayo had to comply with the demands for Sihayo's sons and the cattle fines within twenty days and assent to the others within thirty days.

Frere did not forward the ultimatum to London until he knew that it would arrive too late for the government to prevent war. Bulwer was pressured by Frere into signing it.[122] The expected swift military victory would remove any chance of censure. On 13 January 1879 Hicks Beach tacitly accepted that, while inconvenient, the war would be finished off sufficiently quickly to avoid problems.[123] Submarine telegraph cables have been characterized as one of the 'tools of empire'.[124] At this stage, however, cables from London reached no nearer than Madeira and St Vincent in the Cape Verde Islands, with steamers carrying news from there to the Cape. It generally took twenty days for telegrams to reach London, not far short of the month it took a letter to travel the same distance.

With no reply to the ultimatum, the British invaded Zululand on 11 January 1879. It was highly unusual in being a colonial campaign initiated by the British at a time and place of their choosing. Cetshwayo refused to hand over Sihayo's sons, not only because Sihayo was a close friend and ally, but also because he understood that nothing would avert invasion. Even the peace party within the kingdom could not contemplate the dismantling of the *amabutho*. The latter increasingly clamoured to avenge the British insult. Cetshwayo tried to deflect the British by begging for more time, but received the response that only unconditional acceptance of all conditions would be entertained. The *amabutho* were summoned once more for an abbreviated version of the first fruits ceremony.

3

Battles

Chelmsford was refused reinforcements in the autumn of 1878, but the government relented in December, sending two more battalions. Already Chelmsford had six battalions at his disposal, including the 1/24th and 2/24th Foot. The 1/24th had been overseas since 1867 and in South Africa since 1875. Long-service men enlisted prior to the introduction of short service comprised a third; another third had enlisted before 1875. Officers and NCOs had considerable continuity of service and the battalion performed well against the Xhosa in 1877–8. While the 2/24th had a higher proportion of short-service soldiers—at least 40 per cent had enlisted in 1877—and only arrived in South Africa in 1878, it had also been tested against the Xhosa.[1] Chelmsford lacked mounted troops and men detached from infantry battalions formed two squadrons of mounted infantry. In addition, Chelmsford drew on colonial volunteer units and the Natal Mounted Police. Other irregular units were raised and men sent ashore from HMS *Active* formed a naval brigade. In all Chelmsford had 5,476 regulars and 1,193 irregular horsemen. This force was still considered insufficient and the Natal Native Contingent was formed from African levies.

Sir Henry Bulwer opposed raising it as an unnecessary provocation to the Zulu and, as a result, it was not recruited until September 1878. Chiefs in Natal owed their positions to the British, each receiving a government stipend, and many were hostile to the Zulu having been driven into Natal in the past.[2] Seven battalions were organized in three regiments. Due to settler concerns, only one in ten was armed and they were older models. The remainder carried traditional weapons: a red headband alone distinguished them from hostile Zulu. Seconded or former regulars were appointed as officers, and other whites as NCOs. Many of the latter were from the dregs of Natal society but several regulars attempted to learn Zulu.[3] Five troops of Natal Native Horse were also raised. Three—descendants of those driven westwards by the *mfecane* and traditional enemies of the Zulu—were known as the Sikali Horse after their chief, Zikhali kaMatiwane. The two others were the Edendale Troop and the Hlubi Troop. The former were Christian converts from the Wesleyan Edendale Mission; the latter was recruited from the Tlokwa, a Basotho subdivision, and led by Hlubi Molife. Only the latter were Basotho but the British referred to the whole as 'Basutos'. Three companies of Natal Native Pioneers were additionally raised, as well as African border guards and a border levy. In all, 9,350 black auxiliaries accompanied the invading columns while over 6,000 were enrolled in border guards and levies.

Chelmsford's great problem was lack of transport. The Victorian army was well used to the application of modern technologies in its campaigns,[4] but the railway inland from Durban did not reach even Pietermaritzburg until October 1880.[5] The only options available in Zululand were oxen or native carriers.[6] Such was the cumbersome nature of ox wagons that Wolseley calculated, during the second invasion of Zululand in May 1879, that Chelmsford's transport stretched out 3–4 miles further than it could travel in a day.[7] Chelmsford hoped to persuade Bulwer to impose martial law, enabling him to commandeer wagons and oxen. When Bulwer refused, there was little option but purchase or hire.[8] This naturally drove up prices. The loss of 132 wagons, hundreds of oxen, and £60,000 worth of supplies at Isandlwana crippled No. 3 Column.

No. 3 Column, which Chelmsford accompanied, was nominally commanded by Colonel Richard Glyn of the 1/24th. Glyn's Column totalled 4,313 combatants and 346 assorted conductors, drivers, and *voorlopers*. The regular infantry comprised seven companies of the 1/24th under Brevet Lieutenant Colonel Henry Pulleine, and eight companies of the 2/24th under Brevet Lieutenant Colonel Henry Degacher. In support, there was N Battery, with its six seven-pounder rifled-muzzle-loading guns, under Brevet Lieutenant Colonel Arthur Harness, and elements of No. 5 Field Company, Royal Engineers. The mounted element consisted of the 1st Squadron, Imperial Mounted Infantry commanded by Brevet Major Cecil Russell, and colonial units—130 men of the Natal Mounted Police under Inspector George Mansel, and 113 men from the Natal Carbineers, Newcastle Mounted Rifles, and Buffalo Border Guard. There were also two battalions of the 3rd Natal Native Contingent, commanded by Commandant Rupert Lonsdale, and a company of Natal Native Pioneers.

Opening Moves

The column crossed the Buffalo at Rorke's Drift on 11 January, leaving B Company, 2/24th as garrison under Lieutenant Gonville Bromhead, the post as a whole being under the command of Brevet Major Henry Spalding of the 104th Foot. It has sometimes been suggested that Bromhead's company was chosen for the assignment because of his deafness, but other companies also remained on detached service. It was intended B Company would join the column in due course.

After a brief action against Sihayo's followers in the Batshe valley on 12 January, Chelmsford decided to make his next camp at Isandlwana, some 10 miles beyond Rorke's Drift. It was the only area in the vicinity which offered sufficient room for transport and animals, while giving its defenders a seemingly reasonable field of fire. It had brushwood for fires and water close at hand. Recent heavy rains made progress hard going and repairs to the track were required to enable the wagons to reach the new camp.

Isandlwana means 'shaped something like a small hut' in Zulu but it was actually named for its similarity to the second stomach of a ruminant. It was variously spelled in British reports, versions including Isandula, Insalwana, Isandlana, Insandwhlana, Insandlwana, Sandoola, Sandula, and Sandhlwana. To the north of the campsite, established

Figure 4. The view from the top of Isandlwana showing the monuments and cairns in the camp area and on the nek. The monument to the South Wales Borderers is to the right with the 'colonial' graves to the left. The memorial to the Natal Carbineers can be seen in the centre middle distance on the forward slope of Black's Kopje.

under the shadow of the high rocky outcrop of Isandlwana, were a series of heights, some 1,500 yards away, and guarding access to the Nqutu plateau. The nearest heights—the iNyoni—rose several hundred feet above the plain. A spur led up from Isandlwana by way of the Tahelane ridge. To the east, out on the wide plain, lay the Conical Kopje (amaTutshane), about 1½ miles distant from the saddle or nek. The latter separated Isandlwana from Mahlabamkhosi, soon known as Black's or Stony Kopje, to the south. The plain stretched 4 miles southwards towards the Malakatha Mountain and the Hlazakazi ridge and 8 miles eastwards to the Magogo and Silutshana hills, and Siphezi Mountain.

The plain appeared to slope gently away from Isandlwana, but it was broken by dongas (gullies), which ran roughly north to south. Many areas of dead ground obstructed the apparent open fields of fire, although Chelmsford was to argue later that 'there never was a position where a small force could have made a better defensive stand'.[9] For the Zulu, 'the rocky broken ground on the flanks was no more serious obstacle than a ploughed field to our soldiers at home'.[10]

There was some difference of opinion on the merits of the site, particularly when Chelmsford declined to laager the wagons. Chelmsford remarked, 'It is not worth while, it will take too much time, and besides the wagons are most of them going back at once to Rorke's Drift for supplies.'[11] Although strongly recommended prior to the campaign by experienced Boers, laagering was hideously complicated. It would have taken a considerable amount of time, and Chelmsford intended to keep moving. Thus, he ignored his own *Regulations for Field Forces in South Africa*, which stated, 'Troops marching through the enemy's country, or where there is any possibility of attack, will, when halting, though but for a few hours, invariably form a wagon laager.' Chelmsford's notes on the later findings of the Isandlwana enquiry stated that a laager was 'never intended to be used as a redoubt, but as protection for the oxen'.[12]

Entrenchment was an alternative but it is not clear that entrenchments would have helped. Glyn's staff officer, Major Francis Clery, told the enquiry that the men were too exhausted to laager or otherwise entrench the camp by the time they reached it on the evening of 20 January. The ground was exceptionally stony but that would have made it possible to construct stone sangars. Chelmsford later suggested that, if tents had been lowered, they would have provided an additional impediment to the Zulu.[13] This is doubtful.

It was assumed that the warning time provided by infantry picquets and mounted vedettes thrown forward of the camp would provide sufficient protection. Mansel said he originally posted his vedettes several miles out, but Clery instructed him to draw them back closer to the camp and, against Mansel's advice, to withdraw that to the rear of Isandlwana altogether: 'My dear fellow, those vedettes are useless there, the rear always protects itself.'[14] There were picquets and vedettes, albeit closer to the camp than Mansel believed necessary, on the Magaga hill, the Nyezi hill, iThusi hill, the Qwabe ridge, and the

Conical Kopje. As it happened, there was also a picquet to the rear of Isandlwana on 22 January.

There was no reason to suppose the Zulu were likely to attack. Russell led out a reconnaissance some 20 miles to the east of the Batshe towards Siphezi on 15 January and saw nothing. Reports were heard of Zulu in the Mangeni gorge to the south, which contained the stronghold of 'Matyana' (Matshana kaSitshakuza of the Mchunu) in the vicinity of Siphezi. Chelmsford, who had ridden out towards the Mangeni on 21 January, resolved to send out a strong reconnaissance party that night. He did not consult either Glyn or Clery, who were unaware of where the party was being sent or for what purpose.[15]

Chelmsford's Foray

Most of the Natal Native Contingent under the command of Lonsdale—only four companies remained in camp—and about 120 of the mounted police and volunteers under a former regular, Major John Dartnell, started well before dawn on 21 January. By mid-afternoon, Dartnell had encountered some 1,500 Zulu near the Siphezi, who deployed threateningly. Zulu boys taken prisoner revealed that the main Zulu *impi* was to the north-east. Calling up Lonsdale to his assistance, Dartnell felt it unwise to proceed. Since it was too late to do more, he stayed where he was on the northern slopes of the Hlazakazi. Dartnell sent a message back to Chelmsford that he would attack in the morning.

At about 01.30 hours on 22 January, Clery took Dartnell's message to Glyn.[16] Having been effectively supplanted by Chelmsford, Glyn simply referred Clery to the general. Dartnell had been expected to return to camp but Chelmsford decided to move out in Dartnell's support since the Mangeni was known as a natural route frequented by *impi* in the past. Chelmsford also intended to select a new campsite. Pulleine would command the camp in the absence of Chelmsford and Glyn. Chelmsford chose not to take a wagon with the reserve ammunition and it was left to be forwarded in due course.

Six companies of the 2/24th, most of the remaining mounted infantry and four guns moved out with Chelmsford at about 03.30 on 22 January. Chelmsford reached Dartnell about 06.30 but, behind him, the force was badly strung out. At about 09.30 Chelmsford stopped for breakfast near Magogo. While there, Chelmsford received a message sent by Pulleine to Clery at 08.05: 'Report just come in that the Zulus are advancing in force from the left front of the camp.'[17] There was no urgency in the note, the force left behind seemed perfectly adequate and no one supposed this could be the main *impi*. Chelmsford did send his naval ADC, Lieutenant Berkeley Milne, to the top of Magogo with his telescope to observe the distant camp.

Milne spent about an hour at his vantage point some 12 miles from the camp, but his view was partially impeded.[18] He could see no evidence of activity and the tents remained standing. Dark patches near the camp were assumed to be oxen. Chelmsford saw no reason to alter his plans. Captain Alan Gardner, attached to the column's staff, was sent back to Isandlwana between 10.00 and 11.00 with orders for Pulleine to strike camp and follow Chelmsford. Gardner subsequently suggested that it was intended to send on only the baggage of those troops out with Chelmsford and that Pulleine was to 'remain himself at his present camp and entrench it'.[19] If ever written, the order was lost amid the camp's fall and it seems unlikely Pulleine was intended to stay at Isandlwana. Gardner was accompanied by Major Stuart Smith of the Royal Artillery, four other officers, and a small escort of mounted infantry. The group arrived at Isandlwana at about 12.00.

When Chelmsford first reached Dartnell, the Zulu encountered on the previous day had vanished but then appeared gradually withdrawing north-eastwards towards Siphezi. At about 14.00 Chelmsford was found by Russell. Russell had seen a Natal Native Contingent officer bearing a message from Hamilton-Browne that the main *impi* was in close proximity to the camp about two hours earlier. The officer had not found Chelmsford or his staff. Subsequently, Russell received a second message from Hamilton-Browne that the camp was under attack. Russell then sent two more officers to find his general. In a statement to the House of Lords in August 1880, Chelmsford only admitted to having personally received Pulleine's first message. This was technically correct since subsequent messages sent from the camp and received at about 15.00 were addressed to and received by Chelmsford's staff.

Hamilton-Browne had been ordered to start his battalion back to the camp at about 09.30. En route, at about 10.00, Hamilton-Browne had taken two Zulu prisoners, who revealed the presence of the *impi* in the vicinity. He sent off a message to Chelmsford. Later, at about 11.00, Hamilton-Browne saw large numbers of Zulu between him and the camp, and could see bursting shells and dark masses on the plateau. Hamilton-Browne sent a second message saying the Zulu were attacking the camp. Getting closer, Hamilton-Browne observed the last stages of the battle through his field glasses, sending off yet another message which did not reach Chelmsford. His men having little ammunition, Hamilton-Browne retired to a rocky area sometime after 13.00 and requested reinforcements, sending back another message—this time oral—by one of his officers, 'For God's sake come back, the camp is surrounded and must be taken unless helped.'[20]

At about 12.45, Harness, who was on the col between Hlazakazi and Magogo, heard artillery; shells could be seen bursting on the plateau. Harness turned his guns, and the two companies of the 2/24th escorting him, back towards the camp but Chelmsford's ADC, Brevet Major Matthew Gosset, directed Harness to resume his march in the general's name. At about 13.15 Chelmsford went up to the Mdutshana hill with some of his staff. Nothing could be seen with certainty. Hamilton-Browne's messages were thought to be exaggerated. Chelmsford then himself decided to return to the camp, with an escort but at a leisurely pace, sometime between 14.00 and 14.45. Chelmsford reached Hamilton-Browne's position at about 15.30, still some 5 miles short of Isandlwana.

According to Hamilton-Browne, when he finally met Chelmsford to tell him the camp had fallen, Chelmsford replied, 'How dare you tell me such a falsehood? Get your men into line at once and advance.'[21] Not long after Chelmsford joined Hamilton-Browne, Lonsdale struggled in with dire news. Feeling ill, Lonsdale, who had been concussed in a bad fall from his horse earlier in January, had ridden back to the camp to arrange for supplies to be sent to his battalion. Lonsdale had ridden into the outskirts of the camp sometime between 14.00 and 14.30 without initially noticing the Zulu were in possession of it. In utter disbelief, Chelmsford is said to have exclaimed, 'But I left over 1,000 men to guard the camp.'[22]

It took until 18.00 before Chelmsford could concentrate his exhausted force, and it was not until 20.15, in the fast fading twilight, that he regained the camp. Only then did the full extent of the catastrophe become apparent. Moving to Rorke's Drift the following morning, Chelmsford's force passed a large body of Zulu returning up the Batshe valley—those who had attacked Rorke's Drift—but both sides were too exhausted to fight after their previous exertions. Chelmsford reached Rorke's Drift at about 08.00 on 23 January, much relieved to find the post still holding out.

Isandlwana

At Isandlwana, Pulleine had five companies of his own regiment—A, C, E, F, and H—plus G Company of the 2/24th. In addition there were two guns of N Battery; some of the 1st Squadron, Imperial Mounted Infantry; colonial volunteers; camp casuals, assorted staff; and four companies of the Natal Native Contingents: in all, over 1,300 men. Clery later wrote that, at the last minute and on his own initiative since he realized nothing had been done, he left orders for Pulleine.[23] These were to assume command of the camp, to draw in the infantry picquets closer to the camp but to keep out the mounted vedettes, and to have a wagon available to be sent forward with ammunition to support Chelmsford if necessary.

Mounted picquets of the Natal Carbineers out on Qwabe hill across the plain beyond the Conical Kopje, and on the Nyezi feature, another 2 miles or so beyond that, reported Zulu approaching from the north-east between 07.00 and 07.30. Pulleine had the camp stood to at 08.00 and sent his first message to Chelmsford. The defenders were drawn out on the eastern side of the camp inclined towards the iNyoni. The oxen were brought in closer to the wagons, while a messenger was sent to bring in F Company men employed on improving the road back to Rorke's Drift. Some forty or so wagons, intended to start back to Rorke's Drift, remained at the rear of the camp, their oxen yoked, to await a safer moment to start. At about 09.00, a few Zulu appeared on the plateau but soon vanished. It was reported that some were retiring to the north-east but others moving to the north-west. No alarm was felt for, as Lieutenant Henry Curling of N Battery was to write, no one 'dreamed they would come on'.[24] Large groups of Xhosa had often been seen during the Ninth Frontier War without anything developing.

Sometime between 10.00 and 10.30, Brevet Colonel Anthony Durnford arrived with about 450 men from No. 2 Column, Pulleine having been told to expect him. The camp was stood down for a combined breakfast and lunch. Durnford's column comprised the five troops of the Natal Native Horse and two companies from the 1st Natal Native Contingent. In addition, there was No. 11 Rocket Battery, Royal Artillery under Major Francis Russell, mostly manned by privates drawn from the 24th. The Hale's rocket, a nine-pounder weapon with a range of 1,300 yards, launched from a tube, was more notable for the supposed psychological effect of its noise than as a munition. Durnford, colonial engineer in Natal on and off since 1873, had long been an advocate of using African manpower. No. 2 Column was tasked initially only with border defence. Chelmsford was wary of Durnford's supposed recklessness, the latter having lost the use of his left arm when leading colonial volunteers against Langalibalele back in 1873. Durnford was certainly driven by his perceived past failure. When he moved his column down to the Tugela in response to a rumour about Zulu movements, he had to be sharply ordered back by Chelmsford, who threatened to remove him from command.[25] At about 02.00 on 21 January, Chelmsford then ordered Durnford up to Isandlwana with the force immediately at his disposal.

Chelmsford had not left any precise indication of who was to command once Durnford, four years senior to Pulleine, arrived. Later, Chelmsford's acerbic assistant military secretary, Lieutenant Colonel John North Crealock, claimed Durnford had been ordered to take command. Crealock also suggested that the orders Clery issued to Pulleine to defend the camp were binding upon Durnford. The actual instructions to Durnford were later found in Crealock's order book, recovered from the battlefield in June 1879. They merely ordered Durnford up to the camp without any instructions either to reinforce it or to assume command.[26]

Aware of a Zulu presence, but unclear as to the situation from the confused reports, Durnford sent men to the top of Isandlwana. They could see nothing. Durnford then indicated he would not stay in the camp but head off any possible Zulu attempt to get behind Chelmsford since the reports seemed to suggest the Zulu were retiring in that direction. According to Durnford's staff officer, Lieutenant William Cochrane, Durnford asked Pulleine for two companies of the 24th but Pulleine declined on the grounds that his orders were to defend the camp. Acquiescing, Durnford remarked, 'Very well, perhaps I had better not take them. I will go with my own men.'[27] Nevertheless, he also said, 'If I get into difficulties, I shall rely on you to support me.'[28]

At about 11.00 Captain George Shepstone—one of Theophilus Shepstone's sons acting as Durnford's political officer—accompanied two of the Sikali troops under Lieutenants Charles Raw and Joseph Roberts, up towards the Nqutu plateau. At around 11.15, Durnford headed across the plain with the Edendale and Hlubi troops. They were trailed at about 11.30 by Russell's rocket battery, the rocket troughs carried on mules. Captain Charles Nourse's company of the 1/1st Natal Native Contingent accompanied Russell as escort. At about the same time, Captain Charles Cavaye's E Company of the 1/24th was sent up on to the Tahelane ridge about 1,200 yards from the camp to reinforce and replace the picquets from the Natal Native Contingent, who moved forward after Roberts and Raw. This appears to have been in accordance with Pulleine's desire to support Durnford.[29]

Up on the plateau, Roberts moved to the north while Raw went eastwards. According to Donald Morris, sometime between 11.15 and 11.45 some of Raw's men saw and gave chase to a few Zulu herding cattle. In Morris's dramatic prose, one rode up to a crest of the Ngwebeni valley known as Mabaso: 'Then, in astonishment, he stared into the ravine itself. Closely packed and sitting in utter silence, covering the floor of the ravine and perched on the steeply rising sides, stretched as far as the eye could see in both directions, were over 20,000 Zulu warriors.' Morris said that the patrol dismounted and fired one volley before hastily retiring.[30] In reality, Raw merely reported later that, as his men followed up groups of Zulu, the whole *impi* showed itself 'from behind the hill in front where they had evidently been waiting'.[31] Conductor James Hamer of the Army Commissariat and Transport Department, accompanying Shepstone, reported chasing cattle over a ridge and seeing the Zulu 'in front of us, in perfect order as quiet as mice & stretched across in an even line'.[32] An African NCO, Nyanda, also spoke of cresting a ridge.[33] Shepstone sent off men to warn Durnford out on the plain and himself returned to the camp to warn Pulleine. Having seen the Zulu from a greater distance, Lieutenant Durrant Scott of the Natal Carbineers on vedette duty also sent two Natal Carbineers to warn Durnford.

The position of the Zulu bivouac prior to Isandlwana has become a matter of debate, as has the position where the *impi* was discovered. Zulu accounts are contradictory. The traditionally accepted bivouac site is the Ngwebeni valley behind Mabaso. Ron Lock has argued that the *impi* did not camp in one location but by regiments along the Nqutu plateau.[34] The evidence suggests that the traditional site remains the most likely since the ravine below Mabaso was sufficiently large to contain the *impi* and sufficiently concealed from the vedettes' viewpoints.[35] It is again traditionally implied that the discovery of the *impi* occurred at Mabaso although a general Zulu presence in the area had been evident from the first reports almost five hours earlier. Analysis of reports and surviving contemporary annotated maps by Lock, Peter Quantrill, and Keith Smith suggest, however, that the *impi* was not discovered, as Morris claimed, still at its bivouac in the Ngwebeni but as some Zulu were moving forward from the Ngwebeni into the dead ground between the Mabaso and iThusi hills en route towards the rear of Isandlwana. Earlier, the Natal Carbineers had observed some of these movements, prompting the first stand-to in the camp at 08.00. A reasonably convincing case, based on the maps and the presumed timings and distances, can be made for Raw to have encountered the main *impi* at iTusi Hill.[36]

Out on the plain, Russell ignored the warning of two more Carbineers, who rode by on their way back from observing the Zulu. Hearing the firing on the plateau, Russell moved off to the left to ascend. At about 12.30 his rocket battery was overwhelmed about 2 or 3 miles from the camp some way beyond the Conical Kopje, possibly moving up the feature known as the 'Notch' to the left of iThusi, although this is disputed. Russell managed to get off three rockets.

Figure 5. Looking out from the upper slope of Isandlwana towards the distinctive Conical Kopje with iTusi beyond to its left.

Russell and five of his ten men were shot down, the others—one his soldier servant—managing to get away.[37] The battery's mules scattered and Nourse's company disintegrated.

Possibly 4 or 5 miles from the camp and opposite the Nyesi ridge, Durnford was confronted with large numbers of Zulu to his front, at about the same time Russell was overrun. He retreated to the Nyanga donga, where he was reinforced by some of the Natal Carbineers from the Conical Kopje. Retiring steadily, they came across and collected Nourse and five of his men. Durnford continued his retreat to another donga—the Nyogane—about a mile from the camp. By remaining so long at the Nyogane donga, Durnford contributed to the overextension of the defensive line. But his men's horses were blown: they had been almost constantly on the move since leaving Rorke's Drift between 07.30 and 08.00.

The Zulu, some 20,000–24,000 strong, were led by Ntshingwayo kaMahole of the Khoza, who was almost 70, and the 45-year-old Mavumengwana kaNdlela of the Ntuli. The scouts were led by Zibhebhu kaMaphitha of the Mandlakazi. The *impi* left Ulundi on 17 January and, by short marches, reached Siphezi on 20 January, joined en route by local contingents. Apparently, there was some disagreement with Matshana on the best approach to the British camp. Matshana was not altogether trusted as he was a 'Natal Kaffir', who had settled back in Zululand in 1858 and become a royal favourite. The British believed Matshana might come over to them, the possibility encouraging Chelmsford's moves towards Mangeni. In the event, on 21 January, the *impi* moved westwards in small groups to the Ngwebeni, some 4 to 5 miles north-east of Isandlwana, with the intention of working their way around the rear of the British column. Matshana was to rendezvous with the *impi* at Siphezi but Ntshingwayo moved forward without waiting for him and it was Matshana's initial movement that was detected by Dartnell. Matshana himself mistook the Natal Native Contingent for men from the *impi* and only just escaped pursuit. Although one Zulu flanking party was spotted, Zibhebhu's scouts successfully masked the main body from Dartnell passing in the opposite direction. Fourteen Zulu horsemen were seen on Mabaso by vedettes on 21 January but no importance was attached to the sighting.[38] No fires were lit and the Zulu remained concealed although, as suggested earlier, some were moving forward when observed by the vedettes at about 07.00.

Since 22/23 January marked a new moon, when the omens would be more propitious, Colonel Evelyn Wood of No. 4 Column later suggested that the original Zulu intention was to fall on the rear of the camp on 23 January. The Zulu themselves suggested they would not have attacked on a day as inauspicious as that of the 'dead moon' unless discovered. It is equally possible, however, that the Zulu intended to attack later on 22 January.[39] After all, Matshana's followers continued the engagement with Chelmsford that day and the Zulu also attacked Pearson's column at Nyezane on 22 January, although that too was an encounter battle.

Another matter of debate is whether Chelmsford was deliberately lured into splitting his force because Matshana staged some kind of deliberate diversion. John Laband believes it a possibility; Ian Knight does not.[40] It is certainly possible that the fires the Zulu lit on the hills around Dartnell's position on the night of 21 January were intended both to mask the movement of the main *impi* and also to enable Matshana to withdraw his warriors. In that sense, they were a decoy, but the Zulu could not have anticipated that Chelmsford would split his force in response to Dartnell's encounter. Cetshwayo later claimed that Ntshingwayo had been instructed to send a peace delegation to Chelmsford before attacking and that his commanders were still debating whom to send when the *impi*'s discovery triggered the battle. This seems unlikely and it served Cetshwayo's interests to say so. Ntshingwayo seems to have been undecided as to his immediate course of action and intended to wait upon events. One argument, that Ntshingwayo attacked because he saw Chelmsford had divided his forces, rests on a 1917 reminiscence of what a Zulu had once said.[41] The contemporary testimony of Sihayo's son, Mehlokazulu kaSihayo, a subordinate commander of the left horn, suggests the Zulu had not observed Chelmsford's departure in the early pre-dawn darkness. Foraging parties had also been sent out, suggesting no real intent to attack, and the Zulu had certainly not begun their customary ritual preparations for battle.[42] Sounds of firing—from Chelmsford's engagement with Matshana—drew the uNokhenke and uMcijo (also known as the uKhandempemvu) regiments forward across the plateau in the belief that the iNgobamakhosi regiment was engaged, but this was not the case and they returned to their billets. They were unsettled, however, and could not be restrained when discovered.

The intended composition of the *impi*'s horns and chest became disrupted by the suddenness with which the action was brought on, the original left horn becoming the right, the right the centre, and the centre the left. Some have argued that the *impi* had been sufficiently doctored before leaving Ulundi to require nothing more. But there were still last-minute purification rituals to undertake, and it was customary to gather around commanders for final instructions. The *izinduna* desperately tried to bring some order to the advance. Some care needs to be exercised in the precise identification of the whereabouts of individual Zulu regiments in the advance. The right horn—assumed to be the uDudubu, iSangqu, and iMbube regiments of the uNodwengu corps and the uNokhenke regiment of the iKhanda corps—and the centre—assumed to be the uMcijo, uMbonambi, and some of the uMxhapho regiment—moved across the plateau. It was the right-horn regiments that had begun to move when encountered by Raw. The left horn—assumed to be the iNgobamakhosi and uVe regiments—moved down towards the Conical Kopje, but with the right wing and centre far ahead of the left. The reserve was successfully held back, although some broke away to join the battle, the regiments being formed in the customary circle with their backs to the enemy to be given instructions and ritually doctored. The uNdi corps of older married regiments that formed the reserve then moved across the plateau behind Isandlwana to cut the main track back to Rorke's Drift, although it is also possible that they moved after the left wing and that the initial pursuit was undertaken by the right wing. Four regiments formed the uNdi corps—the uThulwana, iNdluyengwe, iNdlondlo, and uDloko—under the command of Cetshwayo's younger half-brother, Dabulamanzi kaMpande.[43]

Back in the camp, a new stand-to was ordered at about noon as Shepstone rode in. Possibly ordered by Durnford before he left the camp, Captain William Mostyn's F Company had been sent to reinforce Cavaye when firing was heard from the plateau.[44] Captain A. J. Barry's company of the 2/3rd Natal Native Contingent—originally on picquet duty on the prominent knoll known as the Magaga, and then sent forward after Raw and Roberts—had already broken. Cavaye and Mostyn were deployed in extended order and fired at the Zulu who were about 800 yards away and moving across their front towards the rear of Isandlwana. A section of E Company under Second Lieutenant Edward Dyson was some 500 yards to the left, and Mostyn moved into the gap between Dyson and Cavaye. All were in a shallow valley beyond the crest of the Tahelane and, therefore, not visible from camp.

Although the evidence is disputed, Dyson's section appears to have been overwhelmed at an early stage. George Chadwick, at one time the custodian of the Isandlwana battlefield, believed that burial cairns of Dyson's men were lost when the main battlefield area was fenced off in 1928. He relocated some in 1958 but they have since been lost again.[45] A small party of engineers repairing the road to Rorke's Drift was also overwhelmed by the uNdi corps en route to the outpost. Shortly after Mostyn's deployment, the 1/24th's adjutant, Lieutenant Teignmouth Melvill, sent a message to order the line to fall back slowly as Zulu were appearing to the rear of the camp. The two companies were drawn up at the foot of the plateau, possibly pulling in some of Barry's men. Captain Walter Stafford's company of the 1/1st Natal Native Contingent, which had come with Durnford, and Lieutenant Richard Vause's Natal Native Horse troop, who dismounted, seem to have filled in to Mostyn's left and to the right of Captain Reginald Younghusband's C Company, which was sent out to cover the withdrawal.[46] Raw and Roberts's troops similarly dismounted to join the firing line. At this stage, the Zulu were some 800 yards distant.

The possibility that the Zulu could approach in largely dead ground appears to have persuaded Pulleine to advance well forward of the camp, the two guns being stationed on a rocky knoll about 600 yards out from the nearest tent lines with Lieutenant Francis Porteous's A Company and Captain George Wardell's H Company to left and right respectively along a slight rocky ridge running roughly north-west to south-east. Captain James Lonsdale's company of the 1/3rd Natal Native Contingent, which had been on picquet duty the previous day, was posted about halfway back to the camp from the Conical Kopje on the morning of the battle. Lonsdale pulled back further about the time Durnford arrived in the camp, and may or may not have filled in to the right of Wardell. It is possible that Captain Edward Erskine's company of the 2/3rd Natal Native Contingent was posted to either the left or right of Wardell, but there is no reliable information as to the exact positions occupied by the Natal Native Contingent. As David Jackson has stated, there 'is no evidence whatsoever that the two wings of the 1/24th were separated by a body of native infantry'.[47] Captain Robert Krohn's company of the 1/3rd Natal Native Contingent was certainly held in reserve in front of the tents. Two further companies from the 2/3rd Natal Native Contingent under Captain Orlando Murray may have been sent back to camp with captured cattle on 21 January. Murray was killed at Isandlwana but there is no evidence as to his companies' whereabouts during the action. If any of the regulars were separated from the remainder by the Natal Native Contingent, it was Lieutenant Charles Pope's G Company of the 2/24th off to the extreme right. There may also have been a composite company of additional 2/24th men in the firing line between Pope and the Natal Native Contingent.

Pulleine received Chelmsford's message to strike the camp at about the time George Shepstone reported the *impi*'s discovery. Shepstone and Gardner both advised caution and Pulleine decided it was impossible to comply with Chelmsford's order for the time being, sending off another note to this effect: 'Heavy firing to the left of camp. Cannot move camp at present.' Gardner chose to amplify this further with his own message: 'Heavy firing near left of camp. Shepstone has come in for reinforcements, and reports the Zulus are falling back. The whole force at camp turned out and fighting about one mile to left flank.'[48] Like Pulleine's first message, these conveyed no real sense of danger, particularly given the mistaken emphasis on Zulu withdrawal. As already related, these messages did not reach Chelmsford's staff until about 15.00.

Under the direction of Stuart Smith, the guns opened at once but the effective range of shrapnel was only 1,200 yards and the opening range was about 3,400 yards. Moreover, the seven-pounder had a low muzzle velocity, which made it unsuitable for shrapnel. Smith fired about twenty-five rounds of one kind or another. They did not do much damage: ironically, Roberts of the Natal Native Horse was killed

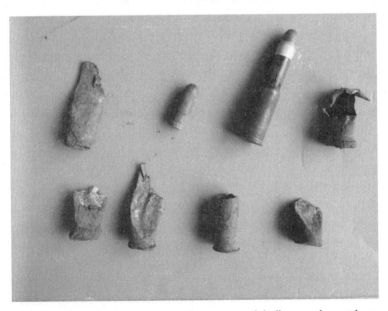

Figure 6. Spent Martini-Henry cartridge cases and bullet together with an unfired round.

by shrapnel while retreating from the plateau. By the time the range was suitable for case shot, the British line was breaking. Zulu accounts suggest they deliberately threw themselves down when they saw the gunners stand away from the guns at the moment of firing. At about 12.15, Smith took one gun off more to the right to try and give supporting fire to Durnford in the Nyogane donga. Pope was extended to cover Durnford's rear although he was still at least 800 yards distant from Durnford's position.

At this stage, the Zulu had reached the ideal range of about 400 yards for the Martini-Henry. Although sighted to 1,000 yards, it was most effective at the shorter range when its heavy 'man-stopping' rounds had a devastating effect. Formally approved for adoption in 1871 as the army's first purpose-built breech-loading rifle, the 0.450 calibre single-shot Martin-Henry began to be issued in October 1874 following extensive trials. The improved Mark II was approved in April 1877: the Mark III was approved in August 1879, too late for the Zulu War. The Zulu were stalled all across the front of the camp. Sometime between 13.00 and 13.30, the British line collapsed. Contemporary (and later) explanations relating to a supposed failure of the ammunition supply on the firing line and the flight of the Natal Native Contingent lack credibility. Primarily, it was the imminent outflanking of Durnford's position in the Nyogane donga that triggered collapse. The uMbonambi may have driven a herd of cattle ahead of them— probably oxen from the camp surrounds—to distract Durnford and mask themselves from Pope's fire.[49] Zulu accounts emphasize the example—at the cost of his life—of Mkhosana kaMvundlana, who was sent down by the Zulu commanders watching from the iNyoni to inspire the uMcijo to renew their effort at the moment of the British retirement.

Durnford's retreat isolated Pope's company as it was further extending. Durnford's retirement may also have persuaded Pulleine to order a general withdrawal on the camp, particularly as many of the camp casuals were apparently leaving in increasing numbers. At the moment when the retirement was ordered—at least two survivors stated that bugles sounded the 'retire'—Wardell, Porteous, and the guns were at least half a mile in front of the camp. It is usually assumed from the discovery of the body of Colour Sergeant Wolfe and about twenty men from Wardell's company on the original firing line that they acted as some kind of rearguard. All subsequent burial parties identified the majority of bodies being in the camp, along the nek, and down the Fugitives' Trail. It is clear that the regulars fell back in relatively good order. At this point, it is possible the Natal Native Contingent broke but whether they were situated in the centre of the firing line or elsewhere cannot be determined. It seems likely that their collapse occurred as a consequence of a general retirement rather than triggering it. The blame attached to the 'cowardly' Natal Native Contingent was the same racial stereotyping that also attributed to them unrestrained killing of wounded Zulu.

Another of Donald Morris's myths was the issue of the ammunition boxes.[50] It featured prominently in the film *Zulu Dawn*, the 'prequel' to *Zulu*, released in 1979. Supposedly, the Mark V ammunition box could not be unscrewed sufficiently quickly. Only one screw actually secured the wedge-shaped wooden panel that formed the lid of each stout box, after which it could be slid off without even removing the copper bands around the ends. A sharp kick or a blow from a rifle butt on the lid's edge could open the box without recourse to the special screwdrivers issued to quartermasters. The tin lining of the box was then drawn back by its attached handle. In the words of David Jackson, 'there is no reliable contemporary evidence that the regulars ran out of ammunition while in the line'.[51] Only Captain Edward Essex, No. 3 Column's transport director, mentioned ammunition to the enquiry, but he did so in the context of organizing casuals to take out ammunition in a cart to Cavaye and Mostyn. Each man carried seventy rounds and it seems unlikely that the additional thirty rounds per man specified by regulations if an engagement was likely were not issued in the period between 08.00 and 12.00. Admittedly, the ammunition carts of the 1/24th, containing the 200 rounds kept in reserve for each man, were about a mile away from Cavaye and Mostyn but, overall, there were 400,000 rounds in the camp since it included all the column's reserve supplies.

Most officers favoured a steady and controlled rate of fire. It was a matter of debate whether independent or volley fire was the best means of achieving this. The manuals suggested an independent rate of fire was almost twice as rapid as volley firing at either long or close range. Frere described the 1/24th in February 1878 as 'old steady shots'.[52] The companies of Cavaye, Mostyn, and Younghusband at least sustained supervised independent fire leading to the supposition that the rate of ammunition expenditure was not excessive. Volley firing is recorded only later in the action when the Zulu came within 400 yards, although it is conceivable that Wardell, Porteous, and Pope adopted it from the beginning. The duration of the main firefight was approximately ninety minutes at most. In other fierce actions during the war the expenditure of ammunition was low—an average of just thirty-three rounds per man over four hours at Kambula and just ten rounds in half an hour at Ulundi. In two hotly contested actions in the Anglo-Transvaal War (1880–1), average expenditure by the infantry was just over seventeen rounds at Laing's Nek (28 January 1881) and just over twenty-two rounds at Ingogo (8 February 1881). In two key actions in Afghanistan, Ahmed Khel (19 April 1880) and Charasia (6 October 1879), expenditure was ten and thirty rounds respectively.[53] Against Mahdists in the Sudan, average expenditure was fifty rounds per man at El Teb in February 1884 and even at Tamai in March 1884, one of the few occasions on which the fabled British defensive square was broken by tribesmen. Because Lieutenant John Chard of the Royal Engineers claimed that only a box and a half of ammunition was left at Rorke's Drift on the morning of 23 January, Morris suggested that 20,000 rounds were fired by the defenders. Even if true, this still equates to only 17.5 rounds per man per hour for ten hours.[54]

All the evidence suggests the 24th were still firing repeatedly at the moment they fell back on the camp. The best known testimony is that of Lieutenant Horace Smith-Dorrien, attached to the column as a transport officer. Smith-Dorrien made no statement on the issue of ammunition to the enquiry and, in a contemporary letter, simply said he was out with the forward companies 'handing them spare ammunition'.[55] In his memoirs, Smith-Dorrien implied he was prevented from handing out ammunition by Quartermaster Edward Bloomfield of the 2/24th. According to Smith-Dorrien, Bloomfield exclaimed, 'For heaven's sake don't take that, man, for it belongs to our battalion,' to which Smith-Dorrien replied, 'Hang it man, you don't want a requisition now do you?' Smith-Dorrien recounted the story because it spoke 'for the coolness and discipline of the regiment'.[56] Smith-Dorrien may have confused Bloomfield with the 1/24th's quartermaster, Pullen. In any case, the exchange may have centred on the ammunition previously loaded for onward transmission to Chelmsford.[57] It mainly reveals the problematic nature of much later recollections.[58]

Despite the considerable degradation of the site over the years, archaeological investigation at Isandlwana has discovered a number of handles from the lining of the ammunition boxes out on the firing line. It has also turned up bent retaining screws, suggestive of boxes broken open with rifle butts. Clearly, ammunition was reaching the firing line.[59] Once the line collapsed, so would the organization of the ammunition supply to the regulars: this would explain Zulu accounts of small groups of the 24th dying in hand-to-hand fighting in the camp once their ammunition was expended. It is entirely feasible that the Natal Native Contingent did find it difficult to replenish their ammunition since those who were armed carried only fifteen rounds per man. Durnford, whose men carried only fifty rounds for their Swinburne-Henry carbines, did run low in the Nyogane donga.

Difficulties could be experienced with the Martini's falling-block lever action, which extracted the spent Boxer rolled brass cartridge, once the weapon became hot. It was not unlike the extractor problems of the Springfield carried by the 7th Cavalry at the Little Big Horn. All recorded examples of rifles jamming relate to the Natal Native Horse and Natal Native Contingent rather than the regulars, who would have been accustomed to rectifying the problem. It might be added that there was also some incompatibility between Martini-Henry and Swinburne-Henry ammunition, which increased the likelihood of jamming if those armed with carbines used the wrong ammunition. It is unlikely, therefore, that this contributed materially to the collapse of the British line. For all its faults, the Martini remained an effective weapon, Edward Hutton writing of Gingindlovu, 'we all had the utmost confidence in our rifles, which were at that time the most perfect weapons in the world'.[60] Only Lock, Quantrill, and Edmund Yorke still lend weight to the difficulty of opening ammunition boxes and/or the subsequent exhaustion of ammunition supply contributing to defeat.[61]

The cartridge's black powder charge produced a large amount of smoke, which could make visibility difficult in the event of rapid or prolonged fire. Volley firing would increase the effect but the evidence suggests this was not adopted until late on. The firing line was also so extended that smoke was probably not a major factor initially. Subsequently, smoke and the dust kicked up by men and animals might have inhibited the final defensive effort, especially as the air was still with little wind to disperse the smoke. Visibility was also arguably affected by a partial eclipse of the sun commencing at about 13.10 and reaching its height at 14.29. At its peak it obscured about 65 per cent of the sun but the sun would have been high. By this time the British collapse was an accomplished fact. Consequently, the partial eclipse is probably more significant for the impact it made upon the Zulu participants, especially in retrospect. A Zulu who spoke to the traveller and novelist Bertram Mitford, in 1882, recalled, 'The sun turned black in the middle of the battle; we could still see it over us, or should have thought we had been fighting till evening.'[62]

A greater factor in the collapse was the extended nature of the British line. Companies were spread out with at least 200–300 yards between them. Each company in extended order covered at least 200 yards in single file. There could be anything between four and ten paces between individual men. The conclusion of William Penn Symons was that, on the right of the guns, the men were probably even further apart. The firing line extended at least 2,000 yards. Archaeological investigations again suggest that the firing line facing towards the iNyoni heights was 200 yards further forward from the camp than usually supposed, probably to make use of the dongas on the northern side of the camp and to deny the Zulu use of more dead ground.[63] Pope's company may also have been initially deployed much further out towards the Conical Kopje.

Pulleine had deployed approximately in line with the instructions Chelmsford had issued to his column commanders in December 1878.[64] British infantry and guns were to be forward, the Natal Native Contingent 'well clear of each flank' and 'well to the rear of each flank' of the regulars, with mounted infantry covering the flanks. The same deployment was more or less employed by Pearson in his action at Nyezane on the same day as Isandlwana. Consequently, the forward deployment was not some whim of an inexperienced Pulleine.

Lieutenant Henry Curling's letters imply that the number of men in the firing line was far fewer than usually supposed. This was because the danger initially seemed slight and it was the intention to break camp. As Curling wrote: 'I suppose that not more than one half the men left in the camp took part in its defence as it was not considered necessary and they were left in as cooks etc.'[65] Other evidence suggests the companies of the 24th deployed with only an average of fifty men each. This would suggest that only 300 or so were in the firing line. It has been plausibly argued that the rest were employed on packing up the camp since Pulleine probably wished to comply as far as possible with Chelmsford's orders.[66] It may also explain why tents were not struck in accordance with the regulations relating to an attack. Normally, packing over 300 tents would have been a lengthy affair. Striking tents would have required re-erecting them before they could be properly packed. Had Pulleine ordered tents to be struck and the Zulu threat not materialized, he would have incurred criticism for the delay in packing the camp as well as appearing alarmist.

The Zulu had never before faced such firepower and it says much for their courage and tenacity that they not only endured it, but also overcame it to push home their attack. Those regiments in the fore-front of the attack were the youngest and least experienced. Zulu battle preparations included the use of stimulants, their snuff contain-ing a particularly potent form of ground cannabis. Coupled with the psychological stimulus of the usual pre-battle rituals, such a powerful drug could have enhanced battle performance. Some Zulu were also likely to be determined to prove equal to the honoured status of *abaqawe* (heroes) by displaying reckless courage. The speed with which the action had begun, however, meant that any customary rituals were swiftly truncated. If anything, such an explanation for Zulu prowess detracts from their achievement.[67]

When the withdrawal was ordered, Pope's company was the most isolated and evidence from the burials in June 1879 suggests few if any reached the camp.[68] Also separated from the rest of the 24th, Young-husband's company retreated up the slope of Isandlwana itself. One of these men was perhaps the last to die, occupying a cave high up on the mountain until shot at about 17.00. Durnford died with sixty or so men on the saddle and slopes of Black's kopje. George Shepstone took some of the Natal Native Contingent—possibly from Erskine's or Murray's companies—to the rear of Isandlwana, trying to hold open the line of retreat. His body was found with about 100 others on the south-western slope of the mountain. There are only fleeting glimpses of others. Many of the 24th were found behind the nek in dongas to the right of the road. Lieutenant Edgar Anstey of F Company and a group of about sixty men were found on the banks of the Manzi-myama stream some 2 miles behind Isandlwana.

The desperate struggle in and around the saddle kept the Zulu horns from closing sufficiently to enable some to flee. The survivors, includ-ing some who decided at an early stage that discretion was the better part of valour, were forced down towards the Buffalo, about 3½ miles distant. What became known as Fugitives' Trail was a nightmare of gullies and broken ground. The Buffalo at Sothondose's Drift (soon to be Fugitives' Drift) was in full spate and included both a whirlpool and a rocky gorge, through which the water took on the characteristics of a torrent. So bad was the ground for horses that Zulu easily kept up with those fleeing on horseback. The artillery galloped through the camp, but one gun overturned and the other was caught in a ravine about 400 yards beyond the nek. There was no time to spike either gun and they were both hauled away by the Zulu.

It is usually suggested that 445 individuals escaped from the field, but this may overestimate the number of African survivors, of whom only eighty-five are definitely known. While the traditional total for European survivors is fifty-five, the actual total appears to be seventy-eight, with a further two probable and fourteen whose fates are unknown.[69] Only five regular officers survived: Essex, Smith-Dorrien, Curling, Gardner, and Cochrane. Just ten members of the 24th escaped the field: four men attached to the mounted infantry, three survivors from Russell's rocket battery, two bandsmen, and Glyn's groom. The Zulu lost at least 1,000 killed or died of wounds. Many more Zulu were horribly wounded. Some were still to be found by travellers like Bertram Mitford in 1882, having survived terrible wounds, but Mitford commented on how few wounded Zulu were to be seen.[70]

Rorke's Drift

As the survivors fled, the uNdi corps—notably the uThulwan—were anxious to gain some kudos for themselves, especially given the prominence of the rival iNgobamakhosi in the battle they had missed: these had been the two regiments that had clashed in 1878. The iNdluyengwe participated in the pursuit down the Fugitives' Trail but the others did not. The Zulu seemingly intended merely a limited incursion to burn farms and lift cattle and then happened upon what appeared to be the tempting target of Rorke's Drift defended by only a few redcoats. Some of the uNdi corps did pursue plunder in the direction of Helpmekaar. Cetshwayo was reportedly angry that his orders not to enter Natal had been ignored. Zibhebhu, slightly wounded in the hand at Isandlwana, turned back when the reserve

Figure 7. A Zulu view of Rorke's Drift from the north showing the rocky ledge that assisted the defence, the reconstructed hospital to the right and the . commissariat store to the left.

reached the Buffalo but the ambitious Dabulamanzi did not. The iNgobamakhosi and uMbonambi also declined to cross the river.[71] In all, about 3,000–4,000 Zulu attacked Rorke's Drift.

Spalding was absent from the garrison at Rorke's Drift, having left to speed along two companies of the 1/24th still at Helpmekaar. Chard had ridden to Isandlwana early that morning to clarify his orders. These had directed him to send up some of his engineers from Rorke's Drift, where he was overseeing the two ponts used to ferry men and supplies across the Buffalo, one actually a cask ferry. Chard arrived at the camp just before Durnford. By this time, Zulu had been seen on the plateau. Worried that there might be a 'dash at the ponts',[72] Chard returned to Rorke's Drift passing Durnford on the track and told Spalding what he had seen. Leaving Chard in command, Spalding departed about 14.00 with the immortal words, 'nothing will happen and I shall be back again this evening early'.[73] That morning NCOs on top of the Oskarberg had heard gunfire but could see nothing. The

Revd George Smith, Surgeon Reynolds, and (supposedly) Otto Witt went up during the early afternoon and saw what they assumed to be Natal Native Contingent columns approaching the Buffalo from the direction of Isandlwana. As the columns came closer it was apparent they were Zulu. They also saw riders coming on in great haste and hurried back down to see what it portended.

Once on the Natal bank after crossing the river, Gardner conferred with Essex and Cochrane and sent a message to Rorke's Drift and another to Helpmekaar, going on to the latter himself. Two privates from the mounted infantry squadron carried Gardner's message to Rorke's Drift although it was a Natal Carbineer who arrived first. Another of those who reached Rorke's Drift was Lieutenant James Adendorff of Krohn's Natal Native Contingent Company at about 15.15. Adendorff, who claimed to have escaped Isandlwana 'by the road', met up with Lieutenant Vaines of the Natal Native Contingent, who had escaped down the Fugitives' Trail. Vaines appears to have ridden direct to Pietermaritzburg while Adendorff arrived at Rorke's Drift accompanied by Trooper Sibthorpe of the Carbineers.[74] Adendorff encountered Chard by the ponts shortly before Bromhead summoned Chard back to the post. Other survivors continued to pass. Lieutenant Alfred Henderson arrived with some of the Hlubi Troop at about 15.30. At Chard's request, Henderson threw out his men as advanced picquets. On the first appearance of the Zulu at about 16.20, they rapidly fled. Their flight had an immediate knock-on effect upon Captain William Stevenson and his large company of the 2/3rd Natal Native Contingent, which had been stationed at Rorke's Drift to undertake labouring tasks. One of Stevenson's fleeing white NCOs was shot down by the outraged defenders.

According to Chard's official report, Adendorff remained to assist in the defence, thus theoretically being the only man to fight at both Isandlwana and Rorke's Drift. Considerable doubt has always surrounded Adendorff's role. Some believe Chard mistakenly attributed to Adendorff actions undertaken by Corporal Francis Attwood of the Army Service Corps. It is also suggested that Vaines and Adendorff were subsequently arrested, but that no further action was taken, possibly because proceedings would have reflected adversely upon Chard's report and because Bromhead ordered Vaines to carry a warning to Helpmekaar. Vaines, however, was not among the forty-eight known survivors of Isandlwana who gathered at Helpmekaar.[75] Conductor Bob Hall of the Army Commissariat and Transport Department was the author of the anonymous account in the *Natal Witness* on 18 February 1879 often attributed to Adendorff. Walter Stafford did recall Adendorff telling him in 1883 he had been present but this was in 1928. On the other hand, Adendorff was seen by others, including Harford who sketched him at Rorke's Drift on the morning of 23 January.[76]

Bromhead may have considered evacuating the post or fighting outside it but Acting Assistant Commissary James Dalton, an experienced former NCO, pointed out they could not outrun the Zulu with the hospital patients in wagons. It was resolved to stay put and fortify the post. Another experienced former NCO, Assistant Commissary Walter Dunne, helped Dalton prepare the defences. Chard arrived back from the ponts when the defences were already being constructed and shortly before the party returned from the top of the Oskarberg. While Revd Smith stayed to aid the defence so far as he could, Witt departed for Helpmekaar. Recently, it has been suggested by author Katie Stossel that Witt left Rorke's Drift some days before the battle and has been consistently mistaken for another Swede, August Hammar, who was the one present on the morning of 22 January before leaving. Witt's highly embroidered account was pure fiction.[77]

A 4-feet-high wall of mealie sacks and of biscuit and meat boxes was constructed, linking the Commissariat Store in Witt's former mission church and the Hospital in Witt's former home. Two wagons were incorporated into the south wall while the north wall was run along a 5-foot-high rocky ledge that gave additional height to the defence and blunted any Zulu charge at that point. A line of biscuit boxes was laid across the yard between the two buildings as an inner barricade. The hospital was also loopholed. Local South African historian Pat Rundgren has argued that Crealock's sketch of Chelmsford's troops arriving at Rorke's Drift on the morning of 23 January, later reproduced in the *Illustrated London News*, shows much of the north wall incomplete. Rundgren speculated that the Zulu arrived before the defences were finished and that the defence was assisted by the Zulu arriving 'in dribs and drabs' rather than en masse.[78] On the other hand, Captain John Tongue of the 2/24th criticized Crealock's sketch, suggesting the mealie sacks were shown too high and there was a 'low breastwork' connecting the hospital to the rest of the defences.[79] It has been noted previously that the barricade immediately in front of the hospital was not complete since the slope there was not conducive to a mealie bag wall. An inner wall was then constructed but with a mere plank sealing the gap as the Zulu arrived. If the sketch is accurate then there was a far greater gap closer to the

Figure 8. John North Crealock's sketch of the relief of Rorke's Drift as reproduced in the *Illustrated London News*, 8 March 1879.

storeroom. Equally, it has been argued there is evidence that some defences had been constructed at Rorke's Drift by 11 January.[80]

With the Natal Native Contingent's departure, a total of perhaps 139 men remained at Rorke's Drift although the precise number is debated. The majority were from B Company of the 2/24th but there were also other members of the 24th; a few from other regiments; supporting commissary, medical, and hospital staff; some artillerymen and engineers; some Europeans from the Natal Native Contingent and colonial volunteers; and the non-combatant Smith. Twenty were bed patients—although Surgeon Reynolds later suggested only eight to ten were totally incapacitated—and a further fifteen ambulatory patients who could at least assist in the defence so that there were probably 119 actual combatant defenders. Subsequently, there were fraudulent claims by men who said they had been at Rorke's Drift and even impersonations of VC winners.[81] Similarly, there were many who claimed to be witnesses of, or the 'last survivor' from, Custer's Last Stand.[82]

The first attack came at about 16.30, the Zulu from the younger iNdluyengwe directing their attack at the south wall. The iNdluyengwe crossed the Buffalo above Fugitives' Drift where the water was calmer, while the other regiments—all men in their forties—crossed further upstream by forming human chains. Sustained fire halted the iNdluyengwe at about 50 yards and they took cover in the mission station's walled vegetable garden and orchard. As more Zulu arrived they reached the barricade but were forced back, although the compound in front of the hospital was abandoned at about 17.00. The height of the barricades and the reach of the Martini-Henry's 'lunger' bayonet placed the Zulu at a disadvantage. The main body of the Zulu now approached from the forward slopes of the Oskarberg, having circled the post to the west at about 17.30. Some stationed themselves up on the Oskarberg's ledges and in caves to fire down into the post, although without much effect.

Whether the Zulu used Martini-Henrys at Rorke's Drift has been continuously debated. Colour Sergeant Frank Bourne thought so and it is conceivable that some were picked up at Isandlwana either from Dyson's section or perhaps from the engineers overwhelmed on the track behind Isandlwana.[83] Four of the seventeen British fatalities died from gunshot wounds, and ten of the fifteen injured had similar wounds. It has been argued that the bullets' strange noises and the randomness of wounding mentioned in defenders' accounts chime more with obsolete firearms.[84] The surgeon who subsequently examined some of the wounds also said they were 'ordinary round bullets fired from smooth-bored guns' with low powder charges.[85]

There were a series of uncoordinated rushes at the western end of the north wall. At about 18.00 the Zulu almost broke over the south wall and Chard ordered the evacuation of the yard adjacent to the hospital. While concentrating the defence, the order left the hospital and its patients, plus the six men allocated to defend them, vulnerable. Between about 18.20 and 19.15 a desperate hand-to-hand struggle ensued as the Zulu broke into the hospital, which lacked interior doors. With the hospital thatch catching fire—in the prevailing wet conditions it burned slowly—the defenders hacked through the interior walls, dragging what patients they could with them. The patients were lowered into the yard through a window and, with covering fire from the inner barricade, had to cross it to reach safety. Author Neil Thornton has recently concluded from a scrutiny of surviving accounts that Private Henry Hook and one patient, Private Connolly, did not escape into the yard through the hospital's gable end window as the others had, but through the low kitchen extension window. They were therefore actually outside the defensive perimeter before regaining safety.[86] With the Zulu now trying to fire the thatched roof of the storehouse, Chard ordered an additional pile of mealie bags to be heaped in front of the store as a last redoubt, a task undertaken by Walter Dunne.

At dusk one of the defenders thought he saw troops on the Help-mekaar road, the resulting cheering confusing the Zulu. Spalding had started to return with the two missing companies, meeting various fugitives. Riding ahead, and about 3 miles from Rorke's Drift, he saw the hospital in flames and, with Zulu approaching, ordered a with-drawal to Helpmekaar. The Zulu now pressed the attack on the storehouse but were illuminated by the glare of the flames, eventually pulling back at about 20.30. There were intermittent attacks mostly aimed at the cattle kraal until about midnight. There were no more attacks after 04.00 on 23 January and, by 05.00, it was realized the Zulu had gone. A large group was observed at about 07.00, presumed to be separate from those who had attacked Rorke's Drift and those who passed Chelmsford's force as it approached. They also melted away. Chard reported that 351 Zulu were buried on 23 January but it is likely that the Zulu lost about 600 killed and died of wounds, includ-ing those finished off by the British.

Had Rorke's Drift fallen then Helpmekaar might have been aban-doned, although whether the Zulu would have pressed on into Natal is doubtful. Certainly, it would have added to the panic that gripped Natal, with hasty laagers being formed for civilians at a number of locations, forts at others, and plans made to fortify key buildings in Durban. It evinced not just fear of the Zulu but also suspicion of the African population within Natal.[87] There was also the sense of loss given the fatalities among the colonial volunteers and police.[88] A total of fifty-seven volunteers and police died in addition to George Shepstone and seventeen European officers and seventy European NCOs of the native units.[89] The volunteer units invariably drew on some of the most prominent settler families in Natal.[90]

Aftermath

Conceivably, ordinary Zulu did not comprehend the implications of what had happened at Isandlwana and Rorke's Drift. Cetshwayo was deeply shocked by the casualties inflicted by the British even in defeat. He was angered that his commanders had allowed the army to attack before its pre-battle rituals had been properly undertaken and, then subsequently, allowed it to disperse. It was two months before Cetsh-wayo was able to summon the *amabutho* again.

On the same day as Isandlwana, Pearson inflicted a defeat on another Zulu force of 4,000–5,000 men at Nyezane, resulting in perhaps another 300 Zulu dead. Pearson then fortified a position at Eshowe and was effectively besieged there until early April 1879. In the north, Wood carried out a series of raids from his base at Kambula. Wood was worsted in the raid on Hlobane on 28 March when encountering the main *impi* of some 20,000 men. The Zulu assault on Wood's entrenchment the following day resulted in perhaps another 2,000 Zulu dead. Together with the repulse of some 10,000 Zulu sent against Chelmsford's Eshowe relief force at Gingindlovu, which cost another 1,000 or so Zulu dead, Kambula ended any hopes Cetshwayo might have entertained of forcing the British to negotiate. His approaches were rebuffed. Defections increased, notably that of Cetshwayo's brother, Hamu.

With considerable reinforcements received from England, Chelmsford embarked on a second invasion of Zululand on 31 May, spurred on by the knowledge that Wolseley was being sent to supersede him. Wolseley did not reach the Cape until 23 June. Exasperation with Chelmsford increased with the laborious pace of the second advance. Another disaster had already befallen a convoy escorted by a detachment of the 80th Foot at Ntombe on 12 March. On 1 June the Prince Imperial, serving in a voluntary capacity, was killed out on a small patrol, adding to Chelmsford's woes. Pointedly ignoring Wolseley's orders that he halt, Chelmsford's force of some 5,500 men advancing in square formation finally shattered some 20,000 Zulu outside Ulundi on 4 July. Zulu losses may have exceeded 1,500 dead. The intensity of the Zulu attack was still considerable, some reaching within 30 yards of the square despite the overwhelming fire put down. The scale of the final defeat proved fatal to Cetshwayo's authority. Wolseley received the submissions of the chiefs following Cetshwayo's flight and the King was run to ground by a patrol on 28 August 1879.

The British government no longer had any appetite for annexation. The settlement imposed by Wolseley entailed the fragmentation of the Zulu kingdom into thirteen segments under 'reliable' chiefs such as Hamu and John Dunn, although they also included Ntshingwayo and Zibhebhu. Wolseley went on to defeat Sekhukhune of the Pedi, who was captured in December 1879. By the time Wolseley left South Africa in April 1880 the political situation in the Transvaal was fast deteriorating. The Anglo-Transvaal War was to break out in December 1880.

4

Heroes and Scapegoats

The successful defence of Rorke's Drift did not prevent rising criticism of Chelmsford and Frere. Having read Chelmsford's despatch on Isandlwana, one of the officers of the 1/24th, Lieutenant William Lloyd, wrote, 'Ld. C better take care or he may find that certain things he did *not* mention in his drivelling report may come out.'[1] As Richard Stevens of the Natal Mounted Police wrote after his escape from Isandlwana, 'There will be an awful row at home about this.'[2] Conveniently deceased, Durnford was an obvious scapegoat, although there was also an attempt to blame Glyn.

Questions and Enquiries

Chelmsford's Court of Enquiry held on 27 January was deliberately restricted to investigating 'the loss of the camp' and not the 'circumstances of the disastrous affair'. It merely ascertained 'what orders were given for the defence of the camp, and how these orders were carried out'.[3] The three members of the court—Colonel Fairfax Hassard, Chelmsford's commanding Royal Engineer, and Lieutenant Colonels Francis Law and Arthur Harness of the Royal Artillery reached no conclusion: 'instructions on this point were not given to it'.[4] Law and Hassard favoured stating an opinion but Harness resisted.[5] Harness may have been placed on the enquiry to ensure that he could not give evidence himself.

The enquiry recorded the statements of eight individuals: Clery, Glyn, Gardner, Essex, Cochrane, Smith-Dorrien, Curling, and Nourse. Those of Glyn and Smith-Dorrien were so brief as to contribute nothing, while Essex and Curling confined themselves to submitting written statements. Supplementary statements were submitted after the enquiry by Crealock and Cochrane, while Gardner supplied a statement separate from his evidence. Lieutenant Harry Davies of the Edendale Troop completed a statement later in February.[6] Gosset also produced an account, which was appended to a pamphlet, 'The Isandula Disaster', produced by Lieutenant Walter James of the War Office Intelligence Branch.[7] Curling later wrote that he had not anticipated that the proceedings would be published and few of those called had taken the trouble 'to make a readable statement'.[8] Other statements were taken but Harness believed there was no point recording 'statements hardly bearing on the loss of the camp but giving doubtful particulars of small incidents more or less ghastly in their nature'. Harness also discounted evidence that either merely corroborated that already recorded or was 'so unreliable that it was worthless', suggesting that if a 'mass of statements' was intended then it could have been recorded by 'three subalterns or three clerks'.[9]

From what he had been told, Frere already believed on 27 January that the camp had fallen because Durnford had overruled Pulleine, a point also conveyed to the Queen's private secretary, Sir Henry Ponsonby, by Frere's daughter that same day.[10] Writing home on 3 February, Captain Francis Grenfell, Chelmsford's deputy assistant adjutant-general, said Durnford had disregarded the orders to defend the camp.[11] Chelmsford's interpreter, the Hon. William Drummond, was still pulling together statements from native sources on 9 February, yet already emphasizing that Durnford had pulled rank on Pulleine.[12] Colonel William Bellairs, acting deputy adjutant-general at Pietermaritzburg, placed the blame firmly on Durnford, urging Chelmsford to publish the enquiry results quickly 'as calculated to remove many erroneous impressions since entertained'.[13] Chelmsford's own notes on the enquiry, probably written in April, noted that Durnford had been ordered to take command of the camp and ignored instructions by moving out of it.[14]

The military periodical, the *Broad Arrow*, suggested initially that 'strange oversights on the part of certain superior officers and a contemptuous opinion of the enemy's intelligence mainly contributed to the disaster of Isandula; while the blindness of Colonel Durnford and the mistaken generosity of Colonel Pulleine in rushing to succour produced it'. Following the enquiry—'the last chapter of Rasselas over again—a "conclusion" in which nothing is concluded'—it began to hint at Chelmsford's culpability.[15] An internal War Office memorandum as early as 11 February 1879, based on the first reports reaching London, largely ascribed blame to Chelmsford for not fortifying his camp, for not keeping in contact with the enemy, and for being 'decoyed' by the Zulu.[16] The army's commander-in-chief, George, Duke of Cambridge, did his best to defend Chelmsford but wanted answers.

Pressed for more information, Chelmsford tried in April to shift some blame to Glyn: 'it would be hardly fair to saddle me with the responsibility of any neglect of details connected with the command of No. 3 Column, for the performance of which the Officer Commanding the column was held accountable to me'.[17] Crealock wrote to his brother on 2 March that the choice of Isandlwana as camp, the placing of outposts, and all interior arrangements were Glyn's responsibility.[18] Even earlier, on 20 February, Chelmsford wrote to Bellairs that Glyn had not objected to any orders given him and he had not interfered with Glyn as regards 'outposts, patrolling, and the ordinary precautions for the safety of the Camp'.[19]

The wily Clery saw the trap being set for Glyn when he was asked to provide full details of how camp regulations had been carried out. Clery almost certainly wrote Glyn's carefully crafted replies to Bellairs on 26 February.[20] Glyn and Clery 'accepted all responsibility for details, but declined to admit *any responsibility for the movement of any portion of the troops in or out of camp*'.[21] Clery reiterated on 28 April that Glyn was a 'complete cipher', revealing that it was he who had issued the last minute orders to Pulleine to defend the camp when he realized

Chelmsford had left none. Chelmsford expressed his relief that Clery had done so.[22] Clery's supposed written order to Pulleine was never found and it is likely that it was only ever oral, as implied by Cochrane in his evidence to the enquiry.[23] Penn Symons later recalled that Gosset, as well as Crealock, did his best to throw the blame on Glyn and Clery.[24]

On behalf of Cambridge, the adjutant general, Sir Charles Ellice, submitted a detailed list of questions to Chelmsford on 6 March 1879. Why had Rorke's Drift and Isandlwana not been put into a state of defence? What steps had been taken to reconnoitre the area? Why did Chelmsford not respond to Pulleine's messages?[25] Chelmsford's reply, sent through the secretary of state for war, Frederick Stanley, failed to convince Cambridge, who could not understand why the camp had not been fortified according to Chelmsford's own field regulations.[26] Cambridge believed Chelmsford had fatally underestimated the Zulu: the principal blame lay with him.[27]

On returning to Britain, Chelmsford was invited to Balmoral, although Beaconsfield refused to see him at his home at Hughenden, granting only a cursory interview at Downing Street in November 1879. Henry Ponsonby concluded from his conversation with Chelmsford that someone else was always responsible for all that had gone wrong.[28] Nonetheless, the Queen remained supportive. Wood and his second in command, Redvers Buller, followed Chelmsford to Balmoral, both making a very favourable impression. Wood suggested that he and Buller were pleased that Cambridge had shown 'loyalty to his generals' in not superseding Chelmsford immediately after Isandlwana.[29] Yet, they were still highly critical of Chelmsford and Crealock.[30]

Attacked in February 1880 by Archibald Forbes for his conduct of the campaign,[31] Chelmsford responded with a memorandum that repeated the now familiar denigration of Durnford.[32] Harness also defended Chelmsford in *Fraser's Magazine* in response to Forbes, although this served primarily to justify his own part in the enquiry.[33] Chelmsford again defended himself in *The Times* in August 1880.[34]

Figure 9. Riviere and Hersee's 'Grand March, Honor to the Brave' celebrating Chard and Bromhead, 1879.

Chelmsford, however, was never able to shake off the shadow of Isandlwana. He was not entrusted again with a field command.

Durnford's brother, Edward, also a Royal Engineer, had no intention of letting matters rest. In 1880, he published a detailed refutation of Chelmsford's Lords speech.[35] Edward Durnford cooperated with Frances Colenso, who had been romantically involved with Anthony Durnford, on her history of the war and its origins. She referred to the 'undisguised attempts that have been made to throw the blame on the dead', maintaining those who had died were not responsible for the selection of the campsite, the neglect of proper scouting, the subdivision of the force, the refusal to respond to messages from Isandlwana, and the turning back of Harness's force when it might have relieved the defenders.[36]

Edward Durnford then published a memoir of his brother in 1882. Two years later Durnford circulated yet another defence.[37] In 1885, prompted by Frances Colenso, the commanding Royal Engineer in Natal, Colonel Charles Luard, followed enquiries begun by his predecessor. These pursued the rumour originating in 1879 with Seaward Longhurst, veterinary surgeon of the King's Dragoon Guards, that Chelmsford's actual orders to Durnford and other papers had been removed from his body by Captain Theophilus 'Offy' Shepstone Jnr when the burial party returned to the scene in May 1879. The *Natal Witness* on 27 May 1879 reported that papers were removed from Durnford's body. In the midst of the ongoing controversy, as Frances Colenso continued to badger Offy Shepstone and Edward Durnford tracked down Longhurst in India, Shepstone borrowed the newspaper's relevant file in 1882. When it was returned, the report had been cut out 'apparently with a knife'.[38]

Luard's enquiries led him to the brother of a former Natal Carbineer, who had found papers in a portmanteau near Durnford's body. These consisted primarily of the order directing Durnford to move to Rorke's Drift on 19 January, and a copy of Chelmsford's instructions for column commanders. In January 1885 Luard asked the inspector general of fortifications, Sir Andrew Clarke, to order an enquiry and sent him a lengthy statement of the evidence he had collected.[39] Clarke pressed the matter and the enquiry took place in April 1886. While authorized, it became clear that it was not intended to delve too deeply. It was restricted to ascertaining whether papers had been removed from Durnford's body.[40] Shepstone was acquitted of any wrongdoing and Luard forced to apologize. Crealock's order book found on the field had been returned to him in June 1879 but he chose not to divulge its survival until pressed on the point in May 1882. Edward Durnford was shown it in Crealock's house but only when enquiries were made on behalf of Clarke's successor as inspector general, Lothian Nicholson, in July 1886 did Crealock say he would reveal it if officially asked to do so. His interest presumably prompted by the Luard case, Nicholson said the information was for his private use only.[41]

Supposedly, as Clarke requested, it was agreed in 1887 to review the official history, but in 1907 it was reprinted without correction. That official history, *Narrative of the Field Operations Connected with the Zulu War of 1879*, was compiled for the War Office Intelligence Branch in 1881 by Major John Sutton Rothwell. Rothwell derived information from the early report prepared by Walter James and from the enquiry. Rothwell also drew on the candid correspondence received by the head of the branch, Sir Archibald Alison, official despatches, and reports. Dispassionate official history was not intended to raise controversies unnecessarily or to criticize the conduct of operations. Consequently, Rothwell accepted that Durnford took command of the camp on his arrival, having been summoned to Isandlwana for that purpose. The Natal Native Contingent fled and opened up the fatal gap in the defence line.[42]

It was fortunate that Rorke's Drift could be manipulated in an attempt to deflect attention from Isandlwana, much as the defeat of Evelyn Wood at Hlobane on 28 March was to be effectively cancelled out by his crushing victory at Kambula the next day. Speaking in the Lords on 13 February, Beaconsfield characterized Isandlwana as a 'terrible military disaster' but not a defeat arising from anything other than accidental circumstances. Rorke's Drift, on the other hand, proved 'that the stamina and valour of the English soldiery have not diminished'.[43]

The Rorke's Drift VCs

Rorke's Drift was claimed to have saved Natal from a Zulu invasion, although Cetshwayo never had any such intention. Wolseley noted sourly that the situation had left the defenders of Rorke's Drift with no recourse but to fight 'like rats for their lives which they could not otherwise save'.[44] That was the general reaction in South Africa. Clery wrote in May that 'until the accounts came out from England nobody had thought of the Rorke's Drift affair except as one in which the private soldiers of the 24th behaved so well'.[45] Arriving in South Africa with reinforcements, Lieutenant Colonel Philip Anstruther commented that too much was made of Rorke's Drift at home for 'they were fighting for their lives and could not have done anything else'.[46] The defenders might have had no choice, but the Zulu did, and they continued to attack despite their horrific casualties.[47]

The defence of Rorke's Drift became sufficiently important, given the criticism of Chelmsford's conduct of the campaign, for Chard's report to be issued as if it were a general order on 7 February.[48] Chard was pressed to put pen to paper because Chelmsford was 'anxious to send that gleam of sunshine home as soon as possible'.[49] With paper at Rorke's Drift in exceedingly short supply and amid persistent heavy rain, Chard managed to produce a detailed, well-crafted, and coherent account on 25 January. It has been suggested that Clery had a major hand in this report and conceivably also that of Bromhead on 15 February. However, stylometric analysis suggests Chard wrote his original report and also that subsequently submitted to the Queen in February 1880. It still remains entirely possible that Chard was assisted materially by Clery, Crealock, and perhaps Bromhead so that it was effectively a team effort.[50]

While Chard noted the efforts of all leading participants, it was Bromhead who recommended VCs for Corporal William Allen, and Privates Fred Hitch, Henry Hook, Robert Jones, William Jones, and John Williams (whose real name was Fielding). Hook, Robert Jones, and William Jones were three of the six men allocated to defend the hospital. It was generally assumed that a fourth, Joseph Williams, would have received the VC had he survived. As Bromhead's commanding officer, Degacher felt the six all worthy of the award.[51]

Chelmsford nominated Chard and Bromhead directly whereas normally their immediate superiors should have done so. Few had anything good to say about either man. Wolseley presented Chard with his VC in July and Bromhead with his in September. Neither impressed him. Wolseley never saw 'a more uninteresting or more stupid-looking fellow' than Chard, but then concluded Bromhead equally so.[52] Wood and Buller thought Chard 'a dull heavy man who seemed scarcely ever able to do his regular work'. Bromhead 'was fearless but hopelessly stupid'. Both believed the real brain behind the defence had been Dalton.[53] Clery felt there was little to be said of Chard and Bromhead beyond that they were good fellows. Bromhead withdrew into his own world, declining to talk about the action and procrastinating when asked for his report.[54] Curling and a fellow engineer of Chard's, Captain Walter Parke, were just as damning. Parke could not understand why Chard had not approached Chelmsford to ask for a significant new appointment. Instead, Chard 'placidly smokes his pipe and does nothing'.[55] When Chard visited Balmoral, he demonstrated the story on the billiard table with books, boxes, and billiard balls standing in for buildings and defences, but as far as the Queen's assistant military secretary, Lieutenant Colonel Arthur Pickard VC, was concerned, revealed he was 'not a genius and not quick, but a quiet, plodding, dogged sort of fellow'.[56]

Questions were raised in the Commons as to why the nominations were confined to the 24th, and cases were made for Surgeon Reynolds, who was awarded the VC in May; Dalton, who received it in November;

and, finally, Corporal Ferdinand Schiess of the 2/3rd Natal Native Contingent in November. The *Broad Arrow* cautioned on 23 August against the 'lavish prodigality' of VCs, commenting further that the award might be 'cheapened by a too friendly eagerness in Pall Mall to recognise acts of equivocal valour'. Subsequently, it suggested, 'It is a curious historico-physiological fact that the smaller are England's wars the more prolific are England's heroes.'[57] The Distinguished Conduct Medal went to Bourne and four other defenders.

Melvill and Coghill

The adjutant of the 1/24th, Melvill, and Lieutenant Nevill Coghill also became the focus of a campaign for the VC. They had both escaped from Isandlwana, Melvill carrying the Queen's Colour of the 1/24th. At Fugitives' Drift, Melvill's horse lost its feet in the river and Melvill was swept to a rock to which Lieutenant Walter Higginson of the Natal Native Contingent was already clinging. Traditionally, the so-called

Figure 10. Fugitives' Drift seen from the Natal bank of the Buffalo. The prominent 'coffin rock' can be seen middle left.

'coffin rock' has been identified as the site of Melvill and Higginson's struggles but Ian Knight suggests Melvill was much closer to the Natal bank when his horse stumbled.[58]

Melvill lost his grip on the Colour and neither he nor Higginson could retrieve it. Having reached the river ahead of Melvill and having left Isandlwana before him, Coghill rode back in to try and assist. Coghill's horse was immediately shot. Reaching the Natal bank, Higginson ostensibly went to find horses but made off. Melvill and Coghill, who was hindered by a previous leg injury, struggled about half a mile up from the river, to be killed near the top of the heights on the Natal side. Ironically, it is believed that they were killed not by pursuing Zulu, since few ventured to cross the swollen river at that point, but by followers of Sihayo's brother, Gamdana kaXongo, who had pledged allegiance to the British. Some of his followers had been detained as spies but released that morning, while some of the younger warriors did not share their chief's new-found loyalty to the British. Francis Grenfell believed the recently released captives responsible.[59] Alternatively, those responsible may have been followers of Sothondose, Zulus long settled on the Natal bank. They were watching events and were urged to kill survivors by the pursuers calling across the river that they would face retribution if they did not do so. On the other hand, as they had been called upon to supply border levies, they may have been deterred from killing fugitives by fear of British reprisal.[60]

A party led by Major Wilsone Black discovered the bodies of Melvill and Coghill on 4 February. Alongside were those of two dead mounted infantrymen.[61] The remains of two cairns close to Melvill and Coghill's grave were identified in 2009. One of the two was almost certainly Sergeant Thomas Cooper of the 1/24th.[62] Henry Harford found the Colour and its case downstream on the following day.[63] The Regimental Colour of the 1/24th had been back at Helpmekaar. The Colours of the 2/24th were never recovered. A part of one of the staffs was found on Stony Kopje and part of another on the Fugitives' Trail, which might suggest a similar attempt to carry it to safety. Strangely, it was reported in 1894 that

Figure 11. The graves of Melvill and Coghill above Fugitives' Drift.

one of the Colours was in the hands of a Frenchman in Paris but this proved to be a copy, probably made for a bazaar.[64] Frere had a cross placed over Melvill and Coghill's grave in April 1879 when their bodies were placed in coffins. The cross on the rock overlooking the grave was vandalized in 1973 by presumed grave robbers but a new one was provided.

Glyn wrote the principal report on Melvill and Coghill on 21 February, consciously presenting their story in the most heroic light to further help the process of retrieving something from the disaster.[65] There was no actual evidence—other than a letter by an unidentified correspondent in the *Natal Mercury* on 26 February—on which the regimental history of the 24th could have concluded that Pulleine entrusted the Colour to Melvill with the words, 'You, as senior subaltern... will take the Colour and make your way from here.'[66] It has been suggested from one survivor's testimony, that Melvill brought the Colour forward from its guard tent towards the firing line before leaving with it.[67]

Wolseley was again critical of the praise accorded Melvill and Coghill, considering it undesirable to make heroes of men 'who taking advantage of their having horses bolted from the scene of action to save their lives'.[68] Even Chelmsford questioned whether Melvill would have received the VC if he had saved the Colour and himself. While Melvill may have been ordered to leave, 'he no doubt was given the best chance of saving his life which must have been lost had he remained in camp'. Chelmsford did not think Coghill was capable through his injury of having participated in any attempt to save the Colour and must have been 'a drag on poor Melvill' so that Melvill had 'lost his life endeavouring to save Coghill rather than vice versa'.[69]

In any case, the VC warrant did not allow for posthumous awards or, rather, assuming that it did not had become convention. Melvill's father was told in April 1879 that his son would have won the VC had he survived. Melvill's widow also received an annual pension of £100 at the Queen's request. When more cases arose during the South African War (1899–1902), Coghill's father revived the matter. King Edward VII twice refused to relent on the rule, but, when Melvill's widow directly petitioned him in December 1906, changed his mind. The rules were altered in January 1907 with Melvill and Coghill honoured together with four others, two of whose cases dated back to the Indian Mutiny.[70]

Arguments were also made for VCs to be awarded to Gardner, Higginson, Adendorff, and Trooper Barker of the Natal Carbineers, who had given up his horse to Higginson and been deserted by him. Pointedly, Chelmsford rejected any consideration of Adendorff on the grounds that his early arrival at Rorke's Drift meant he had left Isandlwana 'way before he had any right to do so'. Higginson's failure to return to help Melvill and Coghill after he went off for horses ruled him out. As for Gardner, rumours began to circulate that his departure from Helpmekaar had been somewhat hasty, a little ditty going the rounds, 'I very much fear that the Zulus are near. So hang it, I'm off to Dundee.'[71] Evelyn Wood recommended Barker in March 1879 but his action was not deemed to fall under the statutes.[72] The one VC awarded for Isandlwana went to Private Samuel Wassall of the 80th Foot attached to the mounted infantry, for saving the life of Private Thomas Westwood at Fugitives' Drift. An existing VC was killed at Isandlwana, Private William Griffiths of the 2/24th, having been awarded it for saving lives in a storm off the Andaman Islands in May 1867.

The Early Histories

Early histories of the war did not add materially to the contemporary debate on blame. Duncan Moodie's general history of conflict in South Africa—first published in Australia in October 1879—relied entirely on press sources, which included interviews with participants. Son of a prominent Natal official, Moodie moved to Adelaide in 1869 and worked mostly as a journalist both there and when he returned to Natal in 1883. He dabbled in poetry. A rather excruciating example of Moodie's verse, 'Isandhlwana', formed a frontispiece to his history. The book was revised and republished in Cape Town in 1888. It followed a consistent line justifying British policy. The proceedings of the enquiry were included in full with defeat ascribed to a failure to laager the camp and to Durnford disobeying orders.[73] Alexander Wilmot's *History of the Zulu War*, also published in 1880, had no doubt that the war was a means of rolling back the 'tide of savagery'. Curiously, Wilmot made no mention of Coghill in his account of saving the Colours, erroneously claiming they had been wrapped around Melvill's body.[74]

The South African Campaign, 1879, compiled by J. P. Mackinnon and Sydney Shadbolt, followed the findings of the enquiry and suggested Durnford took command of the camp, and that the Natal Native Contingent collapsed. Primarily, it was a eulogy, providing a brief biography of fallen officers and outline service records for all officers and units that served in Zululand.[75] Waller Ashe's history accepted that the war was justified by the dangerous nature of the Zulu kingdom and by Cetshwayo encouraging Sekhukhune's defiance of the British. In this account too Durnford took command of the camp, and the Natal Native Contingent broke at the crucial moment, although Ashe did pass some of the responsibility for not laagering to Glyn and Pulleine.[76]

Interest in the war had waned by the end of the 1880s for it was overtaken by other events in Afghanistan and by the Anglo-Transvaal War in South Africa itself. The onward march of empire—the occupation of Egypt in 1882, the ensuing campaigns in the Sudan in 1884–5 and the death of Charles Gordon at Khartoum, the reconquest of the Sudan, and the South African War—pressed on public attention. It was not until the 1930s that the controversies were briefly revived. W. H. Clements's *The Glamour and Tragedy of the Zulu War* (1936) once more criticized Chelmsford's conduct of the campaign. It is not clear what motivated Clements. Moving to South Africa as a child, he found that that there was 'a hazy idea that once upon a time there was a war between the Zulus and Imperial and Colonial Troops'.[77] As a journalist, Clements relied heavily on earlier journalists' accounts. His judgement was that laagering or forming square would have saved the camp. As the British official historian of the Great War, Brigadier General James Edmonds, put it in reviewing the book, Isandlwana and other Zulu battles 'mean little to the present generation'.[78] While noting that Clements had not apparently consulted Rothwell's official account and got some officers' names wrong, Edmonds was satisfied that it was far more than the 'semi-historical narrative' Clements claimed. Edmonds did not challenge Clements's view that Chelmsford was 'one of the worst misfits the British army ever produced'.[79]

Clements provoked the Hon. Gerald French to publish a robust defence, *Lord Chelmsford and the Zulu War* (1939). French was well used to the exercise of historical defence since he had done the same for his own father, Field Marshal Lord French. Ironically, one of Lord French's own targets in the 'battle of the memoirs' following the Great War was the best known survivor of Isandlwana, Sir Horace Smith-Dorrien, who in 1914–15 commanded successively II Corps and Second Army. Declaring that Clements's book was founded for the most part on 'the worthless tittle-tattle of prejudiced correspondents', French based his book on Chelmsford's papers as arranged by Gosset in 1906.[80] If Clements was repeating the 'same old charges',[81] French followed the familiar defence. Durnford had written orders to take command of the camp in Chelmsford's absence and to act only on the defensive. The Natal Native Contingent had given way, allowing the Zulu to 'burst through the gap'.[82] Those who attacked Chelmsford were 'busybodies, know-alls, and copy-hunters'.[83] French reproduced Walter James's map of the supposed position at Isandlwana at 13.00 as drawn in March 1879 but altered it to show the Natal Native Contingent fleeing rather than the Zulu breaking the firing line.[84] H. J. P. Wilkins also published *The Story of the Blood Drenched Field of Isandhlwana* in South Africa for the sixtieth anniversary but it had nothing new to say.

At that point, with a second global war intervening, the Zulu War once more receded into obscurity.

5

Impacts

Prior to 1879 the Zulu were virtually unknown to the British public. 'Zoolas' were just one 'Kaffir' tribe in the 1843 edition of the *Encyclopædia Britannica*, although they had become Zulu in the 1860 edition.[1] By the 1860s illustrations and some photographs had appeared in published accounts of travellers and big game hunters but the audiences for these and for occasional lectures at London institutes such as the Royal Geographical Society were small.[2] The first mention of Zulu appeared in *The Times* only in 1849. So uncertain was the knowledge of Zululand that the newspaper reported rumours in 1867 that David Livingstone had been murdered by Zulu near Lake Nyasa.[3] As Clements put, 'Probably not one person in ten thousand in the Homeland knew where Zululand was. Judging from comments made in the English Houses of Parliament and published in the press, even members of the House were at sea as to its true geographical locality.'[4] By the following year, Frederick Fynney suggested, Zulu was 'almost a household word'.[5]

A negative image of Shaka as an 'unstructured catalogue of vices' emerged from traders' accounts after his death, albeit one that accorded with that of Shaka's African opponents.[6] Frere's equating of Cetshwayo with Shaka seems to have been based on Nathaniel Isaacs's account, published in 1836.[7] Traders' accounts—invariably drawing from each other—were intended partly to conceal their own disreputable activities as well as to promote the need for annexation. The picture was built upon by missionaries whose work Cetshwayo frustrated, notably the Norwegian Hans Schreuder of the Lutheran Hermannsburger Mission, established in Zululand in 1859, and the Revd Robert Robertson. Originally sent into Zululand by Bishop Colenso in 1859, Robertson became a separate missionary bishop in 1870. He began placing anonymous stories in the Natal press alleging Cetshwayo's supposed atrocities from 1875 onwards.[8] Missionaries established the image of indigenous peoples in metropolitan societies through their fundraising and publications.[9] That of the Zulu was strikingly similar to the negative view of Xhosa culture formed through the 'closing of the missionary mind' as well as hardening settler opinion.[10] The Revd Holditch Mason argued that those in England could 'scarcely realise the idea of human beings suffering torture, too terrible to mention, at the hands of the Zulus'. Cetshwayo intended a 'war of extermination' against Europeans.[11] Ironically, the overthrow of the Zulu polity did not benefit the missionaries: there were fewer mission stations in Zululand in the 1880s than before the war.[12]

The Press

The war occurred as British society became increasingly urbanized and industrialized. Although the Education Act of 1870 and the Scottish Education Act of 1872 promoted literacy, the war occurred at a point where it was still transitioning from functional to habitual literacy.[13] The army's own educational provision had also expanded so that, by 1878, it claimed 46.8 per cent of troops had attained a 'superior level of education', although this was not all it seemed.[14] A survey of the files of sixty-five Rorke's Drift defenders shows that thirty-eight (58 per cent) had attained their certificate of education. Forbes commented that he had never seen as much letter writing by ordinary soldiers as he did in Zululand.[15] Colour Sergeant (later Lieutenant Colonel) Frank Bourne may have written letters for others at Rorke's Drift,[16] but, as the editor of the *South Wales Weekly and Telegram* put it in March 1879, the many letters from ordinary soldiers in Zululand appearing in newspapers were a 'credible specimen of the progress of education in the army'.[17]

It was certainly a public with an increasing thirst for news, even if a penny for a daily newspaper was still beyond the reach of many. The role of the press, therefore, was crucial not only in informing the public but also in sustaining interest in the war.

For much of 1879, the war received far more coverage than that in Afghanistan. Stephen Manning has argued this was due to the time it took for news to reach Britain. Thus, 'perhaps perversely, news items from Afghanistan, because they could be readily and promptly reported, rarely stayed in the newspaper columns for long, as another news item could be expected from Afghanistan the next day'.[18] By September, the massacre of Cavagnari's mission in Kabul restored the interest in Afghanistan for it was the sensational that caught the attention. In his novel *The Light That Failed* (1898), Rudyard Kipling likened the 'specials'— the war correspondents—'to a substitute for the gladiatorial arena, sent out when a war begins, to minister to the blind, brutal, British public's bestial thirst for blood'.[19]

The extension of the global telegraph system revolutionized burgeoning war journalism by creating a race among correspondents to get the first news back to their editors, although the direct cable to South Africa was not completed until after the war. It was epitomized by Archibald Forbes's much eulogized 'Ride of Death', in which he covered 110 miles in fifteen hours to carry the news of victory at Ulundi to the nearest telegraph station. The *Illustrated London News* even proposed Forbes be given the VC.[20] By 1886 W. T. Stead would claim grandiloquently, 'I have seen Cabinets upset...armies sent hither and thither, war proclaimed and war averted, by the agency of the newspaper.'[21]

In February 1878 the War Office recognized that the public 'will not consent to be shut out from the news of the theatre of war; nor is it wise that they should be'.[22] When Sir Edward Selby Smyth, who had previously served at the Cape, offered his services in Zululand, Frederick Stanley immediately rejected the appointment of one who was 'hardly well enough known' to take on the job of reversing Isandlwana.[23] Cambridge was equally attuned to the influence of the domestic press, informing Chelmsford in March 1879, 'in these days the freedom of the press has taken very large dimensions, and anybody that has a relative or friend receives letters and sends them to the press giving his version of events as they believe them to have occurred'.[24] Cambridge repeatedly tried to convey to Chelmsford the need to provide 'carefully worded & good clear despatches'. As he continued, 'The Public at home & Parliament particularly requires this.'[25]

The relief of Pearson's force at Eshowe in April brought a sigh of relief from the Horse Guards. Sir Charles Ellice noted that Wood's victory at Kambula had also been fortuitous following the failures at Hlobane 'or I may much fear the press in this country would have again considered that there had been another disaster'.[26] Press opinion continued to influence Chelmsford's career. Cambridge wanted to offer him a new command in 1881 but ministers feared public reaction, saying he would have to take the matter to Cabinet.[27] Cambridge conceded that Chelmsford could not be given another command in March 1884.[28]

Generally, 'specials' were not overly critical of the army and the relationship was symbiotic: they depended upon soldiers for transport, supplies, information, and the means of communication. Correspondents also shared the dangers.[29] Forbes, a former ranker, believed they should record 'how our countrymen, our dear ones, toil and thole, vindicate British manhood, and joyously expend their lives for Queen and fatherland'.[30] Reportage would rarely convey the totality of colonial warfare.[31] Press criticism, however, was not welcomed by the soldiers, especially if a public debate ensued. Forbes made the point that his critique of Chelmsford's operations only reflected that of the army: 'If a force...has formed an unfavourable opinion of its leader, it laughs to scorn the journalist who would have it believe that its commander is a capable chief'.[32] The fact that Forbes had applied for and been denied the South Africa Medal by Chelmsford doubtless added to his antagonism.[33]

Wolseley's campaign in Asante in 1873–4 had attracted a significant number of 'specials', including Henry Morton Stanley, Melton Prior, and

George Henty.[34] Given the assumption that this new war would amount to little—the Afghan conflict had been underway since November 1878—the only 'special' to accompany the army into Zululand was Norris-Newman although the local Natal press also employed correspondents who remained unidentified. In much the same way, only one correspondent—Mark Kellogg of the *Bismarck Times*—accompanied Custer's expedition and he died with Custer.

The first news of Isandlwana appeared in the London press on Monday 11 February—the news reached Reuters just after midnight on 10 February—and brought a flood of new arrivals including Forbes, who came direct from Burma, and the celebrated William Howard Russell. Officers provided the initial sketches for the British press, the first of Isandlwana by Crealock appearing in the *Illustrated London News* on 8 March. Until then the illustrations of Isandlwana, as the *Illustrated London News* admitted, were 'prepared from descriptions furnished by persons who are well acquainted with the location in question, and who have conversed with survivors of the conflict'.[35] The first sketches from Zululand by a 'special' were those of Melton Prior in the *Illlustrated London News* on 3 May 1879. They were rough and ready and, as a result of the engraving process, the published illustration might bear scant resemblance to the original.[36]

The first means by which the press had had an impact on British public perception of the war was in reinforcing the early traders and missionaries' stereotypical image of the Zulu consistent with Victorian visions of Africa.[37] Frere and Shepstone held different views of Shaka's reign but both visualized the Zulu as a threat to confederation.[38] Led by the Natal press, which took its cue from Frere, the British press repeated the perception of the Zulu threat. Even a Liberal newspaper, the *Daily News*, accepted the Zulu as a 'standing menace', although it claimed the British invasion premature.[39] Another Liberal title, the *Manchester Guardian*, considered that the power of the Zulu had been weighing on the Natal settlers 'like a nightmare'.[40] In reality, Natal did not universally support the war, the supposed Zulu threat alarming urban more than rural areas.[41] The Devon press, whose war coverage has been particularly studied, mostly purported to be politically independent or neutral. It was more sceptical than that of London as to the merits of the war. The admittedly Liberal *Devon Evening Express* suggested British lives would be sacrificed 'for a very questionable benefit'. War was allowing 'the Colonist at the Cape to involve the country in the cost and anxieties of a war from which we shall gain neither honour nor profit'.[42] *The Graphic* had concluded on 1 February that the war was of more importance to the colonies than to Britain and 'we have little doubt that Cetewayo is not altogether in the wrong'.[43] By contrast, a provincial Conservative paper, the *Bucks Herald*, had little doubt Cetshwayo was a 'barbaric despot'.[44]

Confidence on the part of the Conservative press was high, *The Times* predicting on 7 February the complete success of Chelmsford's plans 'and the unconditional surrender of the now haughty chief'.[45] For the *Pall Mall Gazette*, the Zulu were 'probably disciplined just sufficiently to embolden them to come out into the open. Once there we have no doubt as to the result of the encounter.'[46] *The Standard* chose to publish Norris-Newman's prognostications of success even after the first news of Isandlwana arrived since he was the only correspondent on the spot.[47]

It was not the case, therefore, that the press ignored the likelihood and actuality of war but the news of Isandlwana was stunning, and the press struggled to find an explanation for the unexpected defeat. The London correspondent of the *Western Morning News* reported on 11 February that the capital[48]

> is struggling between deep depression and high excitement. Evidence of this depression was palpable enough in the railway trains this morning. Nobody cared to talk. Evidence of the excitement is palpable enough in the streets this afternoon. The papers are selling wildly, and little knots of men were to be found in sheltered corners discussing the news.

In Herefordshire the Revd Francis Kilvert attended a volunteer concert where news of 'the terrible disaster' so much affected the colonel, who had known many of the officers of the 24th, that he had to leave.[49] Both the *Bucks Herald* and the *Exeter and Plymouth Gazette* invoked the loss of Varus and his legions in the Teutoburg Forest in AD 9.[50] The search for an explanation resulted in a number of newspapers reproducing a comment from a Berlin paper that the Zulu had been trained by former members of the British German Legion who had been settled unsuccessfully in Kaffraria after the Crimean War.[51] Some British troops apparently believed Matshana's real name was Mazzini and that white renegades led the Zulu.[52]

Although Isandlwana had a unifying effect, press reaction generally followed party lines. The neutral *Paignton Gazette* cautioned that it 'would be indeed a scandal and an offence if this disquieting period was employed to coin political capital out of this calamity',[53] but steeped in moral indignation of all manifestations of 'Beaconsfieldism', the Liberal press condemned an unnecessary and unjust war.[54] The *Northern Echo* went so far as to extend its criticism to the army's officer class, trusting that in future 'when British armies invade savage States they will not take as their model the luxurious effeminacy of the Oriental'.[55] Others similarly attacked the army's 'old guard' and even the *United Service Gazette* suggested there were too few Staff College graduates in the army.[56] Yet, the *Daily News* trusted that the reinforcements being despatched would be sufficient 'to restore our military renown'. It also praised the defence of Rorke's Drift and eulogized Melvill and Coghill, suggesting their deaths were worthy of the sentiments in Tennyson's recent poetic celebration of the stand of Sir Richard Grenville against the Spanish in 1591.[57] Any suggestion, as in the *Saturday Review*, that there had been panic at Isandlwana was firmly rejected by the military press.[58]

Prestige was all important, as the *Liverpool Mercury* acknowledged: 'England cannot afford to be defeated by native forces anywhere, or the lives of the greater portion of the British army in India or the colonies would not be worth a day's purchase.'[59] *The Times*, which likened Isandlwana to Thermopylae, demanded 'the subjugation of the Zulu power'.[60] Similarly, *The Graphic* believed that failure to crush the Zulu 'will gradually sap the loyalty of other native races, so that the white man, everywhere in a minority in South Arica, may have to fight for bare existence'.[61] Not unexpectedly, there was a great deal of thirsting for revenge, the *Daily Telegraph* demanding the cooling of 'the warlike ardour of the savage warriors'.[62]

Press coverage suggests that reportage of Rorke's Drift was eclipsed by the ongoing Isandlwana debate. Initially, Rorke's Drift was confused with Isandlwana and some even suggested it was a victory for Dartnell and Lonsdale's colonial forces. Only the *Daily Telegraph* really reported on it in a way likely to soften the blow of Isandlwana as the government might have hoped. Isandlwana remained at the forefront of the news because of the lack of military activity for weeks thereafter as well as the search to comprehend what had happened.[63]

The press was eager for first-hand accounts from Isandlwana survivors and Rorke's Drift defenders. Such letters gave immediacy compared to official despatches. While many were widely reproduced and some were anonymous, those from a local soldier connected the public with distant events in a very particular way. Letters were not censored and could be blunt in their judgements. Naturally enough, individuals' perspectives would be limited. Penn Symons noted of the six privates of the 1/24th to escape Isandlwana, 'It was very remarkable how their accounts afterwards varied. Men forgot what they saw and did amidst great excitement, and mixed up what others told them with their own experiences and reminiscences.'[64] Many accounts only appeared years later. Frank Bourne, for example, was interviewed on BBC Radio in December 1935 but only a transcript survives from *The Listener* in 1936: the recording was destroyed in the 1960s.[65]

There was an assumption that men had been where they said. Corporal Wiles of the 2/24th Foot was not a survivor of Isandlwana as claimed in the *Bristol Observer*, having clearly been out with Chelmsford.[66] Similarly, Corporal Price could hardly have been the only man left from B Company of the 2/24th as suggested in the *Bucks Herald*.[67]

Otto Witt was mobbed by reporters on his arrival at Plymouth on 4 March 1879 to the extent that they burst into his cabin while he was still asleep.[68] Chard was much feted on his return to Britain, he and other Rorke's Drift defenders being greeted by the Duke of Cambridge at Portsmouth. Chard visited his sister in Somerset and a crowd

A LESSON.

Figure 12. John Tenniel, 'The Lesson', *Punch*, 1 March 1879.

of 4,000 met him at Taunton: he was borne through the streets in a carriage. There were other appearances at Plymouth, London, and Chatham before he went on to Balmoral.[69] Chard received a presentation sword at Plymouth, while Bromhead received a revolver from the tenants of his family seat. Ordinary soldiers present at Rorke's Drift received a presentation bible from the Ladies' Rorke's Drift Testimonial Fund and a parchment from the mayor of Durban.[70]

Cartoonists had to tread a careful line given the number of deaths at Isandlwana. John Tenniel's famous *Punch* cartoon, depicting a Zulu writing 'Despise not your Enemy' on a blackboard for John Bull, appeared on 1 March 1879. *Punch* offered a phrasebook for generals on 15 March including such gems as 'On receiving the news that the troops under his command have been out-generalled and cut to pieces—Now, who *is* responsible for this?' On 5 April came *Punch*'s amendments for Chelmsford's pre-war pamphlet on how to fight the Zulus. The proposed new chapter would be entitled 'How to Insure a Defeat' with such suggestions as 'Knowing that a strongly fortified camp is the key and nucleus of defence against this vigilant and active enemy, the CO should quietly move off with the bulk of his force, leaving the tents untrenched and the wagons unparked'. Further mocking Frere, a supposed letter from him asked for reinforcements to be unmarried, 'as there is something to be said for a force of celibate man-slaying gladiators, after all'.[71] *Fun* followed suit on 19 March with 'The Difficulties of Some Generals', including the scene, 'Then the enemy's ways were so underhanded. Why, they came upon him *without any warning* when he was having a quiet cigar, and not even thinking of them! No General could deal with enemies like that!' The same issue carried Gordon Thompson's cartoon, 'The Mother's Pet' showing Beaconsfield and Chelmsford weeping.[72] Rorke's Drift by contrast was welcomed by Tenniel's *Punch* cartoon on 22 March—'A Vote of Thanks'—crediting Chard and Bromhead with saving Natal and 'the credit of old England'. Equally, another satirical magazine, *Judy*, proclaimed of Isandlwana, 'Never was there a finer example of steadfast valour.'[73]

Domestic Opposition

The more satirical cartoons hinted at public concerns and the press also proved a vehicle for growing opposition to the war. There was initial backing for the government, but Frere's ultimatum created unease and Isandlwana more so. The Conservative papers supported the government and attacked the partisanship of the Liberal press but they did not defend Frere or Chelmsford. *The Standard* reflected the growing consensus, attacking Chelmsford's competence and querying whether money and lives should be expended in 'seizing territory, not for the purpose of governing the natives in accordance with civilised principles, but to steal portions of the land, and allot them to private individuals'.[74] The *Illustrated London News* parodied Caesar's supposed remark after defeating Pharnaces of Pontus in 47 BC, suggesting Chelmsford's dictum should be 'I went, I did not see, I suffered a defeat.'[75] Another Conservative title, the *Irish Times*, called for Chelmsford's removal as early as 7 March.[76] The radical *Reynolds's Newspaper* believed Isandlwana was due to Chelmsford's 'combined negligence, ignorance and imbecility'. *The Spectator* suggested Chelmsford would have taken more care if he had been riding to hounds in Leicestershire.[77]

There was also opposition to the war beyond the press. Parliament reconvened from its Christmas recess two days after news of Isandlwana reached London. The Irish Nationalist MP for Louth, Alexander Sullivan, maintained on 27 February that Cetshwayo 'only did what Queen Elizabeth did in the case of the Spanish Armada'. On 14 August George Anderson, Liberal MP for Glasgow, praised Cetshwayo as a 'gallant monarch' defending his nation 'against one of the most wanton and wicked invasions that ever could be made upon an independent people'.[78] A similar view was taken by the labour reformer Robert Watson, in his polemic, *History of English Rule and Policy in South Africa* (1879). The Opposition's principal attacks on the government were mounted in the Lords by the Marquess of Lansdowne on 25 March 1879 and in the Commons by Sir Charles Dilke on 27 March. The government won both votes comfortably but the Liberals won the argument by portraying the war as unjust and its conduct as lamentable.[79]

Prominent in opposition to the war were Bishop John Colenso and his daughters, Frances and Harriet. A controversial cleric, Colenso took the side of Langalibalele when he was tried by the Cape authorities in 1874. Colenso's liberal views on incorporating African practices into Christian belief, as well as his casting doubt on biblical truth, led to his excommunication by the Bishop of Cape Town in 1866. Colenso remained bishop of Natal until his death in 1883 while a separate bishopric of Maritzburg was consecrated, the schism in the church in Natal enduring until 1910. Colenso took advantage of the Day of Humiliation prescribed by Sir Henry Bulwer for Natal churches on 12 March 1879 to preach a highly politicized sermon on the injustice of the war. It was heard in absolute silence.[80]

In Britain Colenso enlisted the support of the secretary of the Aborigines' Protection Society, F. W. Chesson, and the Liberal MP for Liskeard, Leonard Courtney, to promote the Zulu cause. Chesson published *The War in Zululand* in March 1879 and Colenso translated and published Cornelius Vijn's memoir of captivity at the hands of Cetshwayo in 1880. Not unexpectedly the Society of Friends and the Peace Society also opposed war. In also opposing war, British Wesleyan Methodists took a diametrically different view from Natal's Wesleyan missionaries who supported it. Generally, Nonconformists opposed the war while the Established Church remained silent.[81] As already related, Frances Colenso published her history of the war and its origins in 1880. The heroic light in which she cast Anthony Durnford both in her history and in an adventure tale, *My Chief and I*, written under the pseudonym Atherton Wylde, presented the contradictions of liberal imperialism. Durnford himself blamed the missionaries for the war but ultimately believed in justice for natives only within the empire.[82]

Popular Culture

By 1879 patterns of British consumption were being transformed by new methods of production, distribution, marketing, and advertising, in which empire proved a versatile device for product promotion.[83] Some historians have questioned the impact of popular imperialism in late Victorian Britain but it has been argued that popular culture became a vehicle for dominant ideas and empire was one such idea.[84] Imperialism was deeply embedded in society even before the growth of the 'new journalism' associated with the appearance of cheap mass-circulation daily newspapers such as the *Daily Mail* in the 1890s.[85]

Popular culture rationalized imperial violence as necessary or undertaken for noble, moral, and humanitarian reasons. It romanticized violence despite the supposed distaste for war and for the common soldier. An army safely distanced from society added to war's romantic appeal.[86] Colonial warfare was 'an atavistic form of war, shorn of guilt by Social Darwinian and racial ideas, and rendered less dangerous by the increasing technological gap between Europe and the rest of the world'.[87] Military and civic spectacle; music hall; theatre and other forms of commercial entertainment; commemorative bric-a-brac; and a wide variety of print media including sheet music, matchbox covers, cigarette cards and postcards; all added to war's impact. It amounted to a 'pleasure culture of war'.[88]

Poetry

As might be expected, Isandlwana and Rorke's Drift were enshrined in popular culture. There was a great deal of indifferent poetry. Just before the Battle of Ulundi, Captain William Montague recorded that lines on Isandlwana penned by Robert Buchanan were seen in an issue of *Contemporary Review*:

> Oh listen to that warning cry,
> 'Fly, British soldiers, fly,

For the dusky foe is nigh
From Isandula!'

It 'put the whole camp into roars of laughter: the sentiment expressed was so truly wonderful, the poetic licence so unchecked'. Private James of the 88th Foot similarly wrote of the gales of laughter greeting poems in the press.[89]

The 'Gallant Twenty Fourth' was a persistent theme, as in the poem by Lee and Green in the Natal press:[90]

In Zululand the Twenty-Fourth, a gallant little band
Of British soldiers bold and true, 'gainst legions made a stand
Surrounded by their dusky foes, shut in both left and right,
'Gainst fearful odds they fought as none but Englishmen can fight.

H. B. Worth's 'In Memory of the Officers, Non-commissioned Officers, and Men of the 24th Regiment' had a comforting sense of victory in death:[91]

Each single man, a hero in the strife,
O'erwhelmed by numbers, dearly sold his life,
Though great our loss, the enemy lost more—
For every Briton slain they counted four.

In his history, Moodie included two Rorke's Drift poems, one from *Truth* and one from the *Transvaal Argus*. The latter concluded,[92]

In the heart-thrill of Nations will live your reward,
Oh! Brave Twenty-Fourth!
Oh! Brave Bromhead and Chard.

Bertram Mitford, too, penned 'The Defence of Rorke's Drift' in 1882:[93]

Yes for old England's honour
And for her perilled might,
We strove with vast and 'whelming odds,
From eve till morning light.

Much poetry drew upon classical allusion as in Albert Bencke's 'Thermopylae BC 480. Rorke's Drift. Natal AD 1879'. It echoed the analogy already evident in the press.[94] On the other hand, there was also William McGonagall's 'The Hero of Rorke's Drift':[95]

> Methinks I see the noble hero, Henry Hook,
> Because like a destroying angel he did look,
> As he stood at the hospital entrance defending the patients there,
> Bayoneting the Zulus, while their cries rent the air,
> As they strove hard the hospital to enter in,
> But he murdered them in scores, and thought it no sin.

Interestingly, while there was little verse on the war after the 1880s, John McCrae, the Canadian doctor killed in the Great War and best known for 'In Flanders Fields', penned some poignant lines in 'Isandlwana' (1910):[96]

> Scarlet coats, and crash o' the band,
> The grey of a pauper's gown,
> A soldier's grave in Zululand,
> And a woman in Brecon Town.

There is comparison with the poetic imagery about the Alamo and Custer's Last Stand. Even Walt Whitman and Henry Wadsworth Longfellow succumbed to clichés on heroic Custer and his savage foes. At the time the *Saturday Review* suggested that Americans 'like ourselves are better at doing things than commemorating them'. That was certainly borne out by the British literary output three years later.[97]

Given the reverse at Isandlwana, the story of Melvill and Coghill became a necessary myth. A spectacularly inaccurate poem by J. E. Carpenter, 'The Saving of the Colours', eulogized Melvill and Coghill and suggested the two artillery pieces were spiked by 'the Colonel', presumably Pulleine. It appeared in *The Graphic* on 15 March alongside the first speculative engravings of the battle for the camp and of their attempts to save the Colour:[98]

> We did not turn—but there we stood till every round was spent,
> And every ball had told its tale until the last was sent,
> And then to right, to left of us they closed—still ten to one,
> As bravest 'mid the rave our Gallant Colonel spiked the gun;
> At eve, at wild Isandula, upon that fatal day,

> Nine hundred British heroes stark beneath the moonlight lay,
> And the one deed of the battle that will shine beyond the rest,
> Was the savings of the Colours, found upon a hero's breast.

Emmeline Canning's 'The Rescued Flag' was penned in April 1879 while Charles O'Conor's 'Melvilles's Ride' appeared in the *Belfast News Letter* on 26 June, its comforting recurring refrain, 'And that God has given England His command to rule the world!'[99] George Boyce's 'The Zulu War' pictured how Melvill and Coghill[100]

> Bore the Colours safe that day;
> Using them for their funeral shroud,
> As they fell, while bearing them away,
> And every one of their deeds are proud.

Known for stirring verse such as 'The Loss of the Birkenhead', 'The Red Thread of Honour', and 'The Private of the Buffs', Sir Hastings Francis Doyle contributed 'The Saving of the Colours'. It invoked David and Jonathan—'In their deaths they were not divided'—and was widely published in the provincial press in March 1879:[101]

> And now, forgetting that wild ride, forgetful of all pain,
> High amongst those who have not lived, who have not died in vain,
> By strange stars watched, they sleep afar, within some nameless glen,
> Beyond the tumult and the noise, beyond the praise of men.

A rival for poetic commemoration was Lieutenant the Hon. Standish Vereker of the 2/3rd Natal Native Contingent. Vereker secured a horse as the firing line gave way but gave it up to a Natal Native Horse trooper who claimed it as his own and thus stayed to die. The *Boy's Own Paper* likened his gentlemanly sacrifice to that of the Elizabethan courtier Sir Philip Sidney, who gave his water up to another wounded soldier at the Battle of Zutphen in 1586. It also printed Isabella Fyvie Mayo's 'A Story of Isandhlwana':[102]

> He could not seize another's
> He could not dream a lie
> These were the hard things for him
> The easy way to die!

Music

Music in its varying forms was a constant soundtrack of empire, and music hall the dominant popular (and patriotic) cultural form.[103] Music hall embraced many different performance types—often combining melodrama, spectacle, and sketches—and many varying venues and entertainment configurations. In October 1880, the comic singer and actor Charles Godfrey combined two of his songs, 'Poor old Benjamin the Workhouse Man' and 'The Dusky Warrior' based on the Zulu War, into a 'dramatic song-scena [sic]' entitled 'On Guard'.[104]

The halls did not tend to offer criticism of the military but George Horncastle's 'Sir Garnet Will Show Them the Way', sung by Sam Torr, suggested,[105]

> Tho' Lord Chelmsford no doubt is a brave honest man,
> And Sir Bartle Frere too I daresay,
> They've not led our soldiers to victory yet
> But Sir Garnet will show them the way.

Another song parodied G. W. Hunt's celebrated composition for 'The Great MacDermott', 'By Jingo', originally sung about the Russian threat to Constantinople in 1878. The new version went,[106]

> Lord Chelmsford is the man,
> To skedaddle if he can,
> And leave our men to be
> Slaughtered by the Zooloos.

Inevitably, sentimental ballads took their place in the halls to commemorate Isandlwana. G. C. Anewick's 'The Noble 24th, or Vanquished not Disgraced' with music by Vincent Davies, was sung by J. W. Rowley:[107]

> A story came one morning,
> From a far and distant land,
> That savages had massacred

Figure 13. G. C. Anewick's *The Noble 24th*, 1879.

A small but gallant band.
'Gainst twenty thousand foreign foes,
'Midst thunder shot, and shell,
Five hundred valiant English fought,
And nobly fighting fell.

In other verses, Anewik emphasized the supposed Welshness of the 24th Foot when only some 14 per cent of the 1/24th had been Welsh. It was higher in the 2/24th at 24 per cent.[108] The depot of what remained the 2nd Warwickshire Regiment was allocated to Brecon in 1873 under 'localization'. It had not recruited specifically in Wales prior to this and those recruits obtained from neighbouring Welsh counties went largely to the 2/24th. It only became the South Wales Borderers when new regimental titles were determined under 'territorialization' in 1881. The number of Welsh defenders at Rorke's Drift appears to have been no more than twenty-seven (of whom sixteen were born in the officially English county of Monmouthshire) and possibly as few as five. Some authors have taken those with Welsh-sounding names to be Welsh, by no means the case. There were certainly thirteen Irishmen.[109]

Various songs were set to music for a wider public beyond the music hall. Chard and Bromhead were lauded in the 'Grand March: Honor [sic] to the Brave' by J. Riviere with lyrics by Henry Hersee. Likewise, Melvill and Coghill were honoured with 'The Saving of the Colours' by the Irish composer Sir Robert Prescott Stewart, with lyrics by Mrs M. Gorges:[110]

Where have they found the colours?
Beneath the blood-stain'd wave
Death? Say rather glory
Within each silken fold.

Entertainment

There was occasional theatrical melodrama with Zulu themes, the annual Drury Lane winter spectacle, which alternated with panto-mime, being devoted to the war in 1881.[111] J. W. Poole's 'The Queen's

Colour' was showing in Leeds in April 1882.[112] Zulu tableaux continued to be presented in the music halls in the 1890s, Frank Celli singing 'Rorke's Drift' and appearing in front of a reproduction of Alphonse de Neuville's painting of Rorke's Drift, while Maynard and Calver appeared as Melvill and Coghill in 'Dying to Save the Queen's Colours'.[113] The Great MacDermott himself was still touring a Zulu sketch, 'Our Lads in Red' at the Britannia Theatre, Hoxton in October 1890.[114] The legitimate theatre, however, did not take much interest in African campaigns and plays were limited to Alfred Cook's *War in Zululand*, *Cetewayo at Last*, and *The Zulu Chief*.[115]

In April 1879 Astley's Amphitheatre offered an entertainment billed as 'The Kaffir War' featuring 'the Zulu hosts contending against British troops'. The Zulu were whites blacked up. Astley's did not pretend otherwise but the Metropolitan Music Hall did try to pass off whites as a Zulu troupe.[116] At the end of March 1879, Hamilton's Amphitheatre in Holborn advertised a painting of Isandlwana 'giving from the most authentic sources a life-like representation of the heroic stand against twenty thousand Zulus by the gallant 24th', a 'quadruple war dance by Zulu warriors', and other related entertainment. Scenes of Rorke's Drift and Melvill and Coghill rescuing the Colour were added in April and the show then toured the provinces from June.[117] Billed as 'Hamilton's Excursions Home and Abroad', it was at Surrey Masonic Hall in Camberwell in July. In August 1880 the Battle of Ulundi was presented as a 'Grand Military Spectacular Entertainment' at Lusby's Summer and Winter Palace in the Mile End Road, although apparently without African performers.[118] Similarly, Poole and Young's 'dioramic excursion' on the war, including Isandlwana and Rorke's Drift, was widely toured, appearing at Bristol's Colston Hall in July 1879 and at Exeter's Royal Public Rooms in October.[119]

It was not long before 'genuine' Zulu began to appear on stage. Exhibiting Africans was not new. The 'Hottentot Venus', a Khoesan woman, was exhibited in London in 1810 and five San appeared in 1846. Charles Dickens was appalled by the 'howling, whistling, clucking, stamping, jumping, tearing savages' of eleven 'Zulu Kaffirs' from Natal at St George's Gallery on Hyde Park Corner in 1853.[120]

A troupe of six 'Zulu' appeared at Brecon on 16 June 1879. In July they were at the Agricultural Hall in Islington, provoking criticism from the Home Secretary, Richard Cross, that it was unseemly. A rejoinder from the *Pall Mall Gazette* suggested he would be better to question 'the vendors of obscene literature who throng about omnibus and railway stations'.[121] Subsequently, the Lord Mayor of London instigated an unsuccessful prosecution of a bookseller, Philpott of Gracechurch Street, for displaying the kind of photographs of semi-naked Zulu women that were very familiar to troops in South Africa.[122] The Great Farini (the former Canadian high-wire walker William Hunt) had brought the Zulu to Britain from Paris, where they performed at the Folies-Bergère for a South African called Culley. Farini organized the show at Islington and took 'Farini's Friendly Zulus' to St James's Hall and then, in September 1880, to the Royal Aquarium in Westminster. Through agents in South Africa, Farrini recruited more Zulu to add to the show, some reputedly followers of Hamu. Six more arrived in December 1879, five in April 1880, and three women and a baby in the winter of 1880, one supposedly Cetshwayo's daughter.[123]

Performing three times a day, they became very popular, as testified by one music hall song, 'Go and See the Zulus'—the work of George Horncastle,[124]

> I'm very glad I took my wife
> To see these wondrous men,
> And she was quite delighted too.
> But I was startled when
> She remarked 'twould give her joy
> And true bliss without alloy
> If we named our baby boy
> After all the friendly Zulus.

Five of the original six performers tried unsuccessfully to challenge their contract in December 1879. Farini paid them only £3 per month plus board and lodging and allowed them out for exercise only under strict supervision. Assisted by Chesson and Colenso's son, they objected to the way in which Culley had them 'sold like cows' to Farini. They were compelled by circumstances to return to performing when their case was dismissed, the same occurring when some again went on strike in April 1880. The press was unsympathetic, the *Daily Telegraph* suggesting in January 1880 that London was 'threatened by an impi of outrageous Zulus determined to live here, but equally determined not to work'. In May 1880 the *Newcastle Courant* deemed them 'spoiled by too much good treatment'.[125] One appeared in court in May 1880 for being drunk and disorderly and another in June for fighting.[126]

P. T. Barnum's $100,000 offer to the British government to allow him to exhibit Cetshwayo was rejected but a rival did secure two of Cetshwayo's supposed nieces. Messrs Pinders' Continental Grand Hippodrome Circus came to Aylesbury in October 1879 with a troupe of Zulu who, supposedly refugees from Cetshwayo's army, 'placed themselves under British protection rather than fight'. As the advertisement put it, 'Do not miss this opportunity of witnessing the representatives of our foes, against whom our gallant forces fought so nobly at Isandhlwana and Ekowe.'[127] A group of Zulu and 'real' soldiers re-enacted Isandlwana and Rorke's Drift for Cooke's Circus and Hippodrome in Manchester in September 1879, for Charlie Keith's Circus at Derby in December, and for Ginnett's Portsmouth Hippodrome Circus in January 1880.[128]

One Zulu troupe even appeared in Prague in November 1879.[129] In 1880–1 Farini took some of his Zulu to New York and in 1893 Farini's Australian circus also presented a Zulu War re-enactment. Those Zulu touring the more racially charged United States sometimes faced physical attack and, as in Britain, there were cases of drunkenness and strikes. African-Americans often performed 'Zulu' songs and ballads and many found employment posing as Zulu (as well as Maori and Aborigines) in American travelling shows and circuses.[130] George Wirth's Australian Circus included Zulu who were required to play Matabele in a re-enactment of the Shangani Patrol in the 1890s. Wirth hired more Zulu to tour South America. There were objections to the Zulu appearing semi-naked in Buenos Aires but, in any case, all soon disappeared, Wirth suspecting they had been enticed or even abducted to work on ranches.[131] A Zulu troupe also appeared over the winter of 1899–1900 as part of 'Savage South Africa' within the Greater Britain Exhibition at Earl's Court and then in the 'Briton, Boer and Black' Exhibition at Olympia. There was controversy as they had been granted passes only to travel to the Kimberley mines and arrived in Britain under false pretences.[132] Madame Tussaud's had waxworks of Cetshwayo and his 'principal wife' on display for most of the 1880s, defying Punch's prediction in September 1879 that interest would only last a month. Tussaud's, however, produced no Zulu War tableaux such as those for the Sudan campaigns and the South African War.[133]

Fascination with Zulu there may have been but it was also potentially risky to be Zulu or, rather, taken to be Zulu. In July 1879 a West Indian seaman was attacked in Sheffield when taken for a Zulu. An Indian variety performer, the 'Original Hindoo Snake-Charmer', was similarly attacked as a Zulu in Nottingham in January 1880, while a 'man of colour' and his family in Glasgow were regularly abused as Zulu in September 1880.[134]

One of the more bizarre manifestations of the interest generated was 'Messrs. Brewers and Rolling's Original Zulus' (later the Sheffield Holmes Zulus), a football team that toured the north of England in late 1879, 'leaving their assegais and spears on the touchline'. The full-back, 'Cetewayo', played especially well in front of some 2,000 spectators at Sheffield's Bramall Lane in November, facing Billy Mosforth, the England international winger in a match raising funds for widows and orphans killed in the war. The team also appeared at Barnsley, Chesterfield, Nottingham, Scarborough, Edinburgh, and Glasgow, never losing a match. They were white players blacked up, many from Sheffield Wednesday, and soon aroused the ire of the Sheffield Football Association as amateurs taking payments for appearances. It banned the England international Jack Hunter from a North versus

South game for participating in the tour and warned them that they would be prohibited from any representative games or FA Cup ties. According to a Sheffield FA representative,[135]

> The Zulus were going about the country playing matches in a manner which in the opinion of the committee was calculated to degrade the game and bring discredit upon those connected with it; and, further, that these players were receiving payment for playing.

The 1881 Wharncliffe Charity Cup Final was cancelled as too many players were 'Zulu' who were banned for professionalism, and the team was disbanded. Professionalism was legalized in 1885, the first professional team in Sheffield, the short-lived Sheffield Rovers, being formed mainly by the 'Zulu'.[136] The motivation for creating the 'Zulu' football team in the first place cannot be readily explained beyond the war's cultural impact, but it may well be that the issue of professionalism in the sport played its part.

Lectures on the war were soon being presented to the public illustrated by 'dioramic dissolving views' illuminated by 'oxy-hydrogen lime-light', i.e. magic lantern slides. In Buckinghamshire, the Aylesbury mineral-water manufacturer William North gave his show at Aylesbury, Great Missenden, and Waddesdon in November 1879, while Messrs Piggott, photographers from Leighton Buzzard, presented their talk at Aston Abbotts, Princes Risborough, and Weedon in November and December. Archibald Forbes also lectured at High Wycombe in November 1879. North and the Piggotts were still doing the rounds through 1880, as did some others, although a presentation by the Piggotts at Chesham in December 1880 seems to have been the last.[137] In North's talk he 'proceeded to eulogise the Zulu warriors as foemen worthy of the British arms, owing to their indomitable bravery and utter contempt of death'.[138] Lantern slide sets of the war, usually colourized illustrations from the periodicals, were produced by London firms such as Newton & Co. of Fleet Street, and W. C. Hughes of Hoxton Street.

Commercialism featured in other ways. Forbes did well with his tour, trading on the 'Ride of Death', but Otto Witt also drew large

Figure 14. Magic Lantern Slide of the Battle of Isandlwana.

audiences for recounting his fraudulent experiences. An estimated 1,700 heard Witt speak at the Victoria Park Congregational Tabernacle in South Hackney in March 1879 and he repeated the performance at City Temple, Holborn the following day.[139]

Another facet was Great Western Railways' 'Zulu Express' from Paddington to Plymouth introduced in June 1879. In June 1880 the new Paddington to Birkenhead express was called the 'Northern Zulu' or, occasionally, the 'Afghan Express'. That to the West Country still bore the name as late as 1891.[140]

An enterprising Aberdeen grocer was offering 'Rorke's Drift Relief Whisky' in April 1879 at 17s. od. a gallon.[141] Yeatman's Yeast Powder was advertised as that used to supply troops with bread in South Africa.[142] Restaurants offered 'Zulu oysters' while 'Zulu' clay pipes, 'Zulu' antimacassars, and Hogg's 'Zulu Insect Destroying Powder' were all offered for sale.[143] By the 1890s Attwood & Son's Zulu Cycle Works was operating at Wednesbury and the Birmingham City Cycle Company was producing 'Zulu' safety cycles. 'Zulu Safety Matches' were also manufactured.[144] As late as the 1930s Hulse & Co. of Leeds was manufacturing 'Zulu Chimney Cleaner'.[145]

There was renewed interest when Cetshwayo visited England in July and August 1882 to press for the reinstatement of his kingdom. Deported from Zululand to Cape Town after his capture, Cetshwayo was held in Cape Town Castle until released into civil custody in January 1881. Encouraged by Colenso, Cetshwayo sent letters to all and sundry, pleading to be returned to Zululand. The defeat of the Conservatives and the return of the Liberals in April 1880 assisted his cause. Bulwer, now governor of Natal, opposed restoring him, as did Queen Victoria. The government, however, believed that allowing him to visit London to plead his case would buy time, especially given the outbreak of violence in Zululand as Wolseley's post-war settlement unravelled. Cetshwayo arrived at Plymouth on 5 August 1882. There were meetings with the colonial secretary, Lord Kimberley, and an audience with the Queen at Osborne.[146]

During the war Cetshwayo was depicted as a bestial savage but this had now changed.[147] The Queen was taken with Cetshwayo, a 'very fine man' with a 'good-humoured countenance, and an intelligent face'.[148] She commissioned a portrait of Cetshwayo by Carol Sohn and presented him with a silver cup. Generally, Cetshwayo appeared in European clothes, unsettling previous perceptions of a savage despot, although some images of him such as that by 'Spy' in Vanity Fair suggested his awkward appearance in Western guise.[149] Although disliking the experience, Cetshwayo appeared frequently to crowds from the window of the house he stayed at in Melbury Road, Kensington. He also visited Parliament, London Zoo, Crystal Palace, and the Woolwich Arsenal. Cetshwayo's visit coincided with George Bernard Shaw's work on his fourth novel, *Cashel Byron's Profession*, and Cetshwayo was incorporated into the story, the first major contemporary figure to feature in Shaw's work. Byron, a gentleman prizefighter, is presented to Cetshwayo after winning a bout in his presence. Cetshwayo then reappeared in Shaw's play based on the novel *The Admirable Bashville* in 1901, in which Cetshwayo's entourage get caught up in a brawl between rival fans.[150] Cetshwayo left to be restored to a part of his kingdom on 1 September. In October 2006 he received a blue plaque on the Kensington house, only the second for a black person in London, the first having been for the rock guitarist Jimi Hendrix.[151]

Another materialization of the war's impact was provision for widows and dependants of ordinary soldiers. They were not entitled to any state pension provision, although the government agreed to see whether it would be possible to make money available from the Patriotic Fund, originally established during the Crimean War for the maintenance and education of widows and orphans 'unable to maintain or support themselves'. The sympathy aroused by Isandlwana resulted in a major public response. A 'minstrel entertainment' was staged at Leamington in April 1879; an 'Isandula Benefit' concert at the Gaiety Theatre in May; and a Masonic garden party and bazaar at Exeter in July.[152] Lieutenant Charles Curll of the 2/24th contributed to 'a fund for the benefit of the widows of our poor fellows' at Rorke's Drift in February.[153] The National Aid Society also spent a total of £1,727 on medical comforts for the sick and wounded in South Africa.[154] The Lord Mayor's Mansion House Relief Fund for the widows and orphans of the 24th was opened on 29 March and, by 8 April, totalled over £6,000.[155] The separate 'Isandlana and Rorke's Drift Fund for the Relief of Widows and Orphans' had also raised £2,382. 18s. 3d. by 4 April.[156] Later that same month the fund was extended into a general 'Zulu War Fund' administered by the Patriotic Fund commissioners: it eventually raised £25,000.[157]

Art

Isandlwana and Rorke's Drift naturally dominated artistic response although the war did not generate a large number of commercial engravings: most paintings were commissions. The earliest version of Rorke's Drift was exhibited in May 1879 by an artist based in Southsea, W. H. Dugan. Dugan's painting was displayed at the Yorkshire Fine Art Institute at Leeds. It was then purchased by Hamilton's Panorama at Birmingham, which commissioned Dugan to furnish others on both the Zulu and Afghan wars. In 1882 he produced a version of the deaths of Melvill and Coghill, which was exhibited as part of Hamilton's touring Diorama and Panstereorama in Birmingham, Exeter, and Torquay with William Jones VC providing a short talk.[158]

Charles Fripp's painting, *The Last Stand at Isandhula*, was exhibited at the Royal Academy for the first time in 1885. Fripp, who admired Zulu bravery, went out as war artist for *The Graphic* in March 1879 and almost certainly visited the battlefield.[159] His vivid canvas was a particularly accurate rendition of the topography although the last stands took place in the camp area rather than as far forward as implied. Fripp included no officers in his central group, portraying prominently the stock characters of a drummer boy and a sergeant. The calm appearance and obvious steadfastness of the central group in the face of certain death adhered to the approved Victorian ideal of manliness. The well-known military painter Elizabeth, Lady Butler tended to place ordinary soldiers rather than officers at the centre of her work and Fripp was also influenced by her depiction of a British square in *The 28th Regiment at Quatre Bras* (1875).[160] The heroism of ordinary soldiers was now celebrated in a manner that suggested not only the qualities of those following a once despised occupation, but also their active participation in the imperial cause.

Fripp showed one of the Colours erroneously unfurled in the background but depicted Zulu disembowelling a soldier at the extreme right of his painting. Although now one of the best known

Figure 15. Charles Fripp, *The Last Stand at Isandhula* (1885).

of all Victorian battle paintings, by the time Fripp's canvas was exhibited the war was no longer topical. Viewers were more impressed by Godfrey Giles's painting of Tamai, which was exhibited at the same time.[161] Presented to the National Army Museum in 1960, Fripp's canvas is its most popular painting and now seen as 'a key image in the visual history of Empire'. The museum chose to host a Zulu War Dinner in aid of its own building appeal at Whitehall's Banqueting House in February 1969.[162]

There is a familiarity to such 'last stand' imagery. Custer's Last Stand was endlessly depicted, the centrality of a long-haired, buck-skinned, sabre-wielding Custer set in the very first version by William Cary in the New York *Daily Graphic* on 19 July 1876. Where Cary led, others followed. Used as an advertising poster by the Anheuser-Busch Brewing Company, over 200,000 of Otto Becker's well-known lithographs circulated the United States.[163] Bizarrely, Becker seemed to base some improbable shield-bearing Sioux on images of Zulu. For the Alamo there were well-known paintings by Robert Onderdonk (1903) and

Henry McArdle (1905).[164] Consciously echoing Fripp in British last stand iconography were Frank Feller's *The Last Eleven at Maiwand* (1882); Allan Stewart's *To the Memory of Brave Men: The Last Stand of Major Allan Wilson, the Shangani, 4th December 1893* (1897), aka *There Were No Survivors*; William Barnes Wollen's *The Last Stand of the 44th at Gundamuck, 1842* (1898); and Richard Caton Woodville's *All That Was Left of Them* (1902), showing C Squadron, 17th Lancers facing the Boers at Elands River in 1901. George William Joy's celebrated *General Gordon's Last Stand* (1893) tapped the same vein.

Lady Butler noted in her diary on 16 March 1879 that Rorke's Drift would make a 'magnificent' subject and might tempt her to break her rule on depicting contemporary subjects. But she had personal objections to painting conflict per se. Highly successful compositions such as *The Roll Call* (1874), *Balaclava* (1876), and her current canvas *Scotland for Ever* (completed in 1880) did not include any enemy.[165] As she remarked, 'I never painted for the glory of war, but to portray its pathos and heroism. If I had seen even a corner of a real battle-field, I could never have painted another picture.'[166] Lady Butler's sister, the poet Alice Meynell, was a fierce critic of empire while her Irish Catholic husband, Sir William Butler, was a man of radical persuasions despite being one of Wolseley's leading military adherents. William Butler later suggested, 'five sixths of our African wars have their beginnings in wrongs done in the first instance by white men upon natives'.[167]

In June 1879 the Queen decided she wanted a war painting, and commissioned Lady Butler to undertake one for £1,000 although, initially, there was talk of two. Lady Butler suggested the finding of the Prince Imperial's body. This was accepted but the Queen changed her mind. Lady Butler was persuaded to paint Rorke's Drift although she believed it had been given too much attention 'as though it were a second Waterloo'.[168] The army was generally supportive of Lady Butler's work. Veterans from the 24th now stationed at Portsmouth supplied soldiers who had served at Rorke's Drift as models, and even put on a re-enactment in a garden enclosure lined with sacks to look like mealie bags. Chard modelled for her. The Zulu were more of a problem but the family doctor 'got me a sort of Zulu as model from a show in London'.[169] The Queen inspected the canvas at an early stage and was satisfied provided more Zulu were added. Lady Butler found it difficult to deal with illuminating the night scene from the burning hospital. Her canvas was a composite of incidents and, as well as Chard and Bromhead, she included Dalton, Hitch, Robert Jones, William Jones, Reynolds, Schiess, Revd Smith, the wounded Corporal Scammell of the Natal Native Contingent, and the death of Acting Storekeeper Louis Byrne. She also pictured Private David Jenkins, once erroneously confused with Private James Jenkins, who was killed in the hospital.[170] The Queen felt Alphonse de Neuville's rival painting 'far less real and effective', viewing Butler's finished canvas at Windsor on 13 July 1880.[171] Hung in poor light when exhibited at the Royal Academy in 1881, Butler's painting was not a critical success but proved highly popular with the public.[172]

As suggested by the Queen's comment, Lady Butler had been beaten to the subject by de Neuville. One of the finest French battle painters, de Neuville made his name with his scenes of the Franco-Prussian War, one depicting the Battle of Le Bourget being widely exhibited in Britain in 1878. In April 1879 de Neuville was commissioned by the

Figure 16. Elizabeth, Lady Butler, *The Defence of Rorke's Drift* (1881).

Fine Art Society to paint Rorke's Drift. An appeal for photographs, artefacts, and first-hand accounts was made in the national and provincial press.[173] In part he drew on sketches of Rorke's Drift by Henry Degacher, who was half-French and had attended the same school at Saint-Omer.[174] De Neuville compressed events as did Lady Butler, as well as taking the opposite angle of view. As this looked towards the hospital, he showed patients being evacuated, although by the time this occurred, the yard was no longer defended. Chard, Bromhead, Dalton, Hitch, Reynolds, Scammell, Schiess, and Revd Smith all duly appeared. Chard, Reynolds, and Smith sat for de Neuville and he used photographs of others. Compared to Lady Butler's version, de Neuville put less emphasis upon facial expressions, since the scene was more distant and most were facing outwards towards the Zulu.[175]

Shown to the Queen at Buckingham Palace on 11 March 1880, and then displayed at the Fine Art Society, it was very favourably received with an estimated 50,000 paying to see it, causing Lady Butler allegedly to feel 'quite sick'.[176] The *Illustrated London News* proclaimed that it had 'succeeded in catching the physiognomy and bearing of the British soldier with a fidelity rarely attained by a foreigner, especially,

Figure 17. Alphonse de Neuville, *The Defence of Rorke's Drift* (1880).

perhaps a Frenchman'.[177] The Fine Art Society sold a range of print versions of different quality ranging from 3 to 15 guineas in price, including at least 1,000 of the deluxe version of Rorke's Drift.[178]

So popular was de Neuville's canvas that the newly opened Art Gallery in New South Wales was desperate to acquire it, its cost offset through allowing the Fine Art Society to continue to produce prints. It went on show in Sydney in 1882. Some in Australia still criticized the cost but it proved immensely popular, providing Australians with vicarious participation in an imperial event. Lady Butler's *The 28th Regiment at Quatre Bras* was acquired for Melbourne's public gallery and the two canvases were exchanged for display in the 1890s as well as being shown together in Adelaide. Prints were widely displayed in homes and public places throughout Australia, and it figured prominently in a booklet sold in aid of wounded Anzacs in 1915.[179] In 1913 Revd Smith visited Sydney and was much feted when viewing the painting.[180] The war entered Australian popular culture in much the same way as it did British, with Zulu artefacts displayed in the Victoria public museum, a Melbourne football team dubbing itself the 'Prince Imperials', and the winners of the Melbourne Cup being 'Zulu' in 1881 and 'Martini-Henry' in 1883.[181] In May 1881, too, W. H. Thompson's *Colossal Mirror of the Zulu War in South Africa* was shown in Garner's Theatre, Adelaide. Unfortunately, some of the 8,000 miniature wooden figures worked from under the stage 'stuck fast and refused to proceed on the warpath'.[182]

De Neuville produced two more paintings in 1882 commemorating Melvill and Coghill, both commissioned by J. G. Murdoch of the National Fine Art Association. *Saving the Queen's Colour* showed them leaving the camp, while *The Last Sleep of the Brave* depicted the discovery of their corpses, the Colour draped across them. In each case, de Neuville showed the Regimental Colour and not the Queen's Colour, and of course the Colour was not retrieved from beside their bodies. The pictures were not particularly well received, although they were both engraved for sale by Messrs Dowdeswell's gallery in New Bond Street. One Russian military artist characterized them as showing

'Frenchmen dressed up in British uniforms, and instead of Zulus, the ordinary Parisian negro-models'.[183] Charles Fripp also produced a large-scale watercolour, *Dying to Save the Queen's Colours*, earlier in 1881, a print of which appeared in *The Graphic*.

Other paintings and watercolours were produced of Ulundi and the death of the Prince Imperial but Fripp's canvas on Isandlwana was almost anachronistic for the public had moved on. Other than Fripp's, the last painting on the theme of Isandlwana appeared in 1883, Richard Moynan's *The Last of the 24th Isandula, 1879*. An Irish artist, Moynan, exhibited it at Dublin's Royal Hibernian Academy, winning the Albert Scholarship. He depicted the end of the soldier of the 24th believed to have held out in the cave on Isandlwana until dusk. The soldier, whose uniform was accurate down to his long service and good conduct stripe, had a touch of martyrdom about his pose.[184]

Juvenile Literature

The war also took its place in the canon of popular literature. Children's fiction such as that by Frederick Marryat in the 1830s and 1840s had long espoused heroic masculinity, and the theme would be continued by illustrated publications for boys such as *Boy's Own Paper* (1879), *Boys' World* (1879), *Union Jack* (1880), and *Chums* (1892). The formulaic stories for boys of the former soldier and war correspondent George Henty, who took over the editorship of *Union Jack* in 1880, epitomized the late Victorian adventure genre with all its inbuilt assumptions of the chivalric ideal, moral certainty, manliness, and imperial destiny.[185]

Henty's only story touching on the Zulu War was *The Young Colonists* (1885), which also covered the Anglo-Transvaal War. Tellingly, Henty wrote,[186]

> After having written upwards of fifty records of almost unbroken success to the British arms in almost all parts of the world, I have found it painful to describe these two campaigns in which we suffered defeat. I trust, however, that this story will prove of great interest to the reader because of the characteristic English pluck and daring of its hero.

Dick and Tom Humphreys, emigrants to Natal from Derbyshire, are hired as transport drivers. Henty demonstrated fidelity to known facts but the story was hopelessly implausible. Having climbed Isandlwana before the battle, Dick and Tom hide on its top but sleep through Chelmsford's return. Captured by Mbilini, they are rescued at Hlobane and thus witness Kambula and, later, Ulundi. In the Anglo-Transvaal War they manage to be present at nearly all major actions. At war's end they return to farming. The Henty titles that carried the name of an imperial figure sold better than those which did not.[187] The war did not offer an obvious title figure and Isandlwana was not to be celebrated per se. Henty, who saw Zulu as preferable to Boers, was most exercised by the humiliation of Majuba but blamed Isandlwana on 'the blunder, made by the General in command, of dividing his army and marching away with the greater portion without troubling himself to keep up communication with the force left behind'.[188]

After Henty's death in 1902 his natural successor was a former army doctor, Frederick Brereton. One of Brereton's first stories was *With Shield and Assegai* (1900). Donald Stewart is the son of the Scottish doctor living near Ulundi. Sent back to school in Britain, he is falsely accused of theft and enlists. As he speaks Zulu, he is sent out to Natal as a mounted infantryman. Chelmsford receives news of the attack on Isandlwana and Stewart is sent back to tell Pulleine that help is on its way! He sees the camp's fall but, on his way back to warn Chelmsford, is wounded and forced into the Buffalo, fetching up at Rorke's Drift in time to help its defence. Sent to Durban to recover, he learns his father has escaped from Zululand, but his sister and her friend have been captured. Donald rescues them, reaching Chelmsford's force just before Ulundi. He marries the sister's friend and returns to Scotland to train as a doctor.[189] Similar adventurous tales set in Zululand were Henry Adams's *Perils in the Transvaal and Zululand* (1887) and Constantine Ralli's *The Strange Case of Falconer Thring* (1902).

Not all stories were uncritical of British actions. Ernest Glanville's *The Lost Heiress* (1891) had a notably anti-war theme, while Bertram

Mitford's quartet of novels narrated through the Zulu character, Untuswa, who fights at Isandlwana—*The King's Assegai* (1894), *The White Shield* (1895), *The Induna's Wife* (1898), and *The Word of the Sorceress* (1902)—was highly sympathetic to the Zulu.[190]

Rorke's Drift found its place in compilations for young readers such as James Macaulay's *True Tales of Travel and Adventure, Valour and Virtue* (1884); William Knollys and William Elliott's *Battlefield Heroes* (1900); Alfred Miles's *A Book of Heroes* (1907); Charles Michael's *Brave Deeds for British Boys* (1908); and H. E. Marshall's *Our Empire Story* (1908). Melvill and Coghill's story appeared in *Peril and Patriotism: True Tales of Heroic Deeds and Startling Adventures* (1901). W. Melville Pimblett's *In Africa with the Union Jack* (1898) characterized the war as one of 'strange contrasts, of melancholy occurrences, of noble deeds against desperate odds' but the 'hordes of barbarians' were intelligent as well as savage.[191] The war did not appeal, however, to the Revd W. H. Fitchett, whose *Deeds That Won the Empire* (1897) 'ignored almost any warfare that had the whiff of conquest about it'.[192] British boys' fiction was not unlike the 'dime novels' churned out in the United States in the late nineteenth century, establishing a basis for the many novels relating to Custer.[193]

Isandlwana and Rorke's Drift featured in other popular compilations such as *Battles of the Nineteenth Century* (1896); James Grant's *Recent British Battles on Land and Sea* (1904); and Sir Evelyn Wood's *British Battles on Land and Sea* (1915). It has been argued that school textbooks stood halfway between popular culture and children's stories. While those published prior to the period 1900–5 generally acknowledged Zulu courage and were sometimes critical of British policy, those after this period were increasingly inaccurate and simplistic in pitting Zulu savagery against British heroism. This endured since many of the texts from the 1920s and 1930s were reprinted in the 1950s and even the early 1960s.[194]

The war was not only reflected in children's literature but also in toys. William Britains Ltd produced its first hollow cast lead alloy figures in 1893. A Boer set was produced in 1899 and other contemporary wars featured thereafter. The only figures of African tribal opponents were a Zulu set in 1908 and a Zulu kraal in 1912. New Zulu sets were produced between 1937 and 1940. No other African set appeared until Abyssinians in 1936, apart from the Arabs intended to complement French Foreign Legion figures in 1911. Even the Zulu disappeared from the sets produced between 1945 and 1966 when the production of lead soldiers was ended. Britains resumed issuing 'collectors' metal soldiers in 1993, including an extensive Zulu War range.[195] There were other toy soldier manufacturers, such as the former employees of Britains, the Hanks Brothers, who set up on their own in 1897, and John Hill & Co., who set up in 1898. Both produced Zulus, Hanks as early as 1904. In the 1920s a Zulu Toy Company operated in the United States.[196] There are at least nine contemporary companies producing Zulu War sets in metal or plastic at 54 mm or more, and over forty ranges of smaller figures available for wargames under 30 mm. There are also a number of downloadable Zulu War computer games. Meccano introduced its clockwork 'Zulu Trains' range as a follow-up to its 'Hornby' range in 1922.

Adult Literature

Turning to the adult market, novels showed the same transition as other forms of cultural output from the liberal orthodoxy of anti-militarism in the early Victorian period to an imperial mindset more attuned to evolving popular taste by the last quarter of the nineteenth century.[197] Henty had a specific juvenile audience but Henry Rider Haggard was to project a particular image of the Zulu as well as his robust imperialism to a far wider readership. For Haggard the Zulu were 'the finest savage race in the world' in much the same way that, for Mitford, they were 'the finest and most intelligent race of savages in the world'.[198]

Ironically, Haggard did not actually set foot in Zululand until 1914, but he had been in South Africa from 1875 to 1881 and had helped hoist the Union Jack over the Transvaal in April 1877. Employed as clerk to the Transvaal colonial secretary, Haggard was appointed adjutant of the Pretoria Horse, raised after Isandlwana. It was intended to join Colonel Frederick Weatherly's Border Horse in Zululand but was retained in Pretoria, thereby avoiding the destruction of the Border Horse at Hlobane. When he finally did get to Zululand, Haggard was especially moved by Isandlwana: 'This must be a quiet place for man's eternal sleep. But the scene which went before that sleep!'[199]

Haggard's *Cetywayo and His White Neighbours* coincided with Cetshwayo's visit to London in 1882. While justifying the war as inevitable, it criticized Wolseley's settlement, for Haggard always favoured annexation. Haggard also contributed the story of Isandlwana and Rorke's Drift to Andrew Lang's *The True Story Book* (1893), using in part the testimony of his friend, Edward Essex, and in which he noted his friendship with Coghill. In a nuanced account reflecting his sympathies for the Zulu, Haggard largely put the blame on Durnford. Haggard saw the war as but a scene in 'the building up of a great Anglo-Saxon empire in Africa' and one 'begotten by the genius and courage of individual Englishmen'.[200] Haggard said that the final sentences of his account for Lang 'were written with a pen that was found among the bones of the dead at Isandlwana'.[201]

Of the subsequent novels only *The Witch's Head* (1884) was set during the Zulu War, and it included a depiction of Isandlwana. The second of the three volumes of *The Witch's Head* features a unit clearly based on the Border Horse but which is destroyed at Isandlwana. The hero, Ernest Kershaw, escapes, only to be blinded later by lightning. The remainder of the novels all had Zulu characters, notably that of Umslopogaas in *Allan Quatermain* (1887) and the entire cast in *Nada the Lily* (1892). Umslopogaas was actually based on a Swazi Haggard encountered in the Transvaal in 1877.[202] 'Kukuanaland' in *King Solomon's Mines* (1885) was clearly meant to be Zululand and was depicted as sufficiently civilized under its intelligent and aristocratic rightful ruler as to require no European intervention. In *Allan Quatermain* the inhabitants of Kukuanaland are identical in lifestyle and outlook to the lost white civilization of the Zu-Vendi.[203] Yet Haggard always maintained a 'sharp division' between savagery and civilization.[204]

Haggard's nostalgic and elegiac view of the Zulu past was in the comfortable knowledge that the old Zulu order was gone. For many, the Zulu were ever after cast as Haggard depicted them.[205] Haggard returned to the war in *Black Heart and White Heart: A Zulu Idyll* (1896), and in the final volume of a trilogy on the kingdom's history, *Finished* (1917). In *Finished*, Allan Quatermain is with Durnford but escapes and hides at the top of Isandlwana, seeing the death of the last man of the 24th in the cave below. Zulu moving about prevent him from joining Chelmsford's force on its return and he makes his way to the north, taking no further part in the war.

Commemoration

Attention has been drawn to the common celebration of imperial heroes in street furniture and street names.[206] There is an Isandula Road in Nottingham as well as others named for Bulwer, Chard, Chelmsford, Durnford, Ekowe, and Pearson.[207] Zulu Mews is in Battersea. Similarly, there are roads named Rorke's Drift in Ash, Camberley, and Mychett in Surrey. Plots at Ash were being advertised as early as April 1880.[208] Farms named Rorke's Drift are found near Harrogate and at Romsey in Kent. At least twenty individual properties in the UK are also named Rorke's Drift. In March 2017 a new street in Lichfield was named after Samuel Wassall VC.[209] Then there were new children's names. It was reported in November 1879 that a soldier at Woolwich had christened his son Ketchwayo.[210] This does not seem to have been the case but the 1881 Census does throw up Cetewayo Platt, George Cetewayo Burton, Robert Isandula Jameson, Florinda Isandhlwana Barham, Charles Rorke's Drift Marriner, and Henry Chard Bromhead Gates.

Monuments abounded, some significant in style. One such was that to the 80th Foot in Lichfield Cathedral, which is particularly rich in its symbolism, including the names of the fallen inscribed on approximations of Zulu shields.[211] Of individual monuments, a striking example is the obelisk in Bredgar near Sittingbourne in Kent to

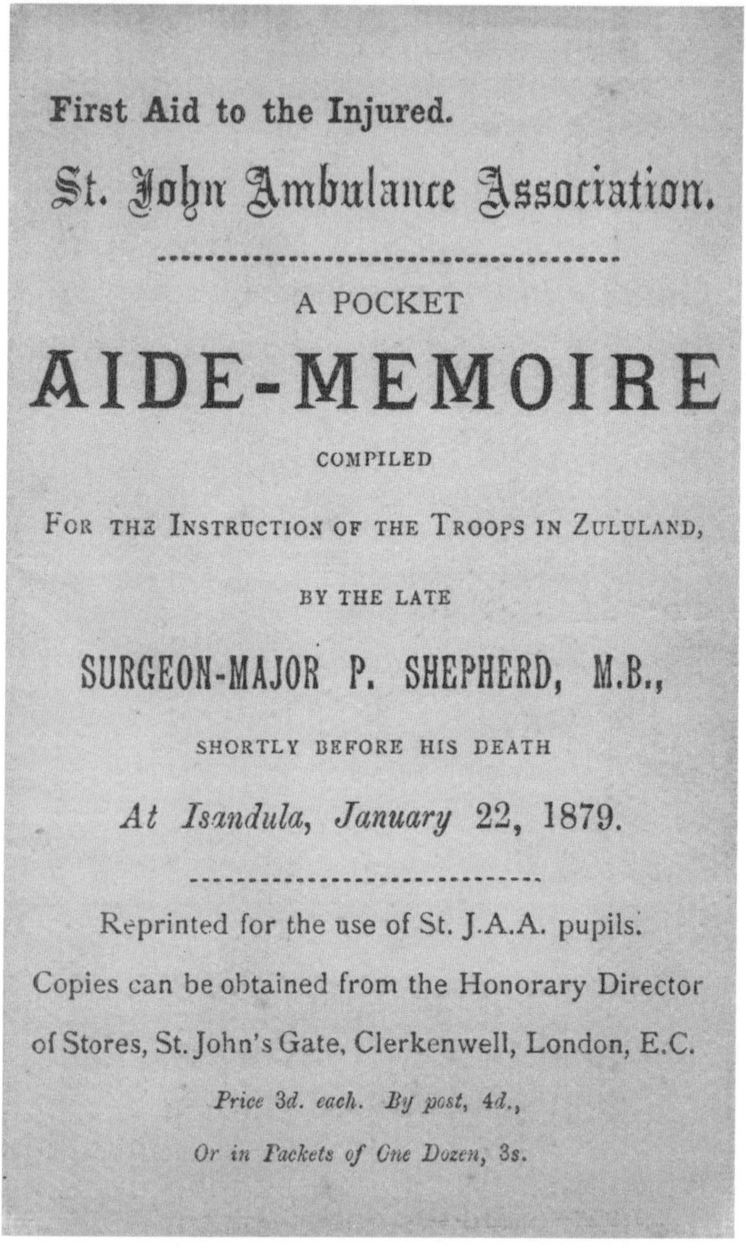

First Aid to the Injured.

St. John Ambulance Association.

∙∙

A POCKET

AIDE-MEMOIRE

COMPILED

FOR THE INSTRUCTION OF THE TROOPS IN ZULULAND,

BY THE LATE

SURGEON-MAJOR P. SHEPHERD, M.B.,

SHORTLY BEFORE HIS DEATH

At Isandula, January 22, 1879.

∙∙∙∙∙∙∙∙∙∙∙∙∙∙∙∙∙∙∙∙∙∙∙∙∙∙∙∙∙∙∙∙∙∙∙∙

Reprinted for the use of St. J.A.A. pupils.

Copies can be obtained from the Honorary Director

of Stores, St. John's Gate, Clerkenwell, London, E.C.

Price 3d. each. By post, 4d.,

Or in Packets of One Dozen, 3s.

Figure 18. Aide-memoire issued by the St John Ambulance Association in memory of Surgeon Major Peter Shepherd, killed at Isandlwana.

Private Ashley Goatham of the 1/24th killed at Isandlwana.[212] In the case of Surgeon Major Peter Shepherd, whose probable grave site has been identified on Fugitives' Trail, the St John Ambulance Association published his pocket aide-memoire for first-aiders in his memory.

At Isandlwana there were initially only the graves. Due to the hardness of the ground and the lack of suitable tools, remains were gathered together and covered with stone cairns in May 1879. The bodies of the 24th were left alone at Glyn's request until the regiment could bury its own, a decision that struck many as strange. Interment of the 24th took place in June. With reports of bones uncovered by rains, Bromhead's elder brother, Major Charles Bromhead, took out another party on 19 September 1879, at which time the staffs and a case from the missing Queen's and Regimental Colours of the 2/24th were found. Bromhead was methodical, but more rains the following summer led to a further burial expedition led by Lieutenant Maurice O'Connell of the 60th Rifles from 14 to 17 March 1880.[213] Relics, including bones, were revealed regularly by the rains, as Mitford witnessed in 1882:[214]

> In spite of a luxuriant growth of herbage the circles where stood the rows of tents are plainly discernible, while strewn about are tent pegs, cartridge cases, broken glass, bits of rope, meat tins and sardine boxes pierced with assegai stabs, shrivelled up pieces of shore-leather, and rubbish of every description; bones of horses and oxen gleam white and ghastly, and here and there in the grass one stumbles upon a half-buried skeleton.

Complaints continued and a Natal official, Alfred Boast, was hired to carry out reburial at deeper level in February and March 1883. Over the course of twenty days, Boast recorded 298 cairns, each with between two and four skeletons.[215] At this time Anstey's body was removed for reburial by his family in Woking: Durnford had been reburied by the Colenso family in Pietermaritzburg in October 1879. Further archaeological examination after erosion that left two cairns close to collapse in 1999 suggested that Boast's cairns have limited value for assessing where the dead fell.[216] There were similar recurring problems from the hasty initial burials of Custer's dead at the Little Big Horn.[217]

The cairns appear only to have been whitewashed after 1900. It was not until 1928 that the area containing most of the cairns was fenced off. Many outside this area were lost over the years, becoming indistinguishable from heaps of stones. Some were reconstructed and others located and recorded in 1958, although, as suggested earlier, these have since been lost. Many of the Zulu dead were buried in dongas, ant bear holes, and the mealie-pits of homesteads in the vicinity. At Rorke's Drift a monument to the defenders was carved immediately after the battle by Bandsman Melsop of the 2/24th, a former stonemason.

Memorials to the colonial units were eventually erected at Isandlwana. That of the Natal Carbineers again invoked Thermopylae:

> Tell It in England Those
> That Pass Us By,
> Here, Faithful to Their Charge,
> Her Soldiers Lie.

An anonymous poem in the *Cape Times* on 20 February 1879 likened the stand of the colonial volunteers to Thermopylae, as did an ode in Latin in the *Natal Witness* on 9 August upon the volunteers' return from the war.[218] The memorial to the Natal Mounted Police was unveiled in 1913. One to the 24th, unveiled by General Sir Reginald Hart VC in 1914, was built over one of the larger original cairns. In unveiling it, Hart, who referred to Smith-Dorrien's memories of the battle, stressed that 'we knew that every man fought his best, and died doing his duty in that state into life to which it had pleased God to call him. Could anyone leave this world in a better way?' The accompanying brochure laid blame on Durnford for not laagering the camp, and on the failure of the ammunition supply.[219] Hart alluded yet again to the example of Thermopylae, a common motif also used for the Alamo and Custer's Last Stand.[220] A monument to the seven Old Boys of Pietermaritzburg High School killed at Isandlwana, including George Shepstone, was only erected in 1969.

There was some early battlefield tourism. Battlefields had a fascination for some in the United States in the 1820s.[221] The field of Waterloo became perhaps the first mass tourist attraction in Europe.[222] As in the case of southern battlefields of the American Revolutionary War in the United States, communications (as well as expense) precluded many visitors from reaching Zululand.

An early pilgrimage was that of the Empress Eugénie who, accompanied by Evelyn Wood, spent April to June 1880 in Zululand to see where her son, the Prince Imperial, had been killed. The group visited Hlobane and Kambula as well as the Prince's death site in the Tshotshosi valley, before returning to Durban via Isandlwana and Rorke's Drift.[223] Another early visitor was Ralph Watts Leyland, a Liverpool shipowner, in 1880. At Isandlwana, Leyland 'walked about in the grass, picking up numbers of bullets, empty cartridges and various other articles. Among them was a small cake of paint in a little tin case, a

Figure 19. General Sir Reginald Hart VC unveiling the Memorial to the 24th, Isandlwana, 4 March 1914.

lead pencil, several uniform buttons, a stud, tent pegs, nails, etc. etc., all lying as thrown down.' He also noted bones protruding from graves.[224] As already indicated, Bertram Mitford visited in 1882. What was described as the 'Pilgrim's Tour' coincided with the fiftieth anniversary in 1929 but it consisted of just one officer, Lieutenant V. J. F. Popham, and two other ranks of the 2nd South Wales Borderers, who joined the commemorations in South Africa.[225]

Zulu War scenes were staples of military re-enactments by regular and auxiliary forces at tournaments and tattoos in the 1890s intended to showcase the army, the Zulu being soldiers blacked up for the purpose. Scenes—usually skirmishes between Zulu and cavalry—featured, for example, at the Biggleswade fete in August 1891; Preston North End Football Ground in October 1892; the Foresters' Fete and Military Tournament at Gloucester in May 1893; the South of Ireland Military Tournament in June 1893; and the Yorkshire Grand Military Tournament in April 1898.[226]

At the annual Royal Military Tournament at the Royal Agricultural Hall in 1892, the Zulu War display 'riveted the attention of the numerous audience, who cheered and laughed by turns, for both troopers and Zulus played their parts with truly marvellous fidelity'. At the same event in 1895 'assegais hurtled through the air, Zulus chanted in savage chorus, machine guns rattled, and a flank attack by Zulus from beneath the Royal Box brought about a hand-to-hand fight which was intensely and strongly realistic'.[227] The Grand Military Fete at Cheltenham's Winter Gardens in February 1895 saw Rorke's Drift staged by the 1st Gloucestershire Engineer Volunteers. The regular adjutant, Captain Cregan, had served in South Africa and visited Rorke's Drift, enabling an artist from Northampton Theatre to produce a realistic backdrop of the mission station. The display was put on twice daily on each of four days with thirty-six soldiers playing the defenders, four the relief column, and fifty-seven the Zulu. Sergeant Major Brown, for example, played Chard and Sapper Moxey played Dabulamanzi. Low-powered blank cartridges were used as well as ball-pointed bayonets on retractable springs and retractable cloth tips to the assegais. All was portrayed to create a picture 'at once peculiarly thrilling and dramatic'.[228] The first re-enactment of Custer's Last Stand close to the battlefield took place in 1909, although William 'Buffalo Bill' Cody made Custer's Last Stand as the climax of his 'Wild West Show' from 1887.[229] William Jones VC briefly toured with Buffalo Bill in Britain in 1887–8.[230]

Tattoos were revived after the Great War, notably the celebrated Aldershot Searchlight Tattoos. 'Zulu' featured at Aldershot in June 1923 but their night attack on the laager of a British convoy 'of the time of the Zulu campaign' brought forth aircraft, tanks, and armoured cars 'by the aid of which the tables are turned upon the attacking hordes, who are scattered, seeking cover in the woods'.[231] Similarly illuminated by searchlights, Zulu were repulsed by machine guns by the 2nd Buffs at Weymouth and Ramsgate in August 1925.[232] More conventionally the Sherwood Foresters re-enacted Rorke's Drift for the North Irish District Tattoo at Londonderry in August 1927. At the Bedford Tattoo in August 1938, the 'Zulu' were recruits from RAF Cardington kitted out in costumes made by Rotarians' wives.[233] There was even a re-enactment of Rorke's Drift by an Australian militia unit in Melbourne in 1934.[234]

The 2nd South Wales Borderers re-enacted Rorke's Drift for the Northern Command Tattoo at Ravensworth Castle in July 1934, attended by the Rorke's Drift defenders, Bourne, Jenkins, and Caleb Wood. There was some controversy, the Newcastle Methodist Synod and local Free Church ministers objecting to portraying Rorke's Drift but 194,000 spectators attended over the six days of the event.[235]

As with the debate on old controversies, war then intervened. In many respects, however, real interest in the Zulu War was but transitory after the early 1880s.

6

Interpretations

A brief revival of interest after the Second World War was sparked by the work of the first professional historian to study Isandlwana, Sir Reginald Coupland, who walked the battlefield with a Zulu veteran and published *Zulu Battle Piece* (1948). While Coupland had written extensively on the history of imperial policy, his study of Isandlwana was 'a pleasant diversion from other work'.[1] Strangely he claimed that Chard and Bromhead were 'both scarcely out of their "teens"'—Chard was 32 and Bromhead 33—although this reflected Chelmsford's citation for their VCs, which suggested they were 'young officers'.[2] Coupland recognized the role of Frere and Shepstone in forcing the issue of war—it was 'Frere's war'—and understood how far the British had underestimated the Zulu. Heavily dependent upon Rothwell's official history, he attributed defeat to the failure to laager the wagons, the collapse of the Natal Native Contingent, and the exhaustion of the ammunition supply on the firing line. While Durnford had taken command of the camp, Coupland did not believe him responsible for all movements since Pulleine must have ordered the deployments to the Tahelane ridge when Durnford was far distant. Tellingly, Coupland suggested that, even if Chelmsford had not managed to divide his force, a Zulu attack on the following day would have been just as successful and even more disastrous. Nor could Chelmsford have saved his camp if he had returned to it on receipt of Pulleine's first message, or avoided an even more comprehensive defeat en route if caught in the open.[3]

Figure 20. Fiftieth Anniversary Commemoration, Isandlwana, January 1929.

The gap between Coupland and the revival in the mid-1960s is related to the loss of interest in imperial themes among military historians following the Second World War and, perhaps, to the process of decolonization. Rupert Furneaux's *The Zulu War: Isandlwana and Rorke's Drift* (1963) merely resurrected the charges against Chelmsford made by Clements thirty years earlier. But then came the juxtaposition of publication of *The Washing of the Spears* and the opening of *Zulu*.

The Washing of the Spears

Born in 1924, Morris was inspired to write on the war by a children's storybook and two South African-set novels—Michael Leigh's *Cross of Fire* (1949), in which a Scot is at both Isandlwana and Rorke's Drift, and T. H. White's *Farewell Victoria* (1933), a mournful tale of a groom's son, Mundy, who takes part in the war.[4] Setting out to write a short story on Isandlwana and Rorke's Drift in 1955, Morris was persuaded by Ernest Hemingway that there was no readable account of the war and none of any kind published in the United States. The main research was undertaken while Morris was stationed in Berlin in 1961–2: having served in the US Navy, he joined the Central Intelligence Agency (CIA) in 1956. Morris was able to see some of Chelmsford's papers but one of his sources was the unreliable 1955 'biography' of Shaka by E. A. Ritter. Morris accepted that the Zulu kingdom's 'irresponsible power posed a considerable threat to the continued existence of the European civilisation in its vicinity'.[5] Morris eschewed any footnotes because he did not 'wish to claim for this work an academic status to which it is not entitled'.[6] As already suggested with reference to such matters as the discovery of the *impi* and the ammunition supply, Morris's well-crafted prose has been very influential. By the time of his death in 2002, it had appeared in seventeen languages and sold in excess of 200,000 copies.[7] As John Laband has written, 'something was brought into being with an indestructible will of its own and has marched remorselessly on, never once out of print'.[8]

Film

It was another writer, John Prebble, whose short story on Rorke's Drift in *Lilliput* magazine in April 1958 led to *Zulu*.[9] Hollywood had not neglected the Zulu, D. W. Griffith having produced *A Zulu's Heart* (1908) with white actors blacked up. This and other early treatments had the Boer 'Great Trek' as the background, a theme suitable for an audience reared on American 'manifest destiny'.[10] The Trek remained central to Hollywood's *Untamed* (1955) and *The Fiercest Heart* (1961). Hollywood's first cinematic version of Custer's Last Stand was in 1909 and of the Alamo in 1911.[11]

The first actual film about the Zulu War was *The Symbol of Sacrifice* (1918) made by F. Horace Rose of African Film Productions in South Africa. The same company had made *De Voortrekkers* (1916). Built around a fictional story and billed as 'The Great National and Patriotic

Drama of the Zulu War of 1879', it featured Isandlwana, Rorke's Drift, Melvill and Coghill, the Prince Imperial and Ulundi, costing some £20,000 to make. The story of the heroine, Marie Moxter, and her fiancé, Preston Fanshall, is seen in parallel to that of a Zulu woman, Melissa, and her lover. Marie saves her faithful servant, Goba, from a cruel German overseer, Carl, who covets Marie for himself just as a witch doctor, Dabomba, covets Melissa. Fanshall escapes Isandlwana to warn Rorke's Drift where he is killed and Marie taken prisoner. Carl allies himself with Dabomba but Marie is saved by Goba. The battle scenes are well done and there is some stress placed on the inability to open the ammunition boxes at Isandlwana. Unfortunately, the historical adviser and Zulu War veteran Johann Colenbrander, playing Chelmsford, was drowned with two others while filming a scene at the Klip River. At one time editor of the *Natal Witness*, Rose was passionately committed to maintaining Natal's links to Britain. The Union Jack was central to the film, which opened with the statement, 'I am the flag that braves the shock of war.' Melvill, kissing the standard wrapped around his body as he died, was the 'symbol of sacrifice'.[12] Patriotism, said Rose, was the root from which 'the greatest and most noble achievements of the human race have sprung'. Thus, the film was also 'to remind the present generation, war-torn and weary as it is, that heroism and devotion are no monopoly of the World's Great War, whose agony has been unfolding before our eyes'.[13] It corresponded with the desire to commemorate the Empire's recently fallen. It was in South Africa that the concept of the two minutes' 'Silence' on Armistice Day originated, the British high commissioner, Sir Percy Fitzpatrick, having witnessed the three-minutes' 'Noon Pause' observed in South Africa each day from July 1916 onwards.

Feature film is fiction but it may capture the surface of reality and serve as a visual recreation of the past. It is also a reflection of popular attitudes and cultural values as a collaborative product of the studio, its producers, director, editor, technicians, writers, and star—and, in that sense, of wider society. Above all, it is driven by commercial pressures and the film that entertains and makes money is likely to be

Figure 21. A scene from *Zulu*, 1964.

one which, through calculation, instinct, or pure luck, best reflects popular collective attitudes. Historical accuracy is not to be expected.

Prebble's article, and the script and screenplay for *Zulu* worked on by Prebble and the director and co-producer, Cy Endfield, from 1959 to 1963, was based upon those sources available at the time.[14] To criticize *Zulu* for its many historical inaccuracies of fact and characterization is pointless. The more trivial include Michael Caine shouting 'Fire!' at one point and showing his amalgam fillings when they would have been gold at the time! As Sheldon Hall has written, errors are not 'of the slightest consequence to serious criticism of *Zulu* either as a work of art (or entertainment), or as a representation of history'.[15]

Zulu reinforced the idea that the Zulu used Martinis at Rorke's Drift but also created its own myths, not least the Zulu salute to brave men at the end of the battle, and the Welshness of the 24th. The garrison famously sing 'Men of Harlech'—the lyrics are peculiar to the film—while awaiting the final Zulu assault. A number of Victorian melodramas had soldiers singing while fighting off natives and

Welshmen sung 'Men of Harlech' when confronted by Apaches in the western *Apache Drums* (1951).[16] Co-producer and star Stanley Baker, for whom *Zulu* was a highly personal project, saw the film as a tribute to the Welsh.[17]

As is well known, *Zulu* was not shot in Zululand but against the spectacular backdrop of the 'amphitheatre' of the Royal Natal National Park in the Drakensbergs between March and June 1963. It had a modest budget of $2 million—it came in at $1.7 million—and, contrary to popular myth, Zulu extras rarely exceeded 240. Most of B Company, 2/24th was played by A Company, 5th South African Infantry Battalion. Interior shots of the defence of the hospital were filmed at Twickenham Studios with West Indian extras.[18] Filming in apartheid South Africa was not without its problems. The part of Cetshwayo was played by Chief (later Prince) Mangosuthu Buthelezi, the maternal great-grandson of Cetshwayo, but the film was deemed 'unfit for black consumption' as an incitement to violence although it was widely seen by whites: it was eventually shown on South African television in 1993. It did less well in the US where racial divisions were also deep.[19] In Britain, the epic nature of the film, the scenery, the opening and ending narration by Richard Burton, and the memorable musical score by John Barry, based on Zulu chants, had an instant impact when it premiered in London on 22 January 1964. Predictably the only purely negative reviews in Britain were in the *Daily Worker* and *The Guardian*.[20]

Zulu had its contemporary parodies but as a production it was an influence on later film-makers.[21] It was given new cinematic releases in 1967, 1972, and 1976 and has been regularly seen on television ever since. By 1989 *Zulu* had grossed $10.1 million worldwide.[22] So well known was it that the apocryphal phrase supposedly uttered by Michael Caine in *Zulu*—'Don't throw those bloody spears at me'—but actually echoing his role in *The Italian Job* (1969), was used by Toyota in 1998–9 for its commercial ident sponsoring ITV movies.[23]

Zulu was ranked as the second-highest placed British film (eighteenth overall) in a satellite television millennium poll of all-time favourite films by 60,000 subscribers; eighth by website users in Channel Four's poll of 100 greatest war films in 2005; and first in the list of favourite films in a poll of Conservative MPs in 2004.[24] In 2008 a survey by the British Forces Broadcasting Service revealed *Zulu* as the most popular film of all time among British service personnel.[25] In the year of its fiftieth anniversary, the *Daily Telegraph* asked rhetorically, 'is this the greatest ever British war film?'[26] Buthelezi attended a fiftieth anniversary showing of the digitally remastered print in London in May 2014. He remarked that the film had been a 'notable piece of PR' for the Zulu nation.[27]

The film's enduring popularity may be owed in part to its hybrid nature, on the one hand looking back to classic imperial adventures such as Alexander Korda's *The Drum* (1938) and *The Four Feathers* (1939), and on the other anticipating the increasingly anti-war mood of the 1960s.[28] Prebble was a former communist and Endfield had been blacklisted in Hollywood. There was an anti-imperialist message, albeit one rendered ambiguous by the emphasis on British valour.[29] Anachronistic lip service was paid to anti-war rhetoric in the screenplay, and class antagonism surfaced between Baker's Chard and Caine's Bromhead. Hook was portrayed as 'an archetypal sixties rebel'.[30] Yet *Zulu* has been increasingly condemned by academic critics uncomfortable with its ambivalence towards imperial themes and for its supposedly liberal ideological veneer.[31] The heroic stature accorded to the Zulu hardly amounts to the racism often alleged. Be it nostalgia for empire or otherwise, the viewing public, for whom *Zulu* retains its special place in British film culture, has largely discounted such critical views.

The cinematic 'prequel' to *Zulu*, in the form of *Zulu Dawn* with Peter O'Toole, John Mills, and Burt Lancaster, appeared in May 1979. It was virulently anti-militarist and not a commercial success.[32] Mills, as Frere, seeks a 'final solution' to the Zulu problem while O'Toole's arrogant Chelmsford is undone by Zulu cunning. While Endfield and Anthony Storey's screenplay was clearly based on Morris, emphasizing the failure of the ammunition supply, Lancaster's Durnford is characterized as a Zulu expert whose knowledge is discounted by

Chelmsford. There is no suggestion that he bears any responsibility for the defeat.

Zulu Dawn began as another project of Endfield and Baker but Baker died in 1976 and the project was taken over by the American producer Nate Kohn, with Douglas Hickox as director. Financial difficulties meant the film went badly over budget. It was filmed in Zululand. Siphezi stood in for Isandlwana and the British crossing of the Buffalo was filmed at Rorke's Drift, albeit with the British crossing into Natal from Zululand rather than vice versa for technical reasons. Buthelezi was given the opportunity to reprise the role of Cetshwayo but his increased political profile precluded it and the part was taken by Simon Sabela, who had been dance leader and stuntman on *Zulu*.[33] As with *Zulu*, there has been detailed criticism of its historical inaccuracies, ranging from the uniforms to how little some actors resemble their characters.[34] While there were some spectacular battle scenes, *Zulu Dawn* was not as good a film as *Zulu* and did not chime with its audience in the same way. As one American critic wrote, 'given the political climate of the audiences at the time these films were made', *Zulu Dawn* could not have been made in 1964 and *Zulu* could not have been made in 1979.[35]

Yet, for all its more politically correct credentials, *Zulu Dawn* still portrayed the Zulu as a savage horde from the perspective of most of its British characters. Hickox equated the invasion of Zululand with Hitler's invasion of Poland but also said that he was influenced by Leni Riefenstahl's *Peoples of Kau* and envisaged the Zulu as 'a sea of black, as African ants'.[36] The opening statement proclaimed that Natal was 'surrounded by a vast and independent Zulu kingdom' as well as suggesting that Isandlwana changed the course of colonial history.[37]

In 1996 Cromwell and Lamancha Productions jointly announced plans for a new film, *The Zulu Wars*, based on the experience of Henry Harford and the 99th Foot. It would be directed by Brian Blessed and financed by crowdfunding. Subscriptions were not as great as anticipated and an agreement could not be reached with the South African government so the project was abandoned.[38]

Figure 22. A scene from *Zulu Dawn*, 1979.

The changing cinematic interpretation over the passage of time bears comparison with treatments of the Alamo and Custer. The classic *They Died With Their Boots On* (1941), starring Errol Flynn as a heroic and flamboyant Custer, can be readily contrasted with Richard Mulligan's characterization of posturing insanity in *Little Big Man* (1970). The imagery of the last stand remained unchanged.[39] Alamo films have had a different trajectory: the Mexican dictator Santa Anna remains as inhumanely callous in *The Alamo* (2004) as in *The Immortal Alamo* (1911). But even John Wayne's *The Alamo* (1960) made some attempt to acknowledge Mexican bravery, and the perspective of Mexicans (Tejanos) who fought with the Texans has been increasingly depicted, as in *Alamo: The Price of Freedom* (1988) and *The Alamo* (2004).[40]

Historiography

Returning to historiography, David Jackson's revisionist 1965 conclusions—on such issues as the supposed ammunition failure and the collapse of the Natal Native Contingent and presented in a specialist military journal—were overshadowed by Morris's bestselling book. Popular accounts appearing in the 1970s added little to Morris and repeated stereotypes of the Zulu hordes. Frank Emery's selection of ordinary soldiers' letters, gleaned from the Victorian provincial press, in *The Red Soldier* (1977), was more original. It was those researches started by *Zulu*, however, that were to do most to add to the historiography. Several authors acknowledged *Zulu* as the inspiration for their interest in the war, including Ian Knight, James Bancroft, Jonathan Hicks, John Young, and Sheldon Hall. Popular accounts of varying value have continued to appear, often connected to anniversaries as in 2004. Some have fallen into stereotypes while some have added telling if relatively minor details. Work by Ron Lock and Peter Quantrill, and most especially by David Jackson, Huw Jones, Julian Whybra, Adrian Greaves, Keith Smith, and Ian Knight has to be taken very seriously. As suggested by the remaining controversies around such issues as the location of the Zulu bivouac, the discovery of the *impi*, Zulu intentions, and ammunition boxes, work by non-academic and academic historians, whether inspired by *Zulu* or otherwise, has continued to unravel the mysteries of Isandlwana and Rorke's Drift.

Increasingly, Africanists have done much to illuminate the Zulu story. In 1979 radicals such as Jeff Guy attacked the commemoration as perpetuating the ideology of white superiority in the centenary academic conference in Durban and notably in the pages of the journal *Reality*. No longer warrior, the Zulu was victim.[41] The interventions were seen by many as unduly divisive when the overall centennial theme was reconciliation.[42] But work by Africanists, especially John Laband and the late Paul Thompson, has been invaluable in analysing Zulu political and strategic decision-making and their operational and tactical methods.

New sources have been identified but significant disagreements remain. Durnford's orders, which had been in the Royal Engineers Museum at Chatham for many years without being noticed, were re-examined in 1990, while Glyn's copy of the orders to column commanders resurfaced in 2003.[43] Curling's letters came to light in 1998. There were also fakes. The account by a Zulu, 'Zabange', unearthed in 1970 was a fabrication.[44] Edmund Yorke reproduced what purported to be a previously unknown message sent by Pulleine to Cavaye at 11.30 ordering him to retire, suggesting that this heralded an attempt to draw back into a defensive laager.[45] It was a forgery produced sometime between 1983 and 1992.[46]

Battlefield archaeology at Isandlwana and Rorke's Drift has assisted reinterpretation to some extent. Excavations and field surveys by Dr Lita Webley at Rorke's Drift in 1988–90 were of limited value. They located a few vestiges of the original foundations of the storehouse and of the hospital, which was smaller than the current structure built by Witt on his return to the site in 1882. Few artefacts were found beyond smashed crockery and fused glass from the fire that consumed the hospital but there was evidence of the over-firing of bullets from older Zulu weapons on the Oskarberg.[47] First mooted in 1989 by the team responsible for the archaeology at the Little Big Horn, excavation at Isandlwana took place in 2000 under the direction of Tony Pollard of the University of Glasgow, following earlier work at Eshowe. As already indicated, artefacts recovered on the firing line had the effect of minimizing the ammunition box controversy as well as fixing the position of the firing line.[48] Finds are still being unearthed. In June 2009 preparations to install a guard hut on Fugitives' Trail turned up a partial skeleton with a general staff button that could only have belonged to Colour Sergeant Keane, Crealock's staff clerk.[49]

Memory

Zulu still exerts its influence in other ways. A limited edition print of De Neuville's painting of Rorke's Drift was thus advertised for the centenary: 'If present enthusiasm is in part a reflection of Stanley Baker's magnificent film "Zulu", in reality the defence remains one of the most glorious of incidents in all the "little wars" of a world painted in British Red.'[50] For that matter, contemporary military artists such as Jason Askew, David Cartwright, and Chris Collingwood have all produced scenes of Isandlwana and Rorke's Drift. While sales of such art might once have been confined to army regiments, its modern profusion suggests not only the popularity of the Zulu War as a subject but also its commercial viability.

The popularity of *Zulu* also created an iconic image for the Martini-Henry, which became highly prized by collectors. In 2008 Mark I Martinis were being offered for sale for £1,100, and in 2011 for £1,350. As one dealer put it, 'The Martini-Henry is a very, very collectable gun—almost entirely due to Michael Caine and the film *Zulu*.' Prices have dropped to around £800 for the later Mark IV of 1886, which is more common than the Mark II used in Zululand, but provenance is all. Spent bullets that may or may not be from the Zulu War are eagerly sought. As another dealer noted, 'It is nothing short of astonishing what collectors—mostly British—are willing to pay for the remains of even a single bullet from a South African battle.'[51] Between 2001 and 2006 there was even a Cardiff-based 'alternative new wave punk' band, 'The Martini-Henry Rifles'. Other artefacts are equally valued. The last Zulu War VC to come on the market—that of Robert Jones—sold in 1996 for £80,000. But even the South Africa Medal awarded Chard's batman, Driver Robson, present at Rorke's Drift, fetched a hammer price of £110,000 in February 2017. It beat the £70,000 paid for the medal of another Rorke's Drift defender, Private Minehan of the 2/24th, in December 2016, and the £60,000 paid in July 2017 for that of Corporal James Bushe of the 2/24th, who was slightly wounded at Rorke's Drift. By contrast, that of Isandlwana survivor Captain Walter Stafford of the Natal Native Contingent fetched only £22,000 in March 2017.[52]

Demand for other artefacts continues to testify to the war's fascination. The cello of Band Sergeant David Gamble of the 1/24th killed on Fugitives' Trail was sold for £6,200 in January 2016, while a letter of Walter Dunne written from Rorke's Drift on 24 January 1879 on the back of a delivery note fetched £15,500 in November 2014.[53] A private collection of over 350 Zulu weapons and artefacts coming to auction in January 2014 was valued at over £100,000.[54] A Zulu shield in good condition can fetch up to £500, and assegais and knobkerries up to £150. William Whitelocke Lloyd's fine wartime watercolours, including scenes at Rorke's Drift, sold for £49,250 in 2012.

It is no exaggeration to suggest that the *Zulu* effect led to the rise of modern battlefield tourism in South Africa, although this was not immediate and only developed in the 1990s with the end of apartheid. David Rattray's Fugitives' Drift Lodge opened in 1989 and Isandlwana Lodge in 1999. Interest was also shown by the creation of the Anglo-Zulu War Historical Society (1997), and by popular video and DVD histories. The Regimental Museums of the Royal Welsh at Brecon—the South Wales Borderers amalgamated with the Welch Regiment as the Royal Regiment of Wales in 1969 and, in turn, amalgamated with the Royal Welch Fusiliers in 2006—and of the Royal Engineers at Chatham have increased footfall through Zulu-themed exhibitions and events. There is a close connection between the Royal Welsh and KwaZulu-Natal. The regiment affiliated to South Africa's Zulu-speaking 121 Motorised Infantry Battalion in 1997. Interestingly, the South African Defence Force awarded the John Chard Medal for long service from 1952 until 2003. Queen Victoria presented a silver wreath of immortelles to the 1/24th on 28 July 1880 and it is still carried on the Queen's Colour of the Royal Welsh, with Coghill's sword still worn by the Queen's Colour ensign. Significant commemorations are observed, as at Brecon Cathedral for the centenary in 1979 and the 125th anniversary in 2004. The regiment is invariably represented at key events at Isandlwana and Rorke's Drift.

Commemorative re-enactments and living history events have become common. Individuals participating in re-enactments strive for authenticity. They often see it as a rediscovery and preservation of the past, and a tribute to those portrayed. For the public it can be educational but commemoration merges into simple entertainment.[55] Prominent in the re-enactment of the 24th Foot has been the Diehard Company of the Victorian Military Society. Originally formed in 1993 to depict the Middlesex Regiment in the late Victorian period, almost from the start the Diehards were called upon to represent the 24th Foot, as in a documentary on Rorke's Drift for Cromwell Productions in 1994.[56] They appeared in South Africa for commemorations in 1999, 2004, and 2009.[57] Most recently, a re-enactment at Cardiff Castle in August 2017 commemorated the 135th anniversary of Cetshwayo's visit to Britain, with both the 'Diehards' and a Zulu '*impi*' that included ten princes of the Zulu royal house.[58]

Isandlwana and especially Rorke's Drift remain metaphors. When England faced Italy in a crucial World Cup-qualifying football match in February 1997, *The Times* commented, 'Whether it is Agincourt, Rorke's Drift, Dunkirk, or the football field, the English remain level-headed in the face of adversity, masters of the tight squeeze.'[59] Italy won 1–0. The origin of the well-known rugby drinking-game song 'Zulu Warrior'—'Drink it down you Zulu Warrior' or 'Hold it down you Zulu Warrior' in some versions—is uncertain. The Students Union at King's College London defeated a motion to ban it in January 2013, the rugby team maintaining it was 'in no way linked to the subjugation of the Zulu'.[60] In August 1977 blacks rioting at the Notting Hill Carnival 'looked and sounded like something out of the film classic *Zulu*', while a notorious, mostly white, football hooligan gang known as the 'Zulu Warriors' associated with Birmingham City Football Club in the 1980s was broken by a police undercover operation after rioting against Leeds United fans in May 1985 that left 500 injured and one dead.[61] In June 2014 an unbeaten century to stave off defeat against Surrey by Gloucestershire's Ian Cockbain 'would certainly have met with the approval of Lieutenant John Chard'.[62] In October 2014 the England Rugby League side wore a commemorative jersey for the centenary of the so-called 'Rorke's Drift Test' against Australia in July 1914, when the British Lions had won 14–6 despite being reduced to ten men by injuries.[63]

In the wake of the Conservative defeat at the May 1997 general election, Peter Brooke, Conservative MP for the Cities of London and Westminster, chose to refer to anticipated constitutional change: 'The people have spoken. The battle of Isandlwana is over and the defence of Rorke's Drift is about to begin.' He was obviously fond of the analogy since he repeated it in July 1998. Now Lord Brooke of Sutton Mandeville, he again spoke—in debates on student tuition fees in November 2002 and May 2004—of previously discussing the issue with a Zimbabwean minister in 'reruns of Rorke's Drift'.[64] More understandably, the fifty-six-day defence of an outpost against the Taliban at Musa Qala in Afghanistan's Helmand Province in 2006 by just eighty-eight men from the Royal Irish Regiment and the Parachute Regiment was also likened to Rorke's Drift.[65]

Thus do Isandlwana and, especially, Rorke's Drift endure in British popular memory, but would it be so without *Zulu*?

7

Zulu Perspectives

The Anglo-Zulu War was a short and limited conflict so far as Britain was concerned, notwithstanding Isandlwana. It was relatively cheap at £5.2 million.[1] By contrast, it was fought on Zulu territory and amongst the Zulu. Given the lack of written records for tribal groups such as the Zulu, much of their story remained inaccessible, although there was, and remains, an oral tradition, to which has been added the imprint of succeeding generations of storytellers. Nonetheless, reconstructing the Zulu perspective is problematic.

Jeff Guy has argued that the war 'meant the disruption and the suspension of fundamental processes of existence, and suffering to all, not just the men responsible for meeting the invaders'.[2] Systematic destruction of kraals and of crops, and large-scale driving off livestock was integral to Chelmsford's strategy. As he wrote in April 1879, 'the more the Zulu nation at large feels the strain brought upon them by the war, the more anxious will they be to see it brought to an end'.[3] The invasion occurred in midsummer when crops would be harvested, leaving the work largely in the hands of women without the assistance of the men on heavier tasks. Food shortages and, potentially, diseases associated with malnutrition were likely.[4] The population of the Nquthu district, where Chelmsford's column crossed into Zululand, was substantially affected, with menfolk joining their *ibutho*, and women, children, and the aged going into hiding. They went into hiding again for the second British invasion in May, and once more in the last months of the war. William Montague noted the area was still deserted and desolated in October 1879. It was then allocated to the outsider, the Sotho Hlubi Molife, in Wolseley's post-war settlement. Hlubi brought in Sotho settlers as well as Natal natives.[5]

Yet, John Laband has cast doubt on the overall impact on the Zulu population, which was in the region of 250,000–300,000 in 1879. The loss of perhaps 6,000 males in their prime equated to 21 per cent of those engaged in the war, but the estimated 14,000 cattle, 1,200 goats, and 3,000 sheep carried off was perhaps only 5 per cent of the total. Equally, while twenty-three of the twenty-four *amakhanda* were torched and perhaps 12,000 huts, this was barely 1 per cent of the total. It is impossible to determine Zulu non-combatant casualties but most civilians encountering the British fled. Many parts of Zululand did not see even a British patrol. Undoubtedly, British actions had serious consequences for many Zulu but most returned to their fields by August and, while many may have gone hungry, the political impact of the dismantling of the Zulu military system was far greater than the war's economic impact.[6]

It has also been suggested that, compared to earlier or later events, the war did not loom large in Zulu history. As J. Y. Gibson, a sympathetic white magistrate, wrote in his history of the Zulu in 1903,[7]

> The war was ended. Many Zulus had been killed. They scarcely knew for what definite cause they fought and died. They had heard of the discussion of various subjects of difference, but as to the exact purport of these differences they were generally ignorant. Some say, metaphorically, that they reached their ears in the crack of rifles.

More to the point, the war did not alter fundamentally the Zulu way of life, whereas the civil war that erupted in the 1880s did. Zulu 'material and social continuity had not been broken by the invasion'.[8]

In fragmenting the Zulu kingdom, Wolseley stressed he was waging war against Cetshwayo and not the Zulu people. By recognizing the chiefs and leaving the economic structure unchanged, the British succeeded in making the Zulu monarchy irrelevant to ordinary Zulu and ambitious chiefs alike.[9] Assisted by a campaign waged by Bishop Colenso and Lady Florence Dixie, as well as by his visit to London in

Figure 23. Cetshwayo in London as seen by 'Spy', *Vanity Fair*, 26 August 1882.

1882, Cetshwayo was allowed to return to Zululand in January 1883. In a partial revision of the post-war settlement, Cetshwayo's authority was restricted to the central part of his former kingdom and individual chiefs' ambitions led immediately to civil war. Cetshwayo was forced to flee by attacks from the other chiefs, notably Zibhebhu. He died at Eshowe in February 1884 while under the protection of the British

Resident. As unrest continued, intervention by the Boers against Zibhebhu ostensibly on behalf of Cetshwayo's son, Dinuzulu, led to the establishment of the Boers' short-lived so-called New Republic in August 1884. British recognition of the New Republic was conditioned by Boer agreement to drop any suggestion of a Boer protectorate over Dinuzulu's territory. The New Republic, however, was too small to survive and it was incorporated into the Transvaal in 1888. Meanwhile Britain had annexed what remained of Zululand in May 1887. The Zulu state existed as an independent entity for little more than sixty years.

Annexation was largely a consequence of the threat of intervention by the Transvaal as suggested by the establishment of the New Republic. The Transvaal itself had regained its independence from British control as a result of the Anglo-Transvaal War. British defeats culminating with that at Majuba on 27 February 1881 had led to Gladstone's Liberal government moving quickly to end hostilities by granting the Transvaal's independence under the convenient fiction of the Crown's continuing suzerainty. The war had been continuing evidence of Frere's mistaken view that the end of Zulu military power would reconcile Boers to confederation, the removal of the perceived Zulu threat having no impact on Boer intransigence. The contest between Britons and Boers would shape South Africa into the twentieth century.

As for the Zulu, British regulars and police were committed against a rebellion by Dinuzulu's supporters in 1888. Dinuzulu was exiled to St Helena in April 1889 but Zibhebhu, who had been driven out of Zululand by Dinuzulu in June 1888, was also barred from returning. The 1880s were far more traumatic than the Zulu War, since Zulu society itself unravelled, opening the way for intervention by the Boers and the British, and to Zulu dispossession. The Zululand Colony was absorbed into Natal in December 1897 and Zululand opened for white settlement in 1902. In February 1906 the Zulu rebelled against the imposition of a capitation (poll) tax. Bhambatha kaMacinza emerged as leader together with Sihayo's son, Mehlokazulu. The rebellion was crushed by British colonial forces from the Cape and Natal by July 1906 with Bhambatha and Mehlokazulu among the dead.

Oral Traditions

Contemporary Zulu accounts of the war were taken down by the British, but filtered in the process. The resulting testimonies reflected both the preconceptions of those interviewing the Zulu and also what their captors wanted to hear. The interviewers—usually Zulu-speaking officials or civilians—showed a 'morbid and recurring fascination' with Isandlwana. Of the forty-five printed Zulu wartime statements—twenty-one in official reports and twenty-four in the press—a total of twenty-five were entirely or extensively related to Isandlwana.[10] Some emphasis was put on what could be discerned of the deaths of officers such as Durnford, Pulleine, and Younghusband.

Some accounts were hearsay and none was from those in significant command positions. However, Zulu testimonies that continued to surface until the 1920s—some were collected on the occasion of the fiftieth anniversary—have still proven valuable, provided care is exercised. Oral tradition was also captured by James Stuart between 1897 and 1924. A colonial official in Natal, Stuart accompanied the South African Native Labour Contingent to the Western Front during the Great War, and also arranged the Zulu representation in the 1924 Wembley British Empire Exhibition. Stuart was supportive of the aims of the Natal Native Congress for a measure of African political representation. In 1913 he published a critique of the policies that had led to the Bhambatha rebellion.[11] Stuart amassed over 200 interviews as well as archival material, although, as with other Zulu voices heard through a white mediator, the material is not without problems.[12] Stuart recorded the testimony of participants such as Mpashana kaSondondo, who had been at Isandlwana. Six oral accounts of the war—four by Zulu, of whom three had been at Isandlwana—were also collected in the 1930s by Denys Bowden, a mining engineer.[13]

Praise songs and poems (izibongo), odes recording the deeds of chiefs like Shaka and the stories of great events in the Zulu past, play a particular role in Zulu oral memory handed down from generation

Figure 24. 120th Anniversary memorabilia, 1999.

to generation. One praise song referring to the deaths of George Shepstone, the colonial volunteers, and the Natal Mounted Police was heard as early as May 1879. Another relating to the last stand of the Natal Carbineers was still being sung by Zulu at Isandlwana at the 125th anniversary in 2004.[14]

Bishop Colenso collaborated on the story of Cornelius Vijn with Magame Fuze, one of his few Zulu converts. Fuze himself wrote a history in the Zulu language: it was privately published in 1922 and in translation in 1979. Another Zulu writer, R. R. R. Dhlomo, contributed a biography of Cetshwayo in the early 1950s but it was almost a Westernized view.[15] The Zulu oral tradition was also reflected in David Rattray's celebrated battlefield tours until his murder in January 2007. Rob Gerrard, who was associated with Isandlwana Lodge, and had a similar delivery style to Rattray, died in September 2016 from injuries in an attack seven months earlier. Symptomatic of continuing violent crime in South Africa, Gerrard's death was the result of a robbery but that of David Rattray may have had wider roots in issues of land distribution.

A contemporary Zulu poet, L. B. Z. Buthelezi, has drawn inspiration from Isandlwana, using traditional forms of expression to invoke the past. Another Zulu poet, L. L. M. Mbatha, penned 'eNtabeni iSandlwana' in 2008, eNtabeni meaning 'Place of the Mountain'. The 'White Zulu', Johnny Clegg, became a cultural figure in South Africa in the 1980s and 1990s. Clegg mixed English and Zulu lyrics and Western and African melodies, and performed Zulu 'war dances' with his bands, Savuka and Juluka. One of his songs, 'Impi YaseSandlwana', commemorating the Zulu victory at Isandlwana, appeared on Juluka's second album in 1982.

The Zulu writer and lyricist Mbongeni Ngema, best known for his work on *Sarafina!* and *Woza Albert!*, produced a storytelling narrative (with music), *The Zulu*, in 2013, based on stories by his great-grandmother, whose husband fought with the iNgobamakhosi. Commenting on the play's production for the Edinburgh Festival in 2014, Ngema said he wanted to tell the story in the UK as well as South Africa because 'it's both our histories: it's the history of South Africa, yet the battle of Isandlwana, in particular, is also the history of the Scottish [sic] people. It will be interesting for me to see how they respond to their own history. Our histories are intertwined by this story.'[16] Coinciding with the 2017 re-enactment at Cardiff Castle, *King Cetshwayo: The Musical* by the Durban-based black director Jerry Pooe, with an all-Zulu cast, was given its world premiere in Brecon. In 2013 Pooe directed another musical in South Africa, *The Last Zulu Warrior*, based on Dinuzulu's life.

Some British officers made ethnographical collections, such as James Bowker, whose collection is at the British Museum, and Henry Feilden, whose collection is divided between the British, Fitzwilliam, and Liverpool museums. Widespread British looting of Zulu artefacts resulted in material in many regimental museums and private collections. Intense interest was shown in Zulu artefacts when displayed at the lectures and lantern slideshows in Britain. Zulu weapons caused 'great excitement' at a Church Missionary Society meeting at Little Horwood in Buckinghamshire in March 1879. Three years later Smith-Dorrien's mother produced Zulu weapons for the Exhibition of Art, Curiosities and Local Handicrafts at Chesham.[17] Albums of Zulu War scenes and of Zulu, not least half-naked women, survive in many collections, although images said to represent Zulu warriors have not always been what they seemed.[18]

Pictorial survivals, once assumed to be near contemporary to the war and by Zulu artists, are engraved cattle horns showing Zulu in action against British soldiers. A number of examples exist in the KwaZulu-Natal Museum, the British Museum, the Smithsonian, and the Carlos Museum in Atlanta. It was thought some were by a single unknown African artist and carved for the 1886 Colonial and Indian Exhibition in London. They are similar to the Indian pictographs depicting Custer's Last Stand.[19] Their interpretation is contested and it has been argued that some were the work of members of the British Naval Brigade at Eshowe.[20] One pair formed part of the 'South Africa: Art of the Nation' exhibition at the British Museum in 2016–17 together with two assegais found piercing Edgar Anstey's body.[21]

One attempt to show the Zulu side of the war was Kenneth Griffith's BBC centenary documentary, *Black as Hell and as Thick as Grass* (1979). A more detached analysis was the Channel Four documentary *Secrets of the Dead: The Mystery of Zulu Dawn* in December 2001. Watched by an estimated 2.2 million viewers, it revealed the results of the archaeology at Isandlwana; demonstrated the ease with which the ammunition boxes could be opened; but also raised the Zulu use of stimulants.[22] In October 2003 BBC Timewatch's *Zulu: The True Story* had dubious reconstructed conversations between Beaconsfield, Queen Victoria, and Chelmsford amid doctored clips adapted from *The Pallisers* (1974). The emphasis was upon Zulu deception of Chelmsford at Isandlwana, the value of Rorke's Drift in saving his face, and the Queen's continued support for him. Such television documentaries, however, reflect British popular interest in the war and cannot really offer a Zulu perspective.

Zulu Identity

Within South Africa, the question and meaning of Zulu identity within the 'Bantustan' of KwaZulu from 1970 until 1994, and within the new South Africa since 1994, has been frequently contested. Differing interpretations of Shaka, Dingane, and Cetshwayo figure largely in the various versions of the Zulu past. One is associated with Mangosuthu Buthelezi. Buthelezi was recognized as chief of the Buthelezi clan—one of those absorbed by Shaka's 'conquest state'—in 1957. He founded the Inkatha Freedom Party (IFP) in 1975, Inkatha being a revival of a 1920s expression of 'Zuluism'. Buthelezi, who broke with the African National Congress (ANC) in 1979, was chief minister of KwaZulu from 1975 to 1994 and minister of home affairs from 1994 to 2004. Buthelezi championed traditional dress, revived some older rituals, and even introduced new ones, such as an annual reed ceremony associated more with the Swazi, which is intended to promote pride in virginity.[23] As indicated earlier, Buthelezi played Cetshwayo in *Zulu*, which helped project his leadership image. He and the IFP had a major role in the centenary commemoration, which included events at Isandlwana, Rorke's Drift, Ulundi, and the death site of the Prince Imperial.[24] Commemorative activities offered opportunities, as at the billed Anglo-Zulu 'Act of Reconciliation' at Isandlwana in January 1992 when Buthelezi issued what was interpreted as a challenge to the ANC: 'There was no new South Africa before the 19th century without having to deal with the Zulu reality. There will be no new South Africa in the last decade of the 20th century without dealing with the Zulu reality.'[25] The background was escalating violence between Inkatha and the ANC, and the direct negotiations on ending apartheid between the latter and the white South African government, which threatened Inkatha's own position.

Reconciliation, however, continued to be stressed in terms of Anglo-Zulu bonds. A Zulu 'priest', Magqubu Ntombela, visited Brecon in September 1987 to lay to rest the sprits of five British soldiers killed by his father at Isandlwana. In 1990 Brecon and Ulundi exchanged gifts in a twinning ceremony, at which Buthelezi stressed reconciliation. Similar sentiments were expressed at the opening of the new gates of the Isandlwana Historic Reserve in January 1993.[26]

The ANC symbolically celebrated Dingane's battle against the Boers at Blood River on 16 December as 'Heroes Day' ('The Day of the Covenant' for Afrikaners), following the launch of its armed wing that day in 1961. By contrast, the IFP's attitude to Dingane as Shaka's murderer was highly ambivalent. From 1972 it celebrated Shaka's death on 24 September as 'Shaka Day', drawing constantly on an idealized version of Shaka's accomplishments. Dingane was rehabilitated periodically as in the development of the Ncome Monument and Museum in December 1998 and November 1999 respectively, but Shaka and Cetshwayo have remained more central to the IFP's vision of 'Zuluness'.[27]

Wider Zulu culture was supposedly reflected in the $6 million South African Broadcasting Corporation television series *Shaka Zulu* (1986) and its sequel, *John Ross* (1987). Whatever the original intentions of *Shaka Zulu*'s white South African director, commercial imperatives privileged the role of white traders beyond their influence on Zulu history. It also misrepresented Zulu society despite claims to historical authenticity.[28] It has been suggested that the series, seen by an estimated 350 million viewers in the United States by 1992, fundamentally shaped the American public's view of African tribal life. Its depiction of Shaka as a 'great man' and of ruthless Zulu militarism suited the IFP as well as the South African government, with which Buthelezi maintained an uneasy alliance in face of the ANC challenge as clashes between rival supporters became increasingly violent into the 1990s.[29] In 1991 some of the sets for *Shaka Zulu* were opened as the Shakaland 'Zulu experience' resort.[30] DumaZulu Cultural Village was also established near Hluhluwe in 1994, again offering a synthetic Zulu experience for tourists. The widespread recognition of Zulu 'warrior' traditions extended to explaining the cricketing prowess of the Zulu-speaking white South African all-rounder, Lance 'Zulu' Klusener, star of the 1999 World Cup, as a product of his youthful experience of Zulu stick-fighting and spear-throwing.[31]

Buthelezi's agenda has not always coincided with that of King Goodwill Zwelithini kaBhekuzulu, who succeeded to the throne in 1968 and whose position as king was recognized in the new South African constitution in April 1994. The IFP has lost much of its political strength since the 2004 elections. Nonetheless, both men have sponsored the commercialization of Zulu heritage through the work of the KwaZulu Monuments Council, renamed Amafa aKwaZulu-Natal (Heritage KwaZulu-Natal) in 1998. KwaZulu-Natal was the first province to pass its own heritage legislation in 1997, predating national legislation by two years. Development has embraced the KwaZulu Cultural Museum at oNdini, inaugurated in February 1985; the King Shaka Interpretive Centre opened at Stanger, close to Shaka's original homestead in September 1995; the Mananga Heritage Centre near Richards Bay in October 1998; and Amafa's flagship Spirit of eMakhosini monument in the Zulu 'valley of kings' in 2003. Amafa has been close to the IFP, which has seen Isandlwana and the other sites as shrines to Zulu nationalism as opposed to the ANC. The latter has a wider Africanist anti-colonial stance. The ANC's interest is memorializing the 'liberation struggle' as in the Pretoria Freedom Park (2004) and Sharpeville Exhibition Centre (2005). Zulu history is not its concern. Interestingly, the statue of a Xhosa warrior erected by the ANC government in 2008 to commemorate the 'Duncan Village Massacre' (1985) was heavily criticized by survivors and the wider community not only as unrepresentative of the event but also as 'Zulu' and 'nothing to do with us'.[32] Zulu cultural hegemony within KwaZulu-Natal's heritage sector is also contested by descendants of groups such as the Ndwandwe, whom Shaka defeated and incorporated within his kingdom.[33]

Tourism and Development

There are always potential clashes between rival political, economic, and community interests in any tourism development based on cultural heritage. Tourism may also require perpetuation of the stereotype as a brand. In endorsing the commercial image of the Zulu warrior, many of the museums in KwaZulu-Natal arguably reinforce rather than challenge stereotypes.[34] One complication was the legacy of the colonial and apartheid past. Prior to 1994, 98 per cent of those monuments recognized through protective legislation reflected white history.[35] It is also the case that new monuments are a fusion of Westernized concepts of memorialization and of traditional African approaches rooted in very different value systems and burial conventions. South African government policies require heritage projects to be 'catalysts for infrastructure development, employment creation, and poverty alleviation to the benefit of previously disadvantaged communities'.[36] It may not be obvious to local communities how a new monument so alien to their own traditions is relevant to them. While many Zulu value the memory of the war, there are political activists who regard the battlefield sites as colonial monuments to be swept away. In April 1994 the statue of a member of the Natal Native Contingent on the Anglo-Zulu War Memorial in Pietermaritzburg was pulled down, although it was not clear whether the vandals necessarily knew its significance. Originally unveiled in October 1883, the memorial was restored in March 1996.[37] Factional and generational divisions have been apparent within African communities.

Perspectives on battlefields in themselves may differ widely. Different visitors will have different motivations and different reactions to what were scenes of death and destruction, irrespective of questions of victory and defeat. Most battlefields in Britain are distanced from their visitors by several centuries and those that have greatest appeal such as Hastings (1066), Bosworth (1485), or Culloden (1746) are those familiarly 'woven into the cultural fabric' of society.[38] More modern conflicts present different presentational challenges, especially where racial issues are involved. If Zulu heritage is contested, it might be noted that the Alamo has become a focus for Hispanic political agitation in the United States, as has the Custer battlefield for Native Americans.[39] An interesting contrast has been drawn between the presentation of the battlefields of Rangiriri (1863) in New Zealand and

Batoche (1885) in Canada. Both saw British and colonial forces defeat indigenous groups—Maori and mixed-race metis respectively—with resulting loss of land and rights. The New Zealand Wars still raise uncomfortable issues and Rangiriri is largely neglected, but Canada has confronted its past and there is a multimillion dollar presentation at Batoche.[40] Isandlwana and Rorke's Drift do not present the same difficulties as the very different perspectives on Blood River apparent in the juxtaposition of the Afrikaner Blood River monument and the Zulu Ncome Museum.[41] Yet, there are questions of presentation and resource management to be faced as with any other battlefields developed for tourism.

As the provincial heritage resource authority, Amafa's responsibilities have expanded without concomitant increase in resources and it has prioritized Isandlwana, Rorke's Drift, and Ulundi over other Zulu War sites. As Rorke's Drift lay in Natal, it was more developed prior to 1994 than Isandlwana, sited in the impoverished KwaZulu 'homeland'. Amafa's relationships with the white-dominated business community have been problematic. It has also sometimes ignored the 'Dundee Diehards', the local equivalent of the UK-based Diehards.[42] Individual tourists may, and tour groups must, use a registered battlefield guide, but there have been tensions on occasions between tour guides and site custodians who can take a proprietorial view of guiding.

Municipalities with which Amafa cooperates have their own priorities while Amafa has also found it difficult to prevent development by the Lutheran Church at Rorke's Drift. Lest Amafa's efforts be unduly criticized, it might be noted that KwaZulu-Natal is not that far behind Britain and the United States in its conscious attempt to preserve battlefields. The Association for the Preservation of Civil War Sites (now the Civil War Trust, part of the American Battlefields Trust) in the United States dates only from 1987, the Battlefields Trust in England from 1993, and the Scottish Battlefields Trust only from 2014, although Historic England Register of Historic Battlefields was established in 1995, and Historic Scotland's Inventory of Historic Battlefields in 2009.

At Isandlwana, Amafa had to negotiate with the Mangwebuthanani Tribal Authority (MTA), which feared loss of, and even expulsion from, land and loss of grazing. MTA receives 25 per cent of all entrance fees at Isandlwana and 3 per cent of the gross profits of Isandlwana Lodge. The community has controlled grazing rights and permission to collect firewood at certain times. A small part of the battlefield was declared a national monument in 1972 and a larger area of 1,976 acres (800 hectares) became a protected historic reserve in November 1989. Some homesteads were moved and no new homesteads are permitted within the reserve. Ezemvelo KZN Wildlife is responsible for nature conservation. A 'Pavilion of Remembrance', with a relief model of the battle, was unveiled in July 1964 but was later demolished. A new visitor centre was inaugurated in January 1992. A memorial to the Zulu dead was erected in January 1999 as a joint project of Amafa and the Zulu people. As with other new monuments, it is a hybrid of Zulu symbolism and Western commemorative mediums. Designed by Gert Swart and taking the form of an *isiqu* (wooden bravery bead necklace), it is close to where many Zulu dead were buried. The *isiqu* is made up of carved wooden blocks, interspersed with acacia thorns and bone carved into the shape of claws, and designed to resemble traditional bull's horns tactics. The surrounding *iziqigi* (sleeping pillows) symbolize the dead but are West African in design and not Zulu.[43] An effort to research the names of the Zulu dead has been underway since 2005.[44]

An aesthetic threat to the site is posed by King Goodwill's controversial plan for a £1.5 million development of an Isandlwana Heritage Village, including a royal palace possibly located over the mass burial pits of the Zulu dead. As a result of environmental and heritage impact surveys in 2016, authorization was granted on condition that a buffer zone be provided for the possible graves.[45] In cutting the battlefield off from the plateau where the first engagement occurred, it raises the wider issue of historically insensitive economic development.

At Rorke's Drift, the local community had no historic tribal status, but the Lutheran Church owned the land and so was involved. Rorke's

Drift was designated a national monument in 1969 and a monument to the Zulu dead was unveiled in 1979. A museum opened in 1992. A further memorial to the Zulu designed by Peter Hall, and in the form of a bronze leopard (the symbol of the iNdluyengwe *ibutho* that had most casualties) lying on top of a pile of war shields (representing loss), was unveiled in 2006. Traditionally, Zulu did not erect memorials to the dead beyond planting *mpafu* thorn bushes for significant leaders, but in this case one was planted behind the memorial.[46] The community at Rorke's Drift has no income from the development as the land is leased to Amafa by the Church, but the Rorke's Drift Zulu Cultural Village has been funded by the Anglo-Zulu War Historical Society since 2007 to showcase Zulu traditions.[47] In 1996 a community hall was built by the students of Southampton University Officers' Training Corps.[48] The restaurant on site is also community-run. New management plans were instituted for Isandlwana in April 2006 and for Rorke's Drift in July 2013.

Land and labour disputes have impacted on tourism development generally. Tourists attending the 139th anniversary commemorations in 2018 were locked in their lodges when protesters complaining that promised electricity supplies had not been connected blocked roads at Rorke's Drift.[49] King Goodwill also used the 2018 commemorative ceremony for Isandlwana at Nquthu to attack ANC plans to take back control of rural land by dissolving the Ingonyama Trust, established in 1994, through which the King administers 2.8 million hectares within KwaZulu-Natal.[50]

Pilfering of Zulu War sites, which was widespread between 1987 and 1991, remains a problem. In March 1991 South African police detained a Zulu caretaker, who received four months' imprisonment for dealing in stolen artefacts. Other homes were raided and a British collector also questioned.[51] There are the influences of local poverty, the belief that valuables are buried with British soldiers, and past encouragement from the prices British and American collectors were prepared to pay for artefacts. Two of the bronze thorns on the Zulu memorial at Isandlwana were sawn off in August 2008. Generally, local communities recognize the value of tourism. The number of foreign visitors to South Africa increased by 10.4 per cent between 1999 and 2003, but by 20 per cent in KwaZulu-Natal, although only 6 per cent of tourists to the latter visited the battlefields. In real terms, this meant visitors to Isandlwana and Rorke's Drift more than doubled between 1994 and 2004.[52] Amafa's last available annual report for 2014–15 showed 16,258 had visited Isandlwana and 13,500 Rorke's Drift.[53] Numbers may have since declined.

Memorialization, be it monument, polemic, art, poetry, or even re-enactment, serves the living rather than the fallen. Its meaning will vary from individual to individual and over time. As the 140th anniversary of Isandlwana and Rorke's Drift approaches, it seems unlikely the war will be forgotten in either country in the way it was between the 1880s and the 1960s. Yet, as Edward Orme has observed, in Western popular imagination and popular culture, the Zulu warrior arguably still 'inhabits the same mental compartment as those other stereotypes of the entertainment world, the Waffen SS officer, the visitor from Outer Space, and the American Cowboy'.[54]

8

Conclusion

Isandlwana derailed British government policy. If not already so, confederation was dead by the time the Boers initiated the Anglo-Transvaal War by ambushing a British column at Bronkhorstspruit on 20 December 1880. In the immediate aftermath of receiving the news of Isandlwana, Beaconsfield feared the 'terrible' news 'will change everything: reduce our continental influence & embarrass our finances'.[1] The American press attacked British imperial policy, notwithstanding some recognition of similarities to the American West. The French and German press were unimpressed by British military performance. One Austro-Hungarian newspaper, however, rejoiced in ultimate British victory as it would turn Britain's attention back to the Russian threat, Austria-Hungary being challenged by Russian ambitions in the Balkans.[2] With subsequent reverses in Afghanistan, and the growing acceptance in Britain that the Zulu War was unjustified, the Conservatives stumbled to defeat at the 1880 general election, although the war did not mean the end of the imperial vision.

Amid the wider conflict between British and Boers and the greater conflicts of the twentieth century, the Anglo-Zulu War was largely forgotten. All that changed with *Zulu*. Isandlwana and Rorke's Drift continue to exert their particular fascination, both being among the most visited heritage sites by British tourists in South Africa.

The war began with an expectation of British victory. The shock of defeat at Isandlwana was then alleviated through an acceptable explanation—the failure of the ammunition supply and the collapse of the Natal Native Contingent—overlaid with a suitably heroic image of British valour in the face of hopeless odds. This image was reinforced by the defence of Rorke's Drift. Ulundi was a satisfactory last battle to demonstrate British superiority. Zulu success was subsumed and, in Britain, Isandlwana is still seen more as a British defeat than as the Zulu victory it undoubtedly was.

The Anglo-Zulu War continues to have multiple meaning. On 22 January 2018 the entrance whiteboard at London Underground's Collis Hill—used for a daily quotation—carried a brief factual statement:

> On this day in history: On the 22–23 January 1879 in Natal, South Africa, a small British garrison named Rorke's Drift was attack [*sic*] by 4,000 Zulu warriors. The garrison was successfully defended by just over 150 British and colonial troops. Following the battle, eleven men were awarded the Victoria Cross.

It was removed when a woman passenger complained it was 'celebrating colonialism'. A pop singer, Lily Allen, chimed in that honouring the colonial past was 'disgusting'. With Transport for London apologizing that the message was 'ill judged', the historian Andrew Roberts lamented, 'It's sad that some members of the public can't differentiate between a factual tribute to an extraordinary example of British heroism, of which everyone should be proud, and the rights and wrongs of a particular period.' The underground worker who had written the message replaced it with a quotation from Martin Luther King, 'We are not makers of history. We are made by history.'[3]

NOTES

Chapter 1

1. Donald Morris, *The Washing of the Spears: The Rise and Fall of the Zulu Nation* (London: Jonathan Cape, 1965), 7.
2. See e.g. James Gump, *The Dust Rose Like Smoke: The Subjugation of the Zulu and the Sioux* (Lincoln, NE: University of Nebraska Press, 1994).
3. Brian Dippie, *Custer's Last Stand: The Anatomy of an American Myth* (2nd edn, Lincoln, NE: University of Nebraska Press, 1994); Frank Thompson, *Alamo: A Cultural History* (Dallas: Taylor Publishing, 2001).
4. Victor Davis Hanson, *Carnage and Culture: Landmark Battles in the Rise of Western Power* (New York: Anchor Books, 2002), 332.
5. Richard Price, *Making Empire: Colonial Encounters and the Creation of Imperial Rule in Nineteenth-Century Africa* (Cambridge: Cambridge University Press, 2008), 2.

Chapter 2

1. Adrian Greaves, *Isandlwana* (London: Cassell, 2001), 209 n. 6.
2. War Office, *Narrative of the Field Operations connected with the Zulu War of 1879* (London: HMSO, 1881), 156–7.
3. John Hussey, *Waterloo: The Campaign of 1815*, ii. *From Waterloo to the Restoration of Peace in Europe* (Barnsley: Greenhill Books, 2017), 247.
4. *Statistics of the Military Effort of the British Empire during the Great War* (London: HMSO, 1922), 253.
5. *The Graphic*, 22 Feb. 1879.
6. Brian Robson, The *Road to Kabul: The Second Afghan War, 1878–1881* (London: Arms and Armour Press, 1986), 239–42.
7. Thomas Ricks Lindley, *Alamo Traces: New Evidence and New Conclusions* (Lanham, TX: Republic of Texas Press, 2003), 139–44.
8. Dippie, *Custer's Last Stand*, 7.
9. R. A. Jonas, *The Battle of Adwa: African Victory in the Age of Empire* (Cambridge, MA: Belknap Press of Harvard University Press, 2011).
10. Ian Knight, *Zulu: Isandlwana and Rorke's Drift, 22–23 January 1879* (London: Windrow & Greene, 1992), 98.

11. Colin de Webb, 'A Zulu Boy's Recollections of the Zulu War', *Natalia* 8 (1978), 6–21, at 13.
12. Knight, *Zulu*, 102.
13. Ian Knight, '"Wet with Yesterday's Blood": The Disembowelling Controversy', *JAZWHS* 6 (1999), 7–11.
14. Frank Emery (ed.), *The Red Soldier: Letters from the Zulu War, 1879* (London: Hodder & Stoughton, 1977), 94, 98; Frédéric Bomy and Julian Whybra, 'The Wrecked Camp at Isandlwana: What the Rear-Guard Saw', in Julian Whybra (ed.), *Studies in the Zulu War 1879*, iv (Writtle: One Slice Books, 2017), 62.
15. Charles Norris-Newman, *In Zululand with the British Throughout the War of 1879* (London: W. H. Allen, 1880), 62–3.
16. Keith Smith, *Studies in the Anglo-Zulu War* (Doncaster: D. P. & G. Military Publishers, 2008), 158–65.
17. Mike Snook, *Like Wolves on the Fold: The Defence of Rorke's Drift* (London: Greenhill Books, 2006), 10–11.
18. John Laband (ed.), *Lord Chelmsford's Zululand Campaign, 1878–1879* (Stroud: Alan Sutton Publishing for Army Records Society, 1994), 87.
19. Bomy and Whybra, 'Wrecked Camp', 45–91.
20. Archibald Forbes, *Memories and Studies of War and Peace* (London: Cassell, 1895), 41–2. The same phrase, 'The clothes had lasted better than the poor bodies they covered' appears in Sir Harcourt Bengough, *Memories of a Soldier's Life* (London: Edward Arnold, 1913), 133.
21. *ILN*, 12 July 1879.
22. Emery (ed.), *Red Soldier*, 96.
23. John Peck, *War, the Army and Victorian Literature* (Basingstoke: Macmillan, 1998), 15–16, 71–93.
24. Christopher Herbert, *The War of No Pity: The Indian Mutiny and Victorian Trauma* (Princeton: Princeton University Press, 2008), 29.
25. Ian Beckett, *The Amateur Military Tradition, 1558–1945* (Manchester: Manchester University Press, 1991), 143–4.
26. Harold Perkin, *The Origins of Modern English Society, 1780–1880* (London: Routledge & Kegan Paul, 1969), 280.
27. Dierk Walter, *Colonial Violence: European Empires and the Use of Force* (London: Hurst, 2017), 231–4; John Lynn, *Battle: A History of Combat and Culture* (Boulder, CO: Westview, 2003), p. xxi.
28. Colonel George Hamilton-Browne, *A Lost Legionary in South Africa* (London: T. Werner Laurie, 1912), 152.
29. Henry Hallam-Parr, *A Sketch of the Kaffir and Zulu Wars: Guadana to Isandhlwana* (London: Kegan Paul, 1880), 263–7.
30. Hamilton-Browne, *Lost Legionary*, 172.
31. Edmund Yorke, *Rorke's Drift, 1879: Anatomy of an Epic Zulu War Siege* (Stroud: Tempus, 2001), 121.

32. Michael Lieven, 'The British Soldier and the Ideology of Empire: Letters from Zululand', *JSAHR* 80 (2002), 128–43.

33. Huw Jones, *The Boiling Cauldron: Utrecht District and the Anglo-Zulu War, 1879* (Bisley: Shermershill Press, 2006), 252–82.

34. John Laband, *Kingdom in Crisis: The Zulu Response to the British Invasion of 1879* (Manchester: Manchester University Press, 1992), 163.

35. Edward Spiers, *The Victorian Soldier in Africa* (Manchester: Manchester University Press, 2004), 49.

36. John Laband and Paul Thompson, *Kingdom and Colony at War: Sixteen Studies on the Anglo-Zulu War of 1879* (Pietermaritzburg: University of Natal Press, 1990), 99.

37. Ian Castle and Ian Knight, *Fearful Hard Times: The Siege and Relief of Eshowe, 1879* (London: Greenhill Books, 1994), 209–10.

38. John Laband, *The Battle of Ulundi* (Pietermaritzburg: Shooter & Shooter, 1988), 37.

39. Keith Smith (ed.), *Select Documents: A Zulu War Sourcebook* (Doncaster: D. P. & G. Military Publishers, 2006), 419.

40. Frank Emery (ed.), *Marching Over Africa: Letters from Victorian Soldiers* (London: Hodder & Stoughton, 1986), 96.

41. Ian Beckett (ed.), *Wolseley and Ashanti: The Asante War Journal and Correspondence of Major General Sir Garnet Wolseley, 1873–1874* (Stroud: History Press for Army Records Society, 2009), 153, 213, 302, 365.

42. David Steele, 'Lord Salisbury, the False Religion of Islam, and the Reconquest of the Sudan', in Edward Spiers (ed.), *Sudan: The Reconquest Reappraised* (London: Frank Cass, 1998), 11–34, at 24.

43. NAM, Charles Gough MSS, 8304-32-221, Gough to wife, 8 Mar. 1880.

44. George MacMunn, *The Martial Races of India* (London: Sampson Low, Marston, n.d. [1933]), 227–8.

45. Winston S. Churchill, *The River War*, 2 vols (London: Longmans Green, 1900), ii. 394.

46. Edward Spiers, 'Dervishes and Fanaticism: Perception and Impact', in Matthew Hughes and Gaynor Johnson (eds), *Fanaticism and Conflict in the Modern Age* (London: Frank Cass, 2005), 19–32.

47. Simon Harrison, 'Skulls and Scientific Collecting in the Victorian Military: Keeping the Enemy Dead in British Frontier Warfare', *Comparative Studies in Society and History* 50 (2008), 285–303; Denver Webb, 'War, Racism, and the Taking of Heads: Revisiting Military Conflict in the Cape Colony and Western Xhosaland in the Nineteenth Century', *JAH* 56 (2015), 37–55.

48. Kim Wagner, *The Skull of Alum Bheg: The Life and Death of a Rebel of 1857* (London: Hurst, 2017), pp. xix–xxii, 6, 191–216.

49. John Pollock, *Kitchener: The Road to Omdurman* (London: Constable, 1998), 149–51.

50. Charles Callwell (ed.), *The Memoirs of Major-General Sir Hugh McCalmont* (London: Hutchinson, 1924), 161–2.

51. Daphne Child (ed.), *Zulu War Journal of Colonel Henry Harford* (Hamden, CT: Archon Books, 1980), 47.

52. Cornelius Vijn, *Cetshwayo's Dutchman, Being the Private Journals of a White Trader in Zululand During the British Invasion* (London: Longmans, Green, 1880), 38.

53. Wagner, *Skull of Alum Bheg*, 205–6.

54. Herbert, *War of No Pity*, 12–17, 64–86, 134–43; Douglas Peers, '"The Blind, Brutal, British Public's Bestial Thirst for Blood": Archive, Memory and W. H. Russell's (Re)making of the Indian Mutiny', in Kaushik Roy and Gavin Rand (eds), *Culture, Conflict and the Military in Colonial South Asia* (Abingdon: Routledge, 2018), 104–30.

55. Robert Johnson, 'General Roberts, the Occupation of Kabul, and the Problems of Transition, 1879–1880', *WH* 20 (2013), 300–22; Robson, *Road to Kabul*, 140–4, 176–8.

56. A. T. Q. Stewart, *The Pagoda War: Lord Dufferin and the Fall of the Kingdom of Ava, 1885–1886* (London: Faber & Faber, 1972), 118–31, 155–6.

57. Adrian Greaves, 'Isandlwana: Affairs at Home', *JAZWHS* 3 (1998), 21–7.

58. Emery (ed.), *Red Soldier*, 22.

59. Emery (ed.), *Red Soldier*, 23–4.

60. Parl. Debs. (series 3), vol. 246, cols 1708–18 (12 June 1879); vol. 247, cols 693–4 and 732–4 (26 June 1879); *Aborigines' Friend*, 1 Dec. 1879.

61. Samuel Martin, 'British Images of the Zulu, c.1820–1879', PhD, Cambridge, 1982, 287.

62. *The Times*, 21 Feb. 1879.

63. *The Graphic*, 16 Aug. 1879.

64. James Froude, *The Earl of Beaconsfield* (London: Sampson Low, Marston, Searle & Rivington, 1890), 213. Following defeat in the Franco-Prussian War, Emperor Napoleon III lived in exile in England, dying in 1873. His only son and heir, Louis, the Prince Imperial, attended the Royal Military Academy at Woolwich, and was allowed to serve in Zululand as a volunteer on Chelmsford's staff.

65. From a substantial literature, see Heather Streets, *Martial Races: The Military, Race and Masculinity in British Imperial Culture, 1857–1914* (Manchester: Manchester University Press, 2004).

66. T. C. McCaskie, 'Cultural Encounters: Britain and Africa in the Nineteenth Century', in Andrew Porter (ed.), *The Oxford History of the British Empire: The Nineteenth Century* (Oxford: Oxford University Press, 1999), 665–89, at 677–8.

67. Catherine Anderson, 'Red Coats and Black Shields: Race and Masculinity in British Representations of the Anglo-Zulu War', *Critical Survey* 20 (2008), 6–28, at 6; Michael Brown, 'Cold Steel, Weak Flesh: Mechanism, Masculinity and the Anxieties of Late Victorian Empire', *Cultural and Social History* 14 (2017), 155–81, at 163–4.

68. Waller Ashe and the Hon. Edmund Wyatt-Edgell, *The Story of the Zulu Campaign* (London: Sampson Low, Marston, Searle & Rivington, 1880), 169, 340.
69. Child (ed.), *Zulu War Journal*, 73.
70. Michael Lieven, 'Heroism, Heroics and the Making of Heroes: The Anglo-Zulu War of 1879', *Albion* 30 (1998), 419–38; Christine Bolt, *Victorian Attitudes to Race* (London: Routledge & Kegan Paul, 1971), 146.
71. Stephanie Barczewski, *Heroic Failure and the British* (New Haven: Yale University Press, 2016), 14, 17–18, 226.
72. James Belich, *The New Zealand Wars and the Victorian Interpretation of Racial Conflict* (Auckland: Penguin, 1988), 311–21.
73. Robson, *Road to Kabul*, 242.
74. Laband, *Chelmsford's Zululand Campaign*, 78.
75. Dippie, *Custer's Last Stand*, 10; Gump, *Dust Rose like Smoke*, 120–2.
76. From an extensive literature, see Gary Gallagher and Alan Nolan (eds), *The Myth of the Lost Cause and Civil War History* (Bloomington, IN: Indiana University Press, 2000).
77. James McPherson, 'American Victory, American Defeat', in Gabor Boritt (ed.), *Why the Confederacy Lost* (New York: Oxford University Press, 1992), 15–42, at 19.
78. Douglas Scott and Richard Fox, *Archaeological Insights into the Custer Battle* (Norman, OK: University of Oklahoma Press, 1987), 108–13.
79. Gump, *Dust Rose Like Smoke*, 9.
80. John Laband, 'Lord Chelmsford', in Steven Corvi and Ian Beckett (eds), *Victoria's Generals* (Barnsley: Pen & Sword, 2009), 92–126, at 102.
81. For the Ninth Cape Frontier War, see Keith Smith, *The Wedding Feast War: The Final Tragedy of the Xhosa People* (London: Frontline Books, 2012). For the Cape Frontier Wars generally, see John Milton, *The Edges of War: A History of the Frontier Wars, 1702–1878* (Cape Town: Juta & Co., 1983).
82. Sonia Clarke (ed.), *Zululand at War, 1879: The Conduct of the Anglo-Zulu War* (Houghton, SA: Brenthurst Press, 1984), 126.
83. KZNA, Wood MSS, II/2/2, Chelmsford to Wood, 23 Nov. 1878.
84. Laband, *Chelmsford's Zululand Campaign*, p. xxxiii.
85. Laband, *Kingdom in Crisis*, 27–9.
86. Laband, *Kingdom in Crisis*, 29–38; Laband and Thompson, *Kingdom and Colony*, 1–25.
87. Richard Cope, *Ploughshare of War: The Origins of the Anglo-Zulu War of 1879* (Pietermaritzburg: University of Natal Press, 1999), 258–9.
88. John Laband, 'Zulu Strategic and Tactical Options in the Face of the British Invasion of January 1879', *Scientia Militaria* 28 (1998), 1–15.
89. Laband, *Kingdom in Crisis*, 57–9.
90. Bruce Collins, 'Defining Victory in Victorian Warfare, 1860–1882', *JMH* 77 (2013), 895–929.

91. John Laband, *The Rise and Fall of the Zulu Nation* (London: Arms and Armour Press, 1997), 212.
92. William Storey, *Guns, Race, and Power in Colonial South Africa* (Cambridge: Cambridge University Press, 2008), 144–209, 287–318.
93. Laband, *Kingdom in Crisis*, 62–5; Jeff Guy, 'A Note on Firearms in the Zulu Kingdom with Special Reference to the Anglo-Zulu War, 1879', *JAH* 12 (1971), 557–70.
94. Ron Lock and Peter Quantrill, *Zulu Victory: The Epic of Isandlwana and the Cover Up* (London: Greenhill, 2002), 63–4.
95. Jack Hogan, '"Hardly a Place for a Nervous Old Gentleman to Take a Stroll": Firearms and the Zulu during the Anglo-Zulu War', in Karen Jones, Giacomo Macola, and David Welch (eds), *A Cultural History of Firearms in the Age of Empire* (Aldershot: Ashgate, 2013), 129–48; Storey, *Guns, Race and Power*, 123–4, 269–74.
96. John Laband, '"Bloodstained Grandeur": Colonial and Imperial Stereotypes of Zulu Warriors and Zulu Warfare', in Benedict Carton, John Laband, and Jabulani Sithole (eds), *Zulu Identities: Being Zulu, Past and Present* (London: Hurst, 2008), 168–76; Laband, 'The War Readiness and Military Effectiveness of the Zulu Forces in the 1879 Anglo-Zulu War', *Natalia* 39 (2009), 37–46.
97. John Laband, '"Fighting Stick of Thunder": Firearms and the Zulu Kingdom—The Cultural Ambiguities of Transferring Weapons Technology', *W&S* 33 (2014), 229–43.
98. Vijn, *Cetshwayo's Dutchman*, 40–1.
99. Laband, *Rise and Fall*, 34–42.
100. Peter Colenbrander, 'The Zulu Political Economy on the Eve of the War', in Andrew Duminy and Charles Ballard (eds), *The Anglo-Zulu War: New Perspectives* (Pietermaritzburg: University of Natal Press, 1981), 78–97.
101. TNA, CO 879/14, Note by Frere, 3 Feb. 1879; Cope, *Ploughshare*, 149.
102. TNA, CO 879/13, Shepstone to Carnarvon, 5 Jan. 1878.
103. Hallam-Parr, *Sketch of Kafir and Zulu Wars*, 125.
104. Charles Callwell, *Small Wars: Their Principles and Practice* (3rd edn, London: HMSO, 1906), 28.
105. Brian Bond, 'The Effect of the Cardwell Reforms in Army Organisation, 1874–1904', *JRUSI* 105 (1960), 515–24, at 523.
106. Edward Spiers, *The Army and Society, 1815–1914* (London: Longman, 1980), 180.
107. Alan Ramsay Skelley, *The Victorian Army at Home: The Recruitment and Terms and Conditions of the British Regular, 1859–1899* (London: Croom Helm, 1977), 235–65; Edward Spiers, *The Late Victorian Army, 1868–1902* (Manchester: Manchester University Press, 1992), 118–51; Brian Bond, 'Recruiting the Victorian Army, 1870–1892', *VS* 5 (1962), 331–8.

108. David French, *Military Identities: The Regimental System, the British Army and the British People, 1870–2000* (Oxford: Oxford University Press, 2005), 16; Bond, 'Recruiting Victorian Army', 334.

109. RA, VIC/MAIN/E/24/78, Stanley to the Queen, 23 May 1879.

110. John Laband, *Zulu Warriors: The Battle for the South African Frontier* (New Haven: Yale University Press, 2014), 7.

111. Jochen Arndt, 'Treacherous Savages and Merciless Barbarians: Knowledge, Discourse and Violence During the Cape Frontier Wars, 1834–1853', *JMH* 74 (2010), 709–35, at 731.

112. John Wright, 'Revisiting the Stereotype of Shaka's "Devastations"', in Carton, Laband, and Sithole (eds), *Zulu Identities*, 69–81.

113. For a summary of the historiography, see Cope, *Ploughshare*, 2–8.

114. Damian O'Connor, 'Imperial Strategy and the Anglo-Zulu War of 1879', *Historian* 68 (2006), 285–304.

115. Graham Dominy, '"Frere's War"? A Reconstruction of the Geopolitics of the Anglo-Zulu War of 1879', *Natal Museum Journal of Humanities* 5 (1993), 189–206, at 196.

116. Norman Etherington, 'Anglo-Zulu Relations, 1856–1878', in Duminy and Ballard (eds), *Anglo-Zulu War*, 13–52; Richard Cope, 'Written in Characters of Blood? The Reign of King Cetshwayo kaMpande, 1872–1879', *JAH* 26 (1995), 247–69.

117. Adrian Preston (ed.), *Sir Garnet Wolseley's South African Diaries (Natal) 1875* (Cape Town: A. A. Balkema, 1971), pp. 134–7.

118. Cope, *Ploughshare*, 127–34.

119. HCCP 1878–9 (C. (2nd series) 2220), 357.

120. Jones, *Boiling Cauldron*, 173–85.

121. HCCP 1878–9 (C. (2nd series) 2220), 273.

122. Adrian Preston (ed.), *Sir Garnet Wolseley's South African Journal, 1879–1880* (Cape Town: A. A. Balkema, 1973), 48.

123. D. P. O'Connor, 'Running for Cover: Parliament and the Anglo-Zulu War, January–March 1879', *JAZWHS* 10 (2001), 30–8, at 30.

124. Donald Headrick, 'The Tools of Imperialism: Technology and the Expansion of European Colonial Empires in the Nineteenth Century', *Journal of Modern History* 51 (1979), 231–63.

Chapter 3

1. F. W. D. Jackson, *Hill of the Sphinx: The Battle of Isandlwana* (London: Westerners Publications, 2002), 7–8.

2. Paul Thompson, *Black Soldiers of the Queen: The Natal Native Contingent in the Anglo-Zulu War, 1879* (Tuscaloosa, AL: University of Alabama Press, 2006), 17–35.

3. Bengough, *Memories*, 103–6.
4. Ian Beckett, 'Victorians at War: War, Technology and Change', *JSAHR* 81 (2003), 330–9.
5. Edward Spiers, *Engines for Empire: The Victorian Army and Its Use of Railways* (Manchester: Manchester University Press, 2015), 60–1.
6. Howard Bailes, 'Technology and Imperialism: A Case Study of the Victorian Army in Africa', *VS* 24 (1980), 83–104.
7. HPL, Wolseley MSS, S.A.2, Wolseley to Stanley, 26 June 1879.
8. John Laband, '"The Danger of Divided Command": British Civil and Military Disputes over the Conduct of the Zululand Campaigns of 1879 and 1888', *JSAHR* 81 (2003), 339–55.
9. Major the Hon. Gerald French, *Lord Chelmsford and the Zulu War* (London: John Lane at the Bodley Head, 1939), 144.
10. George Paton, Farquhar Glennie, and William Penn Symons, *Records of the 24th Regiment: From Its Formation in 1689* (London: Simpson, Marshall, Hamilton, Kent, 1892), 230.
11. Ian Knight, *Zulu Rising: The Epic Story of Isandlwana and Rorke's Drift* (Basingstoke: Macmillan, 2010), 254.
12. Laband, *Chelmsford's Zululand Campaign*, 93.
13. Laband, *Chelmsford's Zululand Campaign*, 93.
14. CC, KCM 89/9/32/1, Mansel to Durnford, 1 Nov. 1879.
15. Clarke (ed.), *Zululand at War*, 100.
16. For caution on timings derived from contemporary accounts, see Smith, *Studies in Anglo-Zulu War*, 13–17.
17. RWM, M1982.82.
18. Ian Knight, '"The Haze Obscures Much!" Where, on the Day of Isandlwana, Did Chelmsford's ADC, Lt. Berkeley Milne Look at the Camp?', *JAZWHS* 41 (2017), 11–17.
19. Smith (ed.), *Select Documents*, 138.
20. Hamilton-Browne, *Lost Legionary*, 132.
21. Hamilton-Browne, *Lost Legionary*, 134.
22. Knight, *Zulu Rising*, 448.
23. Clarke (ed.), *Zululand at War*, 83.
24. Adrian Greaves and Brian Best (eds), *The Curling Letters of the Zulu War: 'There Was Awful Slaughter'* (Barnsley: Pen & Sword, 2001), 92.
25. Laband, *Chelmsford's Zululand Campaign*, 68.
26. Edward Durnford, *A Soldier's Life and Work in South Africa, 1872–1879: A Memoir of the Late Colonel A. W. Durnford* (London: Sampson Low, Marston, Searle & Rivington, 1882), 222.
27. Smith (ed.), *Select Documents*, 122.
28. Paton, Glennie, and Symons, *Records*, 240.
29. F. W. D. Jackson, 'The First Battalion, Twenty-Fourth Regiment Marches to Isandlwana', in Knight (ed.), *There Will Be An Awful Row*, 2–10.

30. Morris, *Washing of Spears*, 360.
31. Smith (ed.), *Select Documents*, 134.
32. Smith (ed.), *Select Documents*, 135.
33. Smith (ed.), *Select Documents*, 137.
34. Ron Lock, *Blood on the Painted Mountain: Zulu Victory and Defeat—Hlobane and Kambula, 1879* (London: Greenhill Books, 1995), 48, 53; Lock, *The Anglo-Zulu War: Isandlwana—The Revelation of a Disaster* (Barnsley: Pen & Sword, 2017), 139–40.
35. Smith, *Studies in Anglo-Zulu War*, 73–7.
36. Smith, *Studies in Anglo-Zulu War*, 78–89; Smith, 'The Annotated Maps of Isandlwana', SOTQ 130 (2007), 22–5; Lock and Quantrill, *Zulu Victory*, 156–7, 184–5; Lock and Quantrill, 'The Encounter with the Zulu Army, 1879', *JSAHR* 83 (2005), 158–64; Lock and Quantrill, 'The Battle of Isandlwana: The Missing Five Hours' (2010), http://www.rorkesdriftvc.com/isandhlwana/isandlwana-the-missing-five-hours.htm.
37. Julian Whybra, 'Gunner William Taylor's Escape from Isandlwana', in Whybra (ed.), *Studies in the Zulu War 1879*, iv. 1–33; William Penn Symons, *Rorke's Drift Diary: An Account of the Battles of Isandlwana and Rorke's Drift Zululand 22nd January 1879* (London: Unicorn Publishing, 2018), 56.
38. Keith Smith, 'The Zulu and the Horse', SOTQ 118 (2004), 19–24.
39. Laband, *Kingdom in Crisis*, 79–81.
40. Laband, *Kingdom in Crisis*, 76; Knight, *Zulu Rising*, 298.
41. Saul David, *Zulu: The Heroism and Tragedy of the Zulu War of 1879* (London: Viking, 2004), 124.
42. Knight, *Zulu Rising*, 340–1, 642–4 n. 34; Knight, '"Guided Rather by Accident": The Opening Zulu Movements at Isandlwana', *JAZWHS* 29 (2011), 11–20.
43. Smith, *Studies in Anglo-Zulu War*, 63–72; Julian Whybra, 'Contemporary Sources on the Composition of the Main Zulu Impi, January 1879', SOTQ 53 (1988), 13–16.
44. Jackson, *Hill of Sphinx*, 28–9.
45. George Chadwick, *The Battles of Isandlwana and Rorke's Drift* (Durban: privately printed, 1981), 18; Ian Knight, 'The Myth of the Missing Companies', *JAZWHS* 9 (2001), 46–50.
46. Thompson, *Black Soldiers*, 52–62.
47. F. W. D. Jackson, 'Isandhlwana, 1879: The Sources Re-examined' *JSAHR* 43 (1965), 30–43, 113–32, 169–83, at 122 n. 43.
48. Knight, *Zulu Rising*, 352.
49. Ian Knight, 'An Examination of Some of the Controversies Which Still Surround the Battle of Isandlwana', in Adrian Greaves (ed.), *Redcoats and Zulus: Myths, Legends and Explanations of the Anglo-Zulu War, 1879* (Barnsley: Pen & Sword, 2004), 53–70; Jennifer Verbeek and V. Bresler, 'The Role of the Ammunition Boxes in the Disaster at Isandhlwana, 22 January 1879', *Journal of the Historical Firearms Society of South Africa* 7 (1977), 22–30.

50. Morris, *Washing of Spears*, 371-3.
51. Jackson, 'Isandhlwana', 123.
52. John Martineau, *The Life and Correspondence of the Rt. Hon. Sir Bartle Frere*, 2 vols (London: John Murray, 1895), ii. 213.
53. Paul Butterfield (ed.), *War and Peace in South Africa, 1879–1881: The Writings of Philip Anstruther and Edward Essex* (Melville, SA: Strydom, 1987), 199, 204–5; Callwell, *Small Wars*, 396.
54. Ian Knight, 'The Martini-Henry Rifle, Rates of Fire and Effectiveness in the Anglo-Zulu War', in Greaves (ed.), *Redcoats*, 182–91, at 190; Adrian Greaves (ed.), *David Rattray's Guidebook to the Anglo-Zulu War Battlefields* (Barnsley: Leo Cooper, 2003), 203–12.
55. Emery (ed.), *Red Soldier*, 87–91.
56. General Sir Horace Smith-Dorrien, *Memories of Forty-Eight Years' Service* (London: John Murray, 1925), 14.
57. Knight, *Zulu Rising*, 379.
58. Michael Lieven, 'A Victorian Genre: Military Memoirs and the Anglo-Zulu War', *JSAHR* 77 (1999), 106–21.
59. Greaves, *Isandlwana*, 120–1.
60. Ian Beckett, 'Retrospective Icon: The Martini-Henry', in Jones, Macola, and Welch (eds), *Cultural History of Firearms*, 233–49, at 249.
61. Lock, *Blood on Painted Mountain*, 59–60; Lock and Quantrill, *Zulu Victory*, 322–7; Yorke, *Rorke's Drift*, 69–75; Yorke, 'Isandlwana, 1879: Reflections on the Ammunition Controversy', *JSAHR* 72 (1994), 205–18; Yorke, *Isandlwana, 1879* (Stroud: Spellmount, 2011), 134–41.
62. Bertram Mitford, *Through the Zulu Country: Its Battlefields and People* (London: Kegan Paul, Trench, 1883), 31; Ian Knight, '"The Sun Turned Black": The Isandlwana Eclipse Debate', *JAZWHS* 7 (2000), 21–2; Knight, '"Fire in the Sky": The Weather at Isandlwana, 22nd January 1879', *JAZWHS* 29 (2011), 28–30.
63. Greaves, *Isandlwana*, 210 n. 10.
64. F. W. D. Jackson and Julian Whybra, 'Isandlwana and the Durnford Papers', in Julian Whybra (ed.), *Studies in the Zulu War 1879*, i (Billericay: Gift Ltd, 2012), 1–53, at 7–19.
65. Greaves and Best (eds), *Curling Letters*, 89.
66. Lock and Quantrill, *Zulu Victory*, 193–5.
67. Smith, *Studies in Anglo-Zulu War*, 307–10.
68. Mike Snook, *How Can Men Die Better: The Secrets of Isandlwana Revealed* (London: Greenhill Books, 2005), 222.
69. Julian Whybra, *The Roll Call: Men Killed in Action and Survivors of Isandlwana and Rorke's Drift* (Reading: Roberts Medals Publications, 1990), 1.
70. Mitford, *Through Zulu Country*, 177.
71. Laband, *Kingdom in Crisis*, 97–9.

72. RA, VIC/MAIN/O/46, Chard Report, 21 Feb. 1880.
73. Adrian Greaves, *Rorke's Drift* (London: Cassell, 2002), 369.
74. Jackson, *Hill of Sphinx*, 41, 44 n. 38.
75. Greaves, *Rorke's Drift*, 107–8, 286–90; Katie Stossel, *A Handful of Heroes: Rorke's Drift—Facts, Myths and Legends* (Barnsley: Pen & Sword, 2015), 74–6; Graham Alexander, 'The Defence of Helpmekaar, 22 January 1879', in Julian Whybra (ed.), *Studies in the Zulu War 1879*, iii (Writtle: One Slice Books, 2016), 41–53.
76. Julian Whybra, 'A Brave Fugitive: An Anonymous Account of Isandlwana', in Whybra (ed.), *Studies in Zulu War*, i. 52–75; Ian Knight, 'The Mysterious Lieutenant Adendorff of Rorke's Drift: Hero or Coward?', *JAZWHS* 5 (1999), 19–24.
77. Stossel, *Handful of Heroes*, 54–66.
78. Pat Rundgren, *What Really Happened at Rorke's Drift* (Dundee, SA: privately published, 2003), 18–22.
79. Ron Sheeley, 'My Escape from the Wily Zulu: Captain Tongue, 24th Regiment at Rorke's Drift', *JAZWHS* 14 (2003), 42–4.
80. Stossel, *Handful of Heroes*, 15–17.
81. Ian Knight, '"There's A Lot of People Who Say They Were at Rorke's Drift": The Problems Which Beset Those Trying to Compile a Definitive List of Defenders', *JAZWHS* 33 (2013), 29–35.
82. Dippie, *Custer's Last Stand*, 76–88.
83. Greaves, *Rorke's Drift*, 135–6, 411–15.
84. Ian Knight, 'Some Reflections on the Battle of Rorke's Drift', in Greaves (ed.), *Redcoats*, 102–15.
85. Greaves, *Rorke's Drift*, 211.
86. Neil Thornton, *Rorke's Drift: A New Perspective* (Oxford: Fonthill, 2016), 62–6, 140–9.
87. John Laband and Paul Thompson, *The Buffalo Border, 1879* (Durban: University of Natal Press, 1983), 51–9; Laband and Thompson, *Kingdom and Colony*, 226–336.
88. Hallam-Parr, *Sketch of Kafir and Zulu Wars*, 275–6.
89. Whybra, *Roll Call*, 19–23.
90. Robert Morrell, *From Boys to Gentlemen: Settler Masculinity in Colonial Natal, 1880–1920* (Pretoria: UNISA, 2001), 143–55.

Chapter 4

1. Jonathan Hicks, 'A Solemn Mockery': The Anglo-Zulu War of 1879—The Myth and the Reality* (Barry: Fielding Publishing, 2006), 37.
2. Emery (ed.), *Red Soldier*, 93.
3. Jackson and Whybra, 'Isandlwana and Durnford Papers', 46.
4. TNA, WO 33/34, Chelmsford to Stanley, 8 Feb. 1879.

5. Sonia Clarke (ed.), *Invasion of Zululand, 1879: Anglo-Zulu War Experiences of Arthur Harness; John Jervis, 4th Viscount St Vincent; and Sir Henry Bulwer* (Johannesburg: Brenthurst Press, 1979), 118–19.

6. Smith (ed.), *Select Documents*, 110–30.

7. TNA, WO 33/33, 'Report on the Isandhlwana Disaster', 21 Mar. 1879.

8. Greaves and Best (eds), *Curling Letters*, 121.

9. Clarke (ed.), *Invasion of Zululand*, 118–19.

10. RA, VIC/ADDE/1/8514, Frere to Cambridge, 27 Jan. 1879; RA, VIC/MAIN/O/ 33/49, Mary Frere to Ponsonby, 27 Jan. 1879.

11. Emery (ed.), *Red Soldier*, 106.

12. NAM, Chelmsford MSS, 6807-386-8, Drummond to Chelmsford, 9 Feb. 1879.

13. NAM, Chelmsford MSS, 6807-386-8, Bellairs to Chelmsford, 5 Feb. 1879.

14. Laband, *Chelmsford's Zululand Campaign*, 92–8.

15. *Broad Arrow*, 8 and 22 Mar. 1879.

16. RA, VIC/MAIN/O/33/92.

17. RA, VIC/ADDE/1/8629, Chelmsford to Cambridge, 15 Apr. 1879.

18. Clarke (ed.), *Zululand at War*, 99.

19. Smith (ed.), *Select Documents*, 230–2.

20. Smith (ed.), *Select Documents*, 233–9.

21. Clarke (ed.), *Zululand at War*, 100–2. Emphasis in original.

22. Clarke (ed.), *Zululand at War*, 128–9.

23. Smith (ed.), *Select Documents*, 112.

24. NAM, Roberts MSS, 7101-23-86, Symons to Chamberlain, 19 Aug. 1888.

25. NAM, Chelmsford MSS, 6807-386-8, Ellice to Chelmsford, 6 Mar. 1879.

26. Smith (ed.), *Select Documents*, 242–4; RA, VIC/ADDE/1/8646, Cambridge to Chelmsford, 1 May 1879.

27. Smith (ed.), *Select Documents*, 244–6.

28. RA, VIC/ADDA36/1663–1664, Ponsonby to wife, 6 and 7 Sept. 1879.

29. NAM, Chelmsford MSS, 6807-386-14, Wood to Chelmsford, 12 Mar. 1879. Emphasis in original.

30. RA, VIC/ADDA36/1668/1669/1681, Ponsonby to wife, 11 and 12 Sept., and 19 Oct. 1879.

31. Archibald Forbes, 'Lord Chelmsford and the Zulu War', *Nineteenth Century* 7 (Feb. 1880), 216–34.

32. French, *Chelmsford and Zulu War*, 333–9.

33. Arthur Harness, 'The Zulu Campaign from a Military Point of View', *Fraser's Magazine* (Apr. 1880), 477–88.

34. Smith (ed.), *Select Documents*, 448–50.

35. Smith (ed.), *Select Documents*, 450–69.

36. Frances Colenso, *History of the Zulu War and Its Origin* (London: Chapman & Hall, 1880), 315, 318.

37. Smith (ed.), *Select Documents*, 470–1.

38. REM, Durnford MSS, 4901.31.8, Luard Dossier.
39. REM, Durnford MSS, 4901.31.1, Luard to Clarke, 22 Jan. 1885.
40. REM, Durnford MSS, 4901.31.6, Luard to Vetch, 8 May 1886; Greaves, *Isandlwana*, 199–202.
41. REM, Durnford MSS, 4901.31.9 and 10.
42. John Laband, *Companion to the Narrative of Field Operations Connected with the Zulu War of 1879* (Constantia, SA: N & S Press, 1989), 11–15.
43. Parl. Debs. (series 3), vol. 243, col. 1042.
44. Preston (ed.), *Wolseley's South African Journal*, 257.
45. Clarke (ed.), *Zululand at War*, 131.
46. Butterfield (ed.), *War and Peace*, 18.
47. Snook, *Like Wolves*, pp. xiii–xiv.
48. Keith Smith (ed.), *Local General Orders Relating to the Anglo-Zulu War 1879* (Doncaster: D. P. & G. Military Publishers, 2005), 84–8.
49. David, *Zulu*, 213.
50. Greaves, *Rorke's Drift*, 174–83, 353–81; Stossel, *Handful of Heroes*, 112–35; David Holmes and Elizabeth Johnson, 'A Stylometric Foray into the Anglo-Zulu War of 1879', *English Studies* 93 (2012), 310–23; David Holmes, 'Who Wrote the Chard Reports? A Stylometric Analysis', *JAZWHS* 32 (2012), 51–63.
51. RA, VIC/MAIN/O/34/19, Degacher to Deane, 3 Feb. 1879.
52. Preston (ed.), *Wolseley's South African Journal*, 57, 112.
53. RA, VIC/ADDA36/1669, Ponsonby to wife, 12 Sept. 1879.
54. Clarke (ed.), *Zululand at War*, 131.
55. Emery (ed.), *Red Soldier*, 241; Greaves and Best (eds), *Curling Letters*, 122.
56. KZNA, Wood MSS, A 598 II/1/6, Pickard to Wood, 14 Oct. 1879.
57. *Broad Arrow*, 23 and 30 Aug. 1879.
58. Ian Knight, 'The Wrong Rock: An Exploration of the True "Claim to Fame" of an Enduring Feature at Fugitives' Drift', *JAZWHS* 26 (2009), 35–40.
59. Greaves, *Isandlwana*, 139.
60. Knight, *Zulu*, 96.
61. Hicks, 'Solemn Mockery', 81.
62. Adrian Greaves, *Fragments and Snippets from the Anglo-Zulu War of 1879* (Tenterden: Debinair Publishing, 2015), 25–7; Stossel, *Handful of Heroes*, 43–6, 160–2.
63. Child (ed.), *Zulu War Journal*, 50–2.
64. *Army and Navy Gazette*, 13 Oct. 1894. The flag is in the RWM.
65. TNA, WO 33/34, Glyn to Bellairs, 21 Feb. 1879.
66. Paton, Glennie, and Symons, *Records*, 268.
67. Snook, *How Can Men Die Better*, 256–7.
68. Preston (ed.), *Wolseley's South African Journal*, 256–7.
69. Knight, *Zulu Rising*, 564.
70. M. J. Crook, *The Evolution of the Victoria Cross: A Study in Administrative History* (Tunbridge Wells: Midas Books, 1975), 68–90; Melvin Smith, *Awarded for*

Valour: A History of the Victoria Cross and the Evolution of British Heroism (Basingstoke: Palgrave Macmillan, 2008), 87–93.
71. Clarke (ed.), Zululand at War, 132.
72. Adrian Greaves, Crossing the Buffalo: The Zulu War of 1879 (London: Weidenfeld & Nicolson, 2005), 149.
73. Zulu War sections of Duncan Moodie's history have been reproduced as Moodie's Zulu War (Cape Town: N & S Press, 1988).
74. Alexander Wilmot, History of the Zulu War (London: Richardson and Best, 1880), pp. v, 60.
75. J. P. Mackinnon and Sydney Shadbolt, The South African Campaign, 1879 (London: Sampson Low, Marston, Searle & Rivington, 1882). Not all biographical and service details were accurate. See Adrian Greaves and Ian Knight, A Review of the South African Campaign of 1879 (Tenterden: Debinair Publishing, 2000).
76. Ashe and Wyatt-Edgell, Story of Zulu Campaign, 16, 47, 51, 63–4.
77. W. H. Clements, The Glamour and Tragedy of the Zulu War (London: Bodley Head, 1936), p. ix.
78. Times Literary Supplement, 12 Sept. 1936.
79. Clements, Glamour and Tragedy, 125.
80. French, Chelmsford and Zulu War, p. xvi.
81. French, Chelmsford and Zulu War, 362.
82. French, Chelmsford and Zulu War, 95.
83. French, Chelmsford and Zulu War, 143.
84. Lock and Quantrill, Zulu Victory, 256, 258–61.

Chapter 5

1. Martin, 'British Images', 1–2.
2. Martin, 'British Images', 99–111, 118–19.
3. Daniel Dodman, 'Race, Respect and Revenge: British Attitudes to the Zulu in the Conflict of 1879', JAZWHS 24 (2008), 11–38, at 12.
4. Clements, Glamour and Tragedy, p. x.
5. Carolyn Hamilton, Terrific Majesty: The Powers of Shaka Zulu and the Limits of Historical Invention (Cambridge, MA: Harvard University Press, 1998), 112.
6. Martin, 'British Images', 28; Hamilton, Terrific Majesty, 36–71; Elizabeth Eldredge, The Creation of the Zulu Kingdom, 1815–1828: War, Shaka and the Consolidation of Power (Cambridge University Press, 2014), 241–51, 293–4.
7. Martin, 'British Images', 57–8.
8. Martin, 'British Images', 226–52.
9. John MacKenzie, 'Introduction', in Mackenzie (ed.), European Empires and the People: Popular Responses to Imperialism in France, Britain, the Netherlands, Belgium, Germany and Italy (Manchester: Manchester University Press, 2011), 1–18.
10. Price, Making Empire, 127–53, 163–9.

11. Revd Holditch Mason, *The Zulu War: Its Causes, and Its Lessons* (London: William Poole, 1879), 3.
12. Cope, *Ploughshare*, 255–6.
13. Stephen Badsey, 'New Wars, New Press, New Country? The British Army, the Expansion of the Empire and the Mass Media, 1877–1918', in Ian Beckett (ed.), *Victorians at War: New Perspectives* (SAHR Special Publication No. 16, 2007), 34–46, at 43.
14. Spiers, *Victorian Soldier*, 3.
15. Emery (ed.) *Marching Over Africa*, 18–19.
16. Lieven, 'British Soldier and Ideology', 128–43.
17. Spiers, *Victorian Soldier*, 9.
18. Stephen Manning, 'Foreign News Gathering and Reporting in the London and Devon Press: The Anglo-Zulu War, 1879—A Case Study', PhD, Exeter, 2005, 188.
19. Michael Paris, *Warrior Nation: Images of War in British Popular Culture, 1850–2000* (London: Reaktion Books, 2000), 48.
20. Roger Stearn, 'War Correspondents and Colonial War, *c.*1870–1900', in John Mackenzie (ed.), *Popular Imperialism and the Military, 1850–1950* (Manchester: Manchester University Press, 1992), 139–61.
21. Roger Stearn, 'War Images and Image Makers in the Victorian Era: Aspects of the British Visual and Written Portrayal of War, *c.*1866–1906', PhD, London, 1987, 149.
22. TNA, WO33/32, 'Newspaper Correspondents with an Army in the Field, and Military Attachés at Headquarters'.
23. RA, VIC/ADDE/1/8596, Stanley to Cambridge, 20 Mar. 1879.
24. RA, VIC/ADDE/1/8593, Cambridge to Chelmsford, 20 Mar. 1879.
25. RA, VIC/ADDE/1/8576, Cambridge to Frere, 6 Mar. 1879.
26. NAM, Chelmsford MSS, 6807-386-7, Ellice to Chelmsford, 2 Apr. 1879.
27. RA, VIC/MAIN/E/26/37, Ponsonby to the Queen, 26 Feb. 1881.
28. RA, VIC/MAIN/E/30/65, Cambridge to the Queen, 3 Mar. 1884.
29. Archibald Forbes, *Memories and Studies of War and Peace* (London: Cassell, 1895), 4–5.
30. Spiers, *Army and Society*, 213.
31. Michael Lieven, '"Butchering the Brutes All Over the Place": Total War and Massacre in Zululand, 1879', *History* 84 (1999), 614–32.
32. John Laband and Ian Knight, *The War Correspondents: The Anglo-Zulu War* (Stroud: Sutton, 1996), p. xiv.
33. Stearn, 'War Images', 182.
34. Ian Beckett, 'Manipulating the Modern Curse of Armies: Wolseley, the Press, and the Ashanti (Asante) War, 1873–1874', in Stephen Miller (ed.), *Soldiers and Settlers in South Africa, 1850–1918* (Leiden: Brill, 2009), 221–34.
35. Peter Harrington, *British Artists and War: The Face of Battle in Paintings and Prints, 1700–1914* (London: Greenhill Books, 1993), 199 n. 2.

36. Laband and Knight, *War Correspondents*, pp. x–xi; John Springhall, 'Up Guards and At Them! British Imperialism and Popular Art, 1880–1914', in Mackenzie (ed.), *Imperialism and Popular Culture* (Manchester: Manchester University Press, 1986), 49–72.

37. Philip Curtin, *The Image of Africa: British Ideas and Action, 1780–1850* (Madison: University of Wisconsin Press, 1964), 479.

38. Hamilton, *Terrific Majesty*, 106.

39. *Daily News*, 21 Feb. 1879.

40. *Manchester Guardian*, 27 Jan. 1879.

41. Edward Orme, 'Victorian Attitudes Towards "Small Wars": The Anglo-Zulu War (1879), A Case Study', MPhil, York, 1984, 91.

42. Manning, 'Foreign News Gathering', 107.

43. *The Graphic*, 1 Feb. 1879.

44. *Bucks Herald*, 1 Feb. 1879.

45. *The Times*, 7 Feb. 1879.

46. *Pall Mall Gazette*, 11 Jan. 1879.

47. Michael Lieven, '"The Honest Representative of True English...Freedom": The Metropolitan Press and the Anglo-Zulu War of 1879', *JAZWHS* 25 (2009), 9–21.

48. Manning, 'Foreign News Gathering', 115.

49. RWM, zb401.

50. *Bucks Herald*, 19 Apr. 1879; Manning, 'Foreign News Gathering', 120.

51. *Pall Mall Gazette*, 15 Feb. 1879; *Sheffield and Rotherham Independent*, 17 Feb. 1879; *Western Times*, 17 Feb. 1879.

52. *Broad Arrow*, 22 Mar. 1879.

53. Manning, 'Foreign News Gathering', 120.

54. *Daily News*, 1 Mar. 1879; *The Spectator*, 1 Mar. 1879.

55. *Northern Echo*, 4 Mar. 1879.

56. Orme, 'Victorian Attitudes', 311, 314.

57. *Daily News*, 20 Feb. and 4 Mar. 1879.

58. Orme, 'Victorian Attitudes', 202.

59. *Liverpool Mercury*, 12 Feb. 1879.

60. *The Times*, 13 Feb. 1879.

61. *The Graphic*, 22 Feb. 1879.

62. *Daily Telegraph*, 11 Mar. 1879.

63. Manning, 'Foreign News Gathering', 123–39.

64. Spiers, *Victorian Soldier*, 40.

65. RWM, 1982.42.

66. Spiers, *Victorian Soldier*, 10.

67. *Bucks Herald*, 22 Mar. 1879.

68. Manning, 'Foreign News Gathering', 126.

69. *Red Earth: The Royal Engineers and the Zulu War, 1879* (Gillingham: Royal Engineers Museum, 1996), 56.

70. Ian Knight, *Nothing Remains But to Fight: The Defence of Rorke's Drift, 1879* (London: Greenhill Books, 1993), 134; RWM, 1993.200. The RWM has several presentation bibles.
71. *Punch*, 1 and 15 Mar., and 5 Apr. 1879.
72. Mark Bryant, *Wars of Empire in Cartoons* (London: Grub Street Publishing, 2008), 74–5.
73. *Punch*, 22 Mar. 1879; *Judy*, 26 Feb. 1879.
74. *The Standard*, 2 May 1879.
75. *ILN*, 8 Mar. 1879.
76. Luke Diver, 'Perceptions Versus Reality? Newspaper Coverage on the Anglo-Zulu War of 1879', MA, NUI Maynooth, 2010, 23.
77. *Reynolds's Newspaper*, 2 Mar. 1879; *The Spectator*, 8 Mar. 1879.
78. Parl. Debs. (series 3), vol. 243, col. 1902; vol. 249, col. 973.
79. O'Connor, 'Running for Cover', 30–7.
80. Anthony W. Henfrey, '"What Doth the Lord Require of Us?": Bishop John Colenso and the Isandlwana Sermon Preached in the Cathedral Church of St Peter, Pietermaritzburg, March 12th, 1879', *JAZWHS* 5 (1999), 34–43; Adrian Greaves, 'Bishop Colenso's Speech', *JAZWHS* 6 (1999), 49–53.
81. Hiroaki Osawa, 'Wesleyan Methodists, Humanitarianism and the Zulu Question, 1878–1887', *JICH* 43 (2015), 418–37; Orme, 'Victorian Attitudes', 155.
82. Michael Lieven, 'Colonel Anthony Durnford: The Imperial Hero and the Contradictions of Liberal Imperialism', *JNZH* 18 (1998), 45–66.
83. Berny Sèbe, *Heroic Imperialists in Africa: The Promotion of British and French Colonial Heroes, 1870–1939* (Manchester: Manchester University Press, 2013), 116–20.
84. John Mackenzie, 'Passion or Indifference: Popular Imperialism in Britain, Continuities and Discontinuities over Two Centuries', in Mackenzie (ed.), *European Empires*, 57–89.
85. Andrew Thompson, *Imperial Britain: The Empire in British Politics, c.1880–1932* (Harlow: Pearson Education, 2000), 36.
86. Paris, *Warrior Nation*, 13–14, 31.
87. John Mackenzie, 'Introduction', in Mackenzie (ed.), *Popular Imperialism and the Military*, 1–24, at 34.
88. Graham Dawson, *Soldier Heroes: British Adventure, Empire and the Imagining of Masculinities* (London: Routledge, 1994), 3–5.
89. William Montague, *Campaigning in South Africa: Reminiscences of an Officer in 1879* (Edinburgh: William Blackwood & Sons, 1880), 219–20; *Contemporary Review* 35 (April 1878), 153–5; RWM, p1948.25a; Orme, 'Victorian Attitudes', 215.
90. John Laband and Jeff Mathews, *Isandlwana* (Pietermaritzburg: Centaur Publications and the KwaZulu Monuments Council, 1992), 79.
91. NAM, 1984-09-33.

92. Moodie, *Moodie's Zulu War*, 70–3, 92–3.

93. H. E. Marshall, *Our Empire Story: Stories of India and the Greater Colonies* (London: Jack, n.d. [1908]), 328–30.

94. Joris Verdonck, '"Those Colours Saved for Better Days": History and Myth in the Poetry of the Battle of Isandlwana, 1879—A New Historicist Reading', *Belgian Journal of English Language and Literature* 4 (2006), 93–108.

95. http://www.mcgonagall-online.org.uk/gems/the-hero-of-rorkes-drift.

96. RWM, zb103c.

97. Thompson, *Alamo*, 105–41; Gump, *Dust Rose Like Smoke*, 120–2, 128–9; Dippie, *Custer's Last Stand*, 12–31; *Saturday Review*, 29 July 1876.

98. *The Graphic*, 15 Mar. 1879.

99. David Truesdale and John Young, *Victoria's Harvest: The Irish Soldier in the Zulu War of 1879* (Solihull: Helion, 2016), 292–4, 297–300.

100. Barczewski, *Heroic Failure*, 148.

101. *Berrow's Worcester Journal*, 22 Mar. 1879; *Sheffield Daily Telegraph*, 22 Mar. 1879; RWM, zb103a.

102. Orme, 'Victorian Attitudes', 213; Robert MacDonald, *The Language of Empire: Myths and Metaphors of Popular Imperialism, 1880–1914* (Manchester: Manchester University Press, 1994), 101.

103. Jeffery Richards, *Imperialism and Music: Britain, 1876–1953* (Manchester: Manchester University Press, 2001), 324.

104. Dave Russell, 'We Carved Our Way to Glory: The British Soldier in Music Hall Song and Sketch, circa 1880–1914', in Mackenzie (ed.), *Popular Imperialism and the Military*, 50–79, at 57.

105. Michael Diamond, 'The Victorian Army as Seen from the Music Hall', *SOTQ* 92 (1998), 18–22.

106. Clements, *Glamour and Tragedy*, p. xv.

107. Michael Diamond, 'Popular Entertainment and the Zulu War', *JAZWHS* 4 (1998), 41–8, at 42; ASKBMC, 389441.

108. Emery (ed.), *Red Soldier*, 112.

109. Norman Holme, *The Noble 24th: Biographical Records of the 24th Regiment in the Zulu War and the South African Campaigns, 1877–1879* (London: Savannah Publications, 1999), 321–69; Greaves, *Rorke's Drift*, 328–9.

110. ASKBMC, 389448; RWM, m1938.3.

111. Jeffrey Richards, 'Popular Imperialism and the Image of the Army in Juvenile Literature', in Mackenzie (ed.), *Popular Imperialism and the Military*, 80–108, at 83.

112. *The Era*, 15 Apr. 1882.

113. Diamond, 'Popular Entertainment', 46.

114. UKC, Theatre Collection, UKC-POS-LDNBRI.0595129.

115. Marty Gould, *Nineteenth Century Theatre and the Imperial Encounter* (Abingdon: Routledge, 2011), 229 n. 15.

116. Diamond, 'Popular Entertainment', 44.

117. Harrington, *British Artists and War*, 188.
118. UKC, Theatre Collection, UKC-POS-LDNLUS.0597388.
119. *Western Daily Press*, 15 July 1879; *Western Times*, 25 Oct. 1879.
120. Bernth Lindfors, 'Circus Africans', *Journal of American Culture* 6 (1983), 9–14; Lindfors, 'Hottentot, Bushmen, Kaffir: Taxonomic Tendencies in Nineteenth Century Iconography', *Nordic Journal of African Studies* 5 (1996), 1–28; Martin, 'British Images', 89–91.
121. Emery (ed.), *Red Soldier*, 144–5.
122. Emery (ed.), *Red Soldier*, 254–5.
123. Erin Bell, 'Beyond the Exhibit: Zulu Experiences in Britain and the United States, 1879–1884', MA, Carleton, 2011, 3.
124. Diamond, 'Popular Entertainment', 45.
125. Martin, 'British Images', 279–80; Bell, 'Beyond the Exhibit', 30–9.
126. Bell, 'Beyond the Exhibit', 72–4.
127. *Bucks Herald*, 4 Oct. 1879.
128. *Manchester Courier*, 15 Sept. 1879; *Derby Daily Telegraph*, 1 Dec. 1879; *Portsmouth Evening News*, 19 Jan. 1880.
129. Emery (ed.), *Red Soldier*, 255.
130. Benedict Carton, 'Introduction', in Carton, Laband, and Sithole (eds), *Zulu Identities*, 3–19, at 15–16; Bell, 'Beyond the Exhibit', 37–44, 53–5, 65–7, 72–4.
131. Peta Tait, *Fighting Nature: Travelling Menageries, Animals Acts and War Shows* (Sydney: University of Sydney Press, 2016), 163–4, 181–4, 187–8.
132. Annie Coombes, *Reinventing Africa: Museums, Material Culture and Popular Imagination in Late Victorian and Edwardian England* (New Haven: Yale University Press, 1994), 86–90.
133. Diamond, 'Popular Entertainment', 46; *Punch*, 27 Sept. 1879; MacDonald, *Language of Empire*, 94–9.
134. *Sheffield and Rotherham Independent*, 15 July 1879; *Nottinghamshire Guardian*, 16 Jan. 1880; *Glasgow Herald*, 24 Sept. 1880.
135. Andrew Ward, 'Extraordinary But True Stories from a Century of Football', *JAZWHS* 19 (2006), 16.
136. http://inbedwithmaradona.com/sheffield-2/2015/11/2/sheffield-zulus-victorian-showmen.
137. *Bucks Herald*, 8, 15, and 29 Nov. 1879; 20 and 27 Dec. 1879; 17 and 31 Jan. 1880; 24 Apr. 1880; 5 June 1880; and 4 Dec. 1880.
138. *Bucks Herald*, 22 Nov. 1879.
139. Martin, 'British Images', 278–9.
140. *Bucks Herald*, 21 Mar. 1891.
141. *Aberdeen Evening Express*, 8 and 15 Apr. 1879.
142. *Belfast Telegraph*, 25 June and 10 Sept. 1880.
143. Orme, 'Victorian Attitudes', 192; *Dundee Advertiser*, 6 Oct. 1879; *Sheffield Daily Telegraph*, 2 Sept. 1882; *Northern Whig*, 9 Aug. 1882.
144. BOD, John Johnson Collection, Labels 12 (31e).

145. https://www.gracesguide.co.uk/F._Hulse_and_Co.
146. Bridget Theron, 'King Cetshwayo in Victorian England: A Cameo of Imperial Interaction', *SAHJ* 56 (2006), 60–87.
147. Jan Pieterse, *White on Black: Images of Africa and Blacks in Western Popular Culture* (New Haven: Yale University Press, 1992), 81.
148. RA, VIC/MAIN/QVJ/1882, 14 Aug.
149. Catherine Anderson, 'A Zulu King in Victorian London: Race, Royalty and Imperialist Aesthetics in Late Nineteenth Century Britain', *Visual Resources* 24 (2008), 299–319.
150. Stanley Weintraub, 'Cetewayo: Shaw's First Hero', *Shaw: The Annual of Bernard Shaw Studies* 19 (1999), 7–22.
151. Ian Knight, 'Blue Plaque for Zulu King's Visit', *SOTQ* 127 (2006), 17–19.
152. *Leamington Spa Courier*, 19 Apr. 1879; Harrington, *British Artists*, 188; *Western Times*, 11 July 1879.
153. Smith (ed.), *Select Documents*, 210.
154. Simon Fowler, '"Pass the Hat for Your Credit's Sake and Pay-Pay-Pay": Philanthropy and Victorian Military Campaigns', *SOTQ* 105 (2001), 2–5.
155. *The Times*, 2, 3, and 8 Apr. 1879.
156. *The Times*, 28 Mar. and 4 Apr. 1879.
157. *The Times*, 24 Apr. 1879; Myna Trustram, *Women of the Regiment: Marriage and the Victorian Army* (Cambridge: Cambridge University Press, 1984), 175, 179.
158. Harrington, *British Artists*, 188; Martin Everett, 'Scenes of Rorke's Drift', *JAZWHS* 18 (2005), 3–4; *Torquay Times*, 5 May 1882; *Western Times*, 19 May 1882. Dugan's painting is now in the RWM.
159. C. E. Fripp, 'Reminiscences of the Zulu War, 1879', *Pall Mall Magazine* 20 (1900), 547–62; R. W. F. Droogleever, 'Charles Fripp and "The Battle of Isandlwana"', *SOTQ* 70 (1992), 5.
160. J. W. M. Hichberger, *Images of the Army: The Military in British Art, 1815–1914* (Manchester: Manchester University Press, 1988), 101; Paul Usherwood, 'Officer Material: Representation of Leadership in Late Nineteenth Century British Battle Painting', in Mackenzie (ed.), *Popular Imperialism and the Military*, 162–78; Anderson, 'Red Coats and Black Shields', 6–28.
161. Paul Usherwood and Jenny Spencer-Smith, *Lady Butler: Battle Artist, 1846–1933* (Gloucester: Alan Sutton Publishing for National Army Museum, 1987), 174.
162. Alison Smith, 'Imperial Heroes', in Alison Smith, David Blayney Brown, and Carol Jacobi (eds), *Artist and Empire* (London: Tate Publishing, 2015), 84–123, at 113; RWM, m1979.447.
163. Dippie, *Custer's Last Stand*, 32–61.
164. James Crisp, *Sleuthing the Alamo: Davy Crockett's Last Stand and Other Mysteries of the Texas Revolution* (New York: Oxford University Press, 2005), 139–78.

165. Elizabeth Butler, *An Autobiography* (London: Constable, 1922), 146, 148.

166. Springhall, 'Up Guards', 66.

167. Usherwood and Spencer-Smith, *Lady Butler*, 79.

168. Butler, *Autobiography*, 148.

169. Butler, *Autobiography*, 149–50.

170. Julian Whybra, 'Private David Jenkins and a Contemporary Roll of Rorke's Drift Defenders', in Whybra (ed.), *Studies in Zulu War 1879*, ii (Billericay: Gift Ltd, 2013), 59–85.

171. Oliver Millar, 'The Defence of Rorke's Drift by Elizabeth Butler: A Victorian Picture in the Collection of Her Majesty the Queen', *JAZWHS* 15 (2004), 25–6.

172. Usherwood and Spencer-Smith, *Lady Butler*, 80.

173. *The Athenaeum*, 3 May 1879; *Bucks Herald*, 10 May 1879.

174. F. W. D. Jackson, 'Zulu War Paintings—Alphonse de Neuville', *JSAHR* 69 (1991), 56–7.

175. Usherwood and Spencer-Smith, *Lady Butler*, 166.

176. Craig Wilcox, *Red Coat Dreaming: How Colonial Australia Embraced the British Army* (Port Melbourne, VIC: Cambridge University Press, 2009), 98.

177. 'The Defence of Rorke's Drift, January 22nd and 23rd, 1879 painted by A. De Neuville', *JAZWHS* 13 (2003), 35–41.

178. Jennifer Verbeek, 'The Paintings of the Zulu War as Historical Documents', *JNZH* 2 (1979), 49–58.

179. Wilcox, *Red Coat*, 99–101.

180. Chris Gosling, 'The Rev. George Smith and Alphonse de Neuville's Painting in Sydney, and an Obituary', *JAZWHS* 22 (2007), 16–18.

181. Wilcox, *Red Coat*, 98–9.

182. http://www.artgallery.sa.gov.au/noye/Lantern/Lan_pano.htm#Zulu%20War.

183. Harrington, *British Artists*, 193–5.

184. Ian Knight, 'R. T. Moynan's Painting "The Last of the 24th Isandlwana"', *JSAHR* 66 (1988), 155–6; Knight, 'The Last of the 24th, Isandlwana', in Knight (ed.), *There Will Be An Awful Row*, 11; Knight, 'The Last of the 24th, Isandlwana', *JAZWHS* 42 (2017), 2–6.

185. Richards, 'Popular Imperialism and Image of Army', 80–108; Richards, 'With Henty to Africa', in Richards (ed.), *Imperialism and Juvenile Literature* (Manchester: Manchester University Press, 1989), 72–106; Patrick Dunae, 'Boys' Literature and the Ideology of Empire, 1870–1914', *VS* 24 (1980), 105–21.

186. George Henty, *The Young Colonists: A Story of the Zulu and Boer Wars* (London: Blackie & Son, 1885), preface.

187. Sèbe, *Heroic Imperialists*, 68–9.

188. Henty, *Young Colonists*, preface.

189. Frederick Brereton, *With Shield and Assegai: A Tale of the Zulu War* (London: Blackie & Son, 1900).

190. Michael Lieven, 'Contested Empire: Bertram Mitford and the Imperial Adventure Story', *Paradigm* 1/25 (1998), online, http://faculty.education. illinois.edu/westbury/paradigm/lieven2.html.
191. W. Melville Pimblett, *In Africa With the Union Jack* (London: J. S. Virtue, 1898), 82–3.
192. Wilcox, *Red Coat*, 113.
193. Dippie, *Custer's Last Stand*, 62–88.
194. Michael Lieven, 'Bias in School History Textbooks: Representations of the British Invasion of Zululand', *Paradigm* 2/1 (2000), online, http://faculty. education.illinois.edu/westbury/paradigm/leiven.html.
195. John Ruddle, *Collectors Guide to Britains Model Soldiers* (Watford: Model and Allied Publications, 1980); Kenneth Brown, 'Modelling for War: Toy Soldiers in Late Victorian and Edwardian Britain', *Journal of Social History* 24 (1990), 237–54.
196. Carton, 'Introduction', 10.
197. Peck, *War, Army and Victorian Literature*, 128–32.
198. Henry Rider Haggard, 'The Zulus: The Finest Savage Race in the World', *Pall Mall Gazette* (June 1908), 764–70; Bertram Mitford, *The Gun Runner: A Tale of Zululand* (London: Chatto & Windus, 1899), p. vi.
199. Stephen Coan, 'Sir H. Rider Haggard and the Anglo-Zulu War in Fact and Fiction', *JAZWHS* 10 (2001), 39–54, at 48.
200. Henry Rider Haggard, 'The Tale of Isandhlwana and Rorke's Drift', in Andrew Lang (ed.), *The True Story Book* (London: Longmans Green, 1893), 151.
201. Coan, 'Haggard and Anglo-Zulu War', 46.
202. Coan, 'Haggard and Anglo-Zulu War', 40.
203. Norman Etherington, 'Rider Haggard, Imperialism and the Layered Personality', *VS* 22 (1978), 71–87.
204. Patrick Brantlinger, *Rule of Darkness: British Literature and Imperialism, 1830–1914* (Ithaca, NY: Cornell University Press, 1988), 192.
205. Hamilton, *Terrific Majesty*, 113–25.
206. Sèbe, *Heroic Imperialists*, 34–9.
207. David Glynne Fox, 'The Roads of War', *JAZWHS* 5 (1999), 5.
208. *Aldershot Military Gazette*, 24 Apr. 1880.
209. *Sunday Mirror*, 19 Mar. 2017.
210. *Bucks Herald*, 1 Nov. 1879.
211. M. Paul Brant, 'The Anglo-Zulu War Memorial in Lichfield Cathedral', in Whybra (ed.), *Studies in the Zulu War*, iii. 13–40.
212. Helen Allison, 'Private Ashley Goatham: Letters from the Zulu War', *JAZWHS* 8 (2000), 12–17.
213. John Laband and Ian Knight (eds), *Archives of Zululand: The Anglo-Zulu War 1879*, 6 vols (London: Archival Publications International, 2000), ii. 216–17.
214. Mitford, *Through Zulu Country*, 17.

215. Knight, *Zulu Rising*, 594.
216. Len van Schalkwyk and Michael Taylor, 'The Excavation and Re-internment of Mortal Remains from Cairn 27, Isandlwana Battlefield, Zululand, South Africa', *JAZWHS* 6 (1999), 12–14.
217. See Richard Hardorff, *Custer Battle Casualties: Burials, Exhumations and Reinterments* (El Segundo, CA: Upon & Sons, 1990).
218. J. Murray, 'An African Thermopylae? The Battles of the Anglo-Zulu War, 1879', *Akroterion* 54 (2009), 51–68.
219. RWM, m1959.356; zwb 3/41.
220. Dippie, *Custer's Last Stand*, 30; Thompson, *Alamo*, 61.
221. See Thomas Chambers, *Memories of War: Visiting Battlefields and Bonefields in the Early American Republic* (Ithaca, NY: Cornell University Press, 2012), 1–16.
222. A. V. Seaton, 'War and Thanatourism: Waterloo, 1815–1914', *Annals of Tourism Research* 26 (1999), 130–58; R. E. Foster, *Wellington and Waterloo: The Duke, The Battle and Posterity, 1815–2015* (Stroud: Spellmount, 2014), 83–7.
223. Ian Knight, *With His Face to the Foe: The Life and Death of Louis Napoleon, The Prince Imperial, Zululand 1879* (Staplehurst: Spellmount, 2001), 1–37, 272–4.
224. Ralph Watts Leyland, *A Holiday in South Africa* (London: Sampson Low, 1882), 1.
225. RWM, c1976.177.
226. *Saffron Walden Weekly News*, 7 Aug. 1891; *Lancashire Evening Post*, 7 Oct. 1892; *Gloucestershire Chronicle*, 27 May 1893; *Cork Constitution*, 5 June 1893; *Yorkshire Evening Post*, 19 Apr. 1898.
227. *Daily Telegraph*, 19 May 1892; *Nottingham Evening Post*, 23 May 1895.
228. RWN, m1959.356; *Gloucester Citizen*, 14 Feb. 1895.
229. Dippie, *Custer's Last Stand*, 92–9; Beth Richards, 'Custer Rides Again: Re-enactments of the Battle of the Little Bighorn and Their Relationship to "Authenticity"', in Rebecca Emmett (ed.), *The Arts and Popular Culture in History* (Plymouth: University of Plymouth Press, 2013), 15–35.
230. Knight, *Nothing Remains*, 153.
231. *The Sphere*, 23 June 1923.
232. *Western Gazette*, 14 Aug. 1925; *Thanet Advertiser*, 22 Aug. 1925.
233. *Derby Daily Telegraph*, 19 Aug. 1927; *Bedfordshire Times and Independent*, 12 Aug. 1938.
234. Wilcox, *Red Coat*, 135.
235. *Sunderland Echo and Shipping Gazette*, 25 May and 16 July 1934.

Chapter 6

1. Sir Reginald Coupland, *Zulu Battle Piece: Isandhlwana* (London: William Collins, 1948), 6.
2. Coupland, *Zulu Battle Piece*, 104.
3. Coupland, *Zulu Battle Piece*, 117.

4. Morris, *Washing of Spears*, 7.
5. Morris, *Washing of Spears*, 12.
6. Morris, *Washing of Spears*, 617.
7. 'Obituary: Donald Morris', *JAZWHS* 13 (2003), ii.
8. John Laband, 'Anglo-Zulu War Studies: Where To From Here?', *JAZWHS* 12 (2002), 44–7, at 44.
9. Prebble's article is reproduced in Sheldon Hall, *Zulu: With Some Guts Behind It—The Making of the Epic Movie* (Sheffield: Tomahawk Press, 2005), 13–24.
10. Peter Davis, *In Darkest Hollywood: Exploring the Jungle of Cinema's South Africa* (Athens, OH: Ravan Press, 1996), 124.
11. Dippie, *Custer's Last Stand*, 97–8; Thompson, *Alamo*, 142, 174–88.
12. Stephen Leech, 'Twentieth Century Images of the "Zulu": Selected Representations in Historical and Political Discourse', MA, UNISA, 1997, 77–8; Ian Knight and Ian Castle, *The Zulu War Then and Now* (London: After the Battle, 1993), 254.
13. Knight, *Nothing Remains*, 154; RWM, 1995.105ii. The RWM has a video copy of the incomplete reconstructed film.
14. Hall, *Zulu*, 418–19.
15. Hall, *Zulu*, 31–6. Hall had in mind John McAdam, 'Observations on the Film *Zulu*', *JAZWHS* 9 (2001), 51–9.
16. Hall, *Zulu*, 37–9.
17. Robert Shail, 'Stanley Baker's "Welsh Western": Masculinity and Cultural Identity in *Zulu*', *Cyfrwng/Media Wales Journal* 1 (2004), 11–25.
18. Hall, *Zulu*, 233–5.
19. Carolyn Hamilton and Litheko Modisane, 'The Public Lives of Historical Films: The Case of *Zulu* and *Zulu Dawn*', in Vivian Bickford-Smith and Richard Mendelsohn (eds), *Black and White in Colour: African History on Screen* (Oxford: James Currey, 2007), 97–119, at 102.
20. Hall, *Zulu*, 319–31; Hall, 'Monkey Feathers: Defending *Zulu*', in Claire Monk and Amy Sargeant (eds), *British Historical Cinema* (Abingdon: Routledge, 2002), 110–28.
21. Hall, *Zulu*, 354–9.
22. Hall, *Zulu*, 315.
23. http://www.hatads.org.uk/catalogue/record/d3fcaco2-b17c-4705-9bd1-cd2b36bb2b60.
24. Hall, *Zulu*, 369–70.
25. 'It's Official: *Zulu* Is the Forces' Favourite War Film', *JAZWHS* 23 (2008), 13.
26. *Daily Telegraph*, 23 Dec. 2014.
27. *Sunday Telegraph*, 25 May 2014.
28. James Chapman, *Past and Present: National Identity and the British Historical Film* (London: Tauris, 2005), 9, 199.
29. Jeffrey Richards, *Visions of Yesterday* (London: Routledge, 1973), 59–61; Richards, 'Imperial Heroes for a Post-imperial Age: Films and the End of

Empire', in Stuart Ward (ed.), *British Culture and the End of Empire* (Manchester: Manchester University Press, 2001), 128–44.

30. Chapman, *Past and Present*, 216.
31. Christopher Sharrett, 'Zulu, or the Limits of Liberalism', *Cineaste* 25 (2000), 28–33; Davis, *In Darkest Hollywood*, 153–62.
32. Hall, *Zulu*, 364–7.
33. Hall, *Zulu*, 186–8, 192–3.
34. John McAdam, 'Zulu Dawn: A Review', *JAZWHS* 11 (2002), 38–45.
35. Hall, *Zulu*, 367.
36. Hamilton and Modisane, 'Public Lives', 105.
37. Leech, 'Twentieth Century Images', 106.
38. *The Zulu Wars: Your Chance To Be There* (Cromwell and Lamancha Productions, 1996).
39. Dippie, *Custer's Last Stand*, 96–7, 115–16, 125.
40. Thompson, *Alamo*, 154–8, 174–88.
41. Jeff Guy, 'The British Invasion of Zululand: Some Thoughts for the Centenary', *Reality* 11 (1979), 8–14.
42. Leech, 'Twentieth Century Images', 120–3.
43. Adrian Greaves, 'Lord Chelmsford's Orders to His Column Commanders', *JAZWHS* 13 (2003), 42.
44. Julian Whybra, 'Zabange: Pure Fiction', in Whybra (ed.), *Studies in Zulu War*, iii. 54–9.
45. Yorke, *Rorke's Drift*, 139–40.
46. Julian Whybra, 'Reading Between the Lines: An Analysis of the Alleged "Pulleine-Cavaye Order" of 22.1.1879', in Whybra (ed.), *Studies in the Zulu War*, ii. 9–18.
47. Greaves, *Rorke's Drift*, 334–45; Greaves, 'Archaeological Investigations at the Battlefield of Rorke's Drift', *JAZWHS* 8 (2000), 1–6; Lita Webley, 'Archaeological Investigations at the Battlefield of Rorke's Drift, Northern Natal', *Southern African Field Archaeology* 2 (1993), 24–34.
48. Andrew Greaves, 'Fieldwork Report: Isandlwana, 2000', *JAZWHS* 8 (2000), 7–11.
49. https://www.heritagekzn.co.za/media-releases/98-grave-excavated-at-isandlwana.
50. *The Defence of Rorke's Drift: A Centenary Limited Edition* (London: The Naval and Military Gallery, 1979).
51. Beckett, 'Retrospective Icon', 234.
52. *Irish Independent*, 19 Dec. 2016; *Scottish Express*, 26 Feb. 2017; *Daily Mirror*, 22 July 2017; *Daily Mirror*, 15 Sept. 2017.
53. https://www.cmuse.org/19th-century-cello-that-went-to-war-sells-for-over-6000-at-auction/; http://www.dailymail.co.uk/news/article-2835921/Incredibly-rare-hand-account-Zulu-battle-written-day-actual-paper-Rorke-s-Drift-sells-15-000.html.

NOTES TO PP. 144-151

54. *Daily Mail*, 10 Jan. 2014.

55. Iain McCalman and Paul Pickering (eds), *Historical Re-enactment: From Realism to the Affective Turn* (Basingstoke: Palgrave, 2010), 1–17.

56. Ian Knight, 'Rorke's Drift Re-enacted', *Colonial Conquest* 10 (1994), 12–14.

57. Ian Knight, 'Isandlwana Re-enacted', *Age of Empires* 15 (1999), 24–7.

58. Tim Rose, '"A Very Disastrous Engagement": The Battle of Isandlwana Re-enactment, 2017', *SOTQ* 168 (2017), 11–18; Ian Knight, 'The Battle of Isandlwana Remembered—at Cardiff Castle', *JAZWHS* 42 (2017), 14–15.

59. *The Times*, 12 Feb. 1997.

60. http://roarnews.co.uk/?p=3135.

61. *Daily Express*, 30 Aug. 1977; https://www.birminghammail.co.uk/news/mid lands-news/police-recall-how-zulu-warriors-9684447.

62. *Bristol Post*, 13 June 2014.

63. *St Helens Star*, 27 Oct. 2014.

64. Parl. Debs. (series 3) vol. 294, col. 309; vol. 315, col. 1211; vol. 641, col. 836; vol. 661, col. 1287.

65. *Daily Mail*, 6 Aug. 2006.

Chapter 7

1. HCCP 1880 (148), 12, Reports of Officers commissioned by Treasury to inquire into recent War Expenditure in S. Africa.

2. Jeff Guy, 'Battling with Banalities', *JNZH* 18 (1998), 156–93, at 191.

3. HCCP 1878–9 (C. (2nd series) 2318), 56, Chelmsford to Stanley, 11 Apr. 1879.

4. Jeff Guy, 'Non-Combatants and War: Unexplored Factors in the Conquest of the Zulu Kingdom', *JNZH* 22 (2004), 53–72.

5. Elaine Unterhalter, 'Confronting Imperialism: The People of Nquthu and the Invasion of Zululand', in Duminy and Ballard (eds), *Anglo-Zulu War*, 98–119; Montague, *Campaigning in South Africa*, 168.

6. John Laband, '"War Can't Be Made with Kid Gloves": The Impact of the Anglo-Zulu War of 1879 on the Fabric of Zulu Society', *SAHJ* 43 (2000), 179–96.

7. Quoted in A. T. Cope, 'The Zulu War in Zulu Perspective', *Theoria* 56 (1981), 41–50, at 44.

8. Jeff Guy, *The Destruction of the Zulu Kingdom: The Civil War in Zululand* (London: Longmans, 1979), 239.

9. Laband and Thompson, *Kingdom and Colony*, 25.

10. Laband and Thompson, *Kingdom and Colony*, 34–44.

11. Hamilton, *Terrific Majesty*, 130–67.

12. C.f. Julian Cobbing, 'A Tainted Well: The Objectives, Historical Fantasies, and Working Methods of James Stuart, with Counter-Argument', *JNZH* 11 (1988), 115–54; and John Wright, 'Making the James Stuart Archive', *History in Africa* 23 (1996), 333–50.

13. Ian Knight '"Kill Me in the Shadows": The Bowden Collection of Anglo-Zulu War Oral History', *SOTQ* 74 (1993), 9–18.

14. Jackson, *Hill of Sphinx*, 80; Snook, *How Can Men Die Better*, 254.

15. Cope, 'Zulu War in Zulu Perspective', 44–8.

16. http://www.internationalartsmanager.com/features/zulu-storyteller.html.

17. *Bucks Herald*, 22 Mar. 1879; 7 Jan. 1882.

18. Jeff Guy, '"A Paralysis of Perspective": Image and Text in the Creation of an African Chief', in Tim Barringer, Geoff Quilley, and Douglas Fordham (eds), *Art and the British Empire* (Manchester: Manchester University Press, 2007), 337–56.

19. Dippie, *Custer's Last Stand*, 36–7.

20. David Fox, 'Zulu Art or Sailors' Scrimshaw: The Decorated "Zulu" Horns of the Anglo-Zulu War, 1879', [South African] *Military History Journal* 13 (2005); Patricia Davison, 'Visual Narratives of the Anglo-Zulu War: Cattle Horns Engraved by an Unknown African Artist', *Southern African Humanities* 28 (2016), 81–101.

21. *The Guardian*, 26 Oct. 2016.

22. Brian Wall and Ian Knight, 'Secrets of the Dead: Two Views', *SOTQ* 108 (2002), 7–13; Ian Knight, 'Secrets of the Dead: The Mysteries of Zulu Dawn—A Consideration of Some Questions Raised by the Recent Television Programme', *JAZWHS* 11 (2002), 34–7.

23. Roger and Pat De la Harpe, Barry Leitch, and Sue Derwent, *Zulu* (Cape Town: Struik, 1998), 37, 100.

24. Leech, 'Twentieth Century Images', 124–6; RWM, p1979.561.

25. *Sunday Telegraph*, 19 Jan. 1992; RWM, zb154.

26. RWM, 1988.12; zb149; 1993.32.

27. Jabulani Sithole, 'Changing Meanings of the Battle of Ncome and Images of King Dingane in Twentieth Century South Africa', in Carton, Laband, and Sithole (eds), *Zulu Identities*, 322–30; Nsizwa Dlamini, 'Monuments of Division: Apartheid and Post-Apartheid Struggles over Zulu Nationalist Heritage Sites', in Carton, Laband, and Sithole (eds), *Zulu Identities*, 383–94; Hamilton, *Terrific Majesty*, 1–3; Daphna Golan, 'Inkatha and Its Use of the Zulu Past', *History in Africa* 18 (1991), 113–26.

28. Hamilton, *Terrific Majesty*, 171–87.

29. Keyan Tomaselli, 'Shaka Zulu, Visual History and Television', *Southern African Humanities* 15 (2003), 91–107; Leech, 'Twentieth Century Images', 138–55.

30. Hamilton, *Terrific Majesty*, 187–205; Benedict Carton and Malcolm Draper, 'Bulls in the Boardroom: The Zulu Warrior Ethic and the Spirit of South African Capitalism', in Carton, Laband and Sithole (eds), *Zulu Identities*, 591–605.

31. Benedict Carton and John Nauright, '"Last Zulu Warrior Standing": Cultural Legacies of Racial Stereotyping and Embodied Ethno-Branding in South Africa', *International Journal of the History of Sport* 32 (2015), 876–98.

32. Sabine Marschall, *Landscape of Memory: Commemorative Monuments, Memorials and Public Statuary in Post-Apartheid South Africa* (Leiden: Brill, 2009), 41–94; Gary Minkley and Phindezwa Mnyaka, 'Seeing Beyond the Official and the Vernacular: The Duncan Village Massacre Memorial and the Politics of History in South Africa', in Derek Peterson, Kodzo Gavua, and Ciraj Rassool (eds), *The Politics of Heritage in Africa: Economies, Histories and Infrastructures* (Cambridge: Cambridge University Press, 2015), 50–69, at 60.

33. Mbongiseni Buthelezi, 'Heritage versus Heritage: Reaching for Pre-Zulu Identities in KwaZulu-Natal, South Africa', in Peterson, Gavua, and Rassool (eds), *Politics of Heritage*, 157–75.

34. Nsizwa Dlamini, 'Failed Experiment? Challenging Homogenous "Zulunisa-tion" in South Africa's Museums', in Carton, Laband and Sithole (eds), *Zulu Identities*, 476–81.

35. Maricki Moeller, 'Battlefield Tourism in South Africa with Special Reference to Isandlwana and Rorke's Drift, KwaZulu-Natal', MPhil, Pretoria, 2005, 68.

36. Sabine Marschall, 'Zulu Heritage Between Institutionalised Commemor-ation and Tourist Attraction', *Visual Anthropology* 21 (2008), 245–65, at 255.

37. Thompson, *Black Soldiers*, p. vii; Mark Coghlan, 'The Last Casualty of the Anglo-Zulu War: Damage to the Anglo-Zulu War Memorial, Pietermaritz-burg', *JAZWHS* 22 (2007), 26–34.

38. Mark Piekarz, 'It's Just a Bloody Field! Approaches, Opportunities and Dilemmas of Interpreting English Battlefields', in Chris Ryan (ed.), *Battlefield Tourism: History, Place and Interpretation* (2nd edn, Abingdon: Routledge, 2007), 29–48, at 40.

39. Randy Roberts and James Olson, *A Line in the Sand: The Alamo in Blood and Memory* (New York: Free Press, 2001), 298–304; Dippie, *Custer's Last Stand*, 133–5; Jerome Greene, *Stricken Field: The Little Big Horn Since 1876* (Norman, OK: Oklahoma University Press, 2008).

40. Chris Ryan, 'The Battles of Rangiriri and Batoche: Amnesia and Memory', in Ryan (ed.), *Battlefield Tourism*, 87–97.

41. Marschall, *Landscape*, 264–86.

42. Moeller, 'Battlefield Tourism', 90, 96–7, 101, 117–18, 122.

43. RWM, p1965.420.111. I owe iconographic clarification to Pat Rundgren. The *isiqu* was adopted by Robert Baden-Powell for the scout movement's wood badge in 1919 but this derived from his experiences in Zululand in 1888.

44. *The Mercury* (SA), 23 Jan. 2015.

45. *News24* (SA), 22 June 2016; *Sunday Times* (SA), 7 May 2017; *Cape Times*, 11 May 2017.

46. Ian Knight, 'New Zulu Memorial at Rorke's Drift', *SOTQ* 126 (2006), 24–5.

47. Adrian Greaves, 'The Rorke's Drift Village Project', *JAZWHS* 20 (2006), 33–5.

48. RWM, 1996.116 'Project Scholastic Acorn'.

49. *Northern KZN Courier*, 25 Jan. 2018.

50. *Sunday Times* (SA), 22 Jan. 2018; *Business Day* (SA), 23 Jan. 2018.

51. RWM, zb152.
52. Moeller, 'Battlefield Tourism', 74–5, 79, 82.
53. https://www.heritagekzn.co.za/reports-publications-policy/annual.
54. Orme, 'Victorian Attitudes', 326.

Chapter 8

1. Cope, *Ploughshare*, 251.
2. Mathew Annis, '"No Sort of Parallel": American Press Coverage of the Anglo-Zulu War', *JAZWHS* 25 (2009), 4–8; Orme, 'Victorian Attitudes', 246–51.
3. *Daily Telegraph*, 25 Jan. 2018; *The Times*, 25 Jan. 2018; *Daily Mail*, 25 Jan. 2018; *Daily Express*, 29 Jan. 2018.

BIBLIOGRAPHY

Primary Sources

Archives

Bodleian Library, Oxford
  Ballad Collection
  John Johnson Collection
Brown University, Providence, Rhode Island
  Anne S. K. Brown Military Collection
Campbell Collections, Pietermaritzburg
  Wood MSS
Hove Pubic Library
  Wolseley MSS
KwaZulu-Natal Archives, Pietermaritzburg
  Wood MSS
National Army Museum, Chelsea
  Chelmsford MSS
  Charles Gough MSS
  Roberts MSS
Royal Archives, Windsor
  Cambridge MSS
  Main Series—South Africa
  Ponsonby MSS
  Queen Victoria's Journal
Royal Engineers Museum, Chatham
  Durnford MSS
Royal Welsh Museum, Brecon
  Zulu War MSS
The National Archives, Kew
  Colonial Office Papers
  War Office Papers
University of Kent, Canterbury
  Theatre Collection

Printed Sources

Beckett, Ian (ed.), *Wolseley and Ashanti: The Asante War Journal and Correspondence of Major General Sir Garnet Wolseley, 1873–1874* (Stroud: History Press for Army Records Society, 2009).

Butterfield, Paul (ed.), *War and Peace in South Africa, 1879–1881: The Writings of Philip Anstruther and Edward Essex* (Melville, SA: Strydom, 1987).

Child, Daphne (ed.), *The Zulu War Journal of Colonel Henry Harford* (Hamden, CT: Archon Books, 1980).

Clarke, Sonia (ed.), *Invasion of Zululand, 1879: Anglo-Zulu War Experiences of Arthur Harness; John Jervis, 4th Viscount St Vincent; and Sir Henry Bulwer* (Johannesburg: Brenthurst Press, 1979).

Clarke, Sonia (ed.), *Zululand at War, 1879: The Conduct of the Anglo-Zulu War* (Houghton: Brenthurst Press, 1984).

Emery, Frank (ed.), *The Red Soldier: Letters from the Zulu War, 1879* (London: Hodder & Stoughton, 1977).

Emery, Frank (ed.), *Marching Over Africa: Letters from Victorian Soldiers* (London: Hodder & Stoughton, 1986).

Froude, James, *The Earl of Beaconsfield* (London: Sampson Low, Marston, Searle & Rivington, 1890).

Greaves, Adrian, and Best, Brian (eds), *The Curling Letters of the Zulu War: 'There Was Awful Slaughter'* (Barnsley: Pen & Sword, 2001).

Laband, John (ed.), *Lord Chelmsford's Zululand Campaign, 1878–1879* (Stroud: Sutton for Army Records Society, 1994).

Laband, John, and Knight, Ian (eds), *Archives of Zululand: The Anglo-Zulu War 1879*, 6 vols (London: Archival Publications International, 2000).

Lock, Ron, and Quantrill, Peter (eds), *The 1879 Zulu War: Through the Eyes of the Illustrated London News* (Kloof, SA: Q-Lock Publications, 2003).

Preston, Adrian (ed.), *Sir Garnet Wolseley's South African Dairies (Natal) 1875* (Cape Town: A. A. Balkema, 1971).

Preston, Adrian (ed.), *Sir Garnet Wolseley's South African Journal, 1879–1880* (Cape Town: A. A. Balkema, 1973).

Smith, Keith (ed.), *Local General Orders Relating to the Anglo-Zulu War, 1879* (Doncaster: D. P. & G. Military Publishers, 2005).

Smith, Keith (ed.), *Select Documents: A Zulu War Sourcebook* (Doncaster: D. P. & G. Military Publishers, 2006).

Statistics of the Military Effort of the British Empire during the Great War (London: HMSO, 1922).

Memoirs and Biographies

Bengough, Sir Harcourt, *Memories of a Soldier's Life* (London: Edward Arnold, 1913).
Butler, Elizabeth, *An Autobiography* (London: Constable, 1922).

Callwell, Charles (ed.), *The Memoirs of Major-General Sir Hugh McCalmont* (London: Hutchinson, 1924).

Drooglever, R. W. F., *The Road to Isandlwana: Colonel Anthony Durnford in Natal and Zululand* (London: Greenhill Books, 1992).

Durnford, Edward, *A Soldier's Life and Work in South Africa, 1872–1879: A Memoir of the Late Colonel A. W. Durnford* (London: Sampson Low, Marston, Searle & Rivington, 1882).

Forbes, Archibald, *Memories and Studies of War and Peace* (London: Cassell, 1895).

Fripp, C. E., 'Reminiscences of the Zulu War', *Pall Mall Magazine* 20 (1900), 547–62.

Grenfell, Field Marshal Lord, *Memoirs* (London: Hodder & Stoughton, n.d. [1925]).

Hallam-Parr, Henry, *A Sketch of the Kafir and Zulu Wars: Guadana to Isandhlwana* (London: Kegan Paul, 1880).

Hamilton-Browne, Colonel George, *A Lost Legionary in South Africa* (London: T. Werner Laurie, 1912).

Knight, Ian, *With His Face to the Foe: The Life and Death of Louis Napoleon, The Prince Imperial, Zululand 1879* (Staplehurst: Spellmount, 2001).

Leyland, Ralph Watts, *A Holiday in South Africa* (London: Sampson Low, 1882).

Martineau, John, *The Life and Correspondence of the Rt. Hon. Sir Bartle Frere*, 2 vols (London: John Murray, 1895).

Mitford, Bertram, *Through the Zulu Country: Its Battlefields and People* (London: Kegan Paul, Trench, 1883).

Molyneaux, William, *Campaigning in South Africa and Egypt* (London: Macmillan, 1896).

Montague, William, *Campaigning in South Africa: Reminiscences of an Officer in 1879* (Edinburgh: William Blackwood & Sons, 1880).

Norris-Newman, Charles, *In Zululand with the British Throughout the War of 1879* (London: W. H. Allen, 1880).

Smith-Dorrien, General Sir Horace, *Memories of Forty-Eight Years' Service* (London: John Murray, 1925).

Symons, William Penn, *Rorke's Drift Diary: An Account of the Battles of Isandlwana and Rorke's Drift Zululand 22nd January 1879* (London: Unicorn Publishing, 2018).

Vijn, Cornelius, *Cetshwayo's Dutchman, Being the Private Journals of a White Trader in Zululand During the British Invasion* (London: Longmans, Green, 1880).

Secondary Sources

Reference Works

Greaves, Adrian, and Knight, Ian, *Who's Who in the Zulu War*, 2 vols (Barnsley: Pen & Sword, 2006–7).

Knight, Ian, *Companion to the Anglo-Zulu War* (Barnsley: Pen & Sword, 2008).

Laband, John, *Historical Dictionary of the Zulu Wars* (Lanham, MD: Scarecrow Press, 2009).

Laband, John, and Thompson, Paul, *The Illustrated Guide to the Anglo-Zulu War* (Pietermaritzburg: University of Natal Press, 2000).

Raugh, Harold E., *Anglo-Zulu War, 1879: A Selected Bibliography* (Lanham, MD: Scarecrow Press, 2011).

Monographs and Booklets

Ashe, Waller, and Wyatt-Edgell, the Hon. Edmund, *The Story of the Zulu Campaign* (London: Sampson Low, Marston, Searle & Rivington, 1880).

Attridge, Steve, *Nationalism, Imperialism and Identity in Late Victorian Culture: Civil and Military Worlds* (Basingstoke: Palgrave, 2003).

Bancroft, James, *Rorke's Drift: The Zulu War, 1879* (Tunbridge Wells: Spellmount, 1988).

Barczewski, Stephanie, *Heroic Failure and the British* (New Haven: Yale University Press, 2016).

Barringer, Tim, Quilley, Geoff, and Fordham, Douglas (eds), *Art and the British Empire* (Manchester: Manchester University Press, 2007).

Barthorp, Michael, *The Zulu War: A Pictorial History* (Poole: Blandford Press, 1980).

Beckett, Ian, *The Amateur Military Tradition, 1558–1945* (Manchester: Manchester University Press, 1991).

Beckett, Ian, *Isandlwana, 1879* (London: Brasseys, 2003).

Beckett, Ian (ed.), *Victorians at War: New Perspectives* (SAHR Special Publication No 16, 2007).

Beckett, Ian (ed.), *Citizen Soldiers and the British Empire, 1837–1902* (London: Pickering & Chatto, 2012).

Belich, James, *The New Zealand Wars and the Victorian Interpretation of Racial Conflict* (Auckland: Penguin, 1988).

Bickford-Smith, Vivian, and Mendelsohn, Richard (eds), *Black and White in Colour: African History on Screen* (Oxford: James Currey, 2007).

Bolt, Christine, *Victorian Attitudes to Race* (London: Routledge & Kegan Paul, 1971).

Boritt, Gabor (ed.), *Why the Confederacy Lost* (New York: Oxford University Press, 1992).

Boyden, Peter, Guy, Alan, and Harding, Marion (eds), *Ashes and Blood: The British Army in South Africa, 1795–1914* (London: National Army Museum, 1999).

Brantlinger, Patrick, *Rule of Darkness: British Literature and Imperialism, 1830–1914* (Ithaca, NY: Cornell University Press, 1988).

Bryant, Mark, *Wars of Empire in Cartoons* (London: Grub Street Publishing, 2008).

Callwell, Charles, *Small Wars: Their Principles and Practice* (3rd edn, London: HMSO, 1906).

Carton, Benedict, Laband, John, and Sithole, Jabulani (eds), *Zulu Identities: Being Zulu, Past and Present* (London: Hurst, 2008).

Castle, Ian, and Ian Knight, *Fearful Hard Times: The Siege and Relief of Eshowe, 1879* (London: Greenhill Books, 1994).

Chadwick, George, *The Battles of Isandlwana and Rorke's Drift* (Durban: privately printed, 1981).

Chambers, Thomas, *Memories of War: Visiting Battlefields and Bonefields in the Early American Republic* (Ithaca, NY: Cornell University Press, 2012).

Chapman, James, *Past and Present: National Identity and the British Historical Film* (London: Tauris, 2005).

Churchill, Winston, *The River War*, 2 vols (London: Longmans Green, 1900).

Clammer, David, *The Zulu War* (Newton Abbot: David & Charles, 1973).

Clements, W. H., *The Glamour and Tragedy of the Zulu War* (London: Bodley Head, 1936).

Colenso, Frances, *The Zulu War and Its Origins* (London: Chapman & Hall, 1880).

Coombes, Annie, *Reinventing Africa: Museums, Material Culture and Popular Imagination in Late Victorian and Edwardian England* (New Haven: Yale University Press, 1994).

Cope, Richard, *Ploughshare of War: The Origins of the Anglo-Zulu War of 1879* (Pietermaritzburg: University of Natal Press, 1999).

Corvi, Steven, and Beckett, Ian (eds), *Victoria's Generals* (Barnsley: Pen & Sword, 2009).

Coupland, Sir Reginald, *Zulu Battle Piece: Isandhlwana* (London: Collins, 1948).

Crisp, James, *Sleuthing the Alamo: Davy Crockett's Last Stand and Other Mysteries of the Texas Revolution* (New York: Oxford University Press, 2005).

Crook, M. J., *The Evolution of the Victoria Cross: A Study in Administrative History* (Tunbridge Wells: Midas Books, 1975).

Curtin, Philip, *The Image of Africa: British Ideas and Action, 1780–1850* (Madison: University of Wisconsin Press, 1964).

David, Saul, *Zulu: The Heroism and Tragedy of the Zulu War of 1879* (London: Viking, 2004).

Davis, Peter, *In Darkest Hollywood: Exploring the Jungle of Cinema's South Africa* (Athens, OH: Ravan Press, 1996).

Dawson, Graham, *Soldier Heroes: British Adventure, Empire and the Imagining of Masculinities* (London: Routledge, 1994).

De la Harpe, Roger and Pat, Leitch, Barry, and Derwent, Sue, *Zulu* (Cape Town: Struik, 1998).

Dippie, Brian, *Custer's Last Stand: The Anatomy of an American Myth* (2nd edn, Lincoln, NE: University of Nebraska Press, 1994).

Doyle, Peter, and Bennett, Matthew (eds), *Fields of Battle: Terrain in Military History* (Heidelberg: Springer, 2002).

Duminy, Andrew, and Ballard, Charles (eds), *The Anglo-Zulu War: New Perspectives* (Pietermaritzburg: University of Natal Press, 1981).

Eldredge, Elizabeth, *The Creation of the Zulu Kingdom, 1815–1828: War, Shaka and the Consolidation of Power* (Cambridge: Cambridge University Press, 2014).

Eldridge, C. C., *England's Mission: The Imperial Idea in the Age of Gladstone and Disraeli, 1868–1880* (London: Macmillan, 1973).

Emery, Frank, *The 24th Regiment at Isandhlwana* (Brecon: Royal Regiment of Wales, 1978).

Emmett, Rebecca (ed.), *The Arts and Popular Culture in History* (Plymouth: University of Plymouth Press, 2013).

Foster, R. E., *Wellington and Waterloo: The Duke, The Battle and Posterity, 1815–2015* (Stroud: Spellmount, 2014).

French, David, *Military Identities: The Regimental System, the British Army, and the British People, 1870–2000* (Oxford: Oxford University Press, 2005).

French, Major the Hon. Gerald, *Lord Chelmsford and the Zulu War* (London: John Lane at the Bodley Head, 1939).

Furneaux, Rupert, *The Zulu War: Isandhlwana and Rorke's Drift* (London: Weidenfeld & Nicolson, 1963).

Gallagher, Gary, and Nolan, Alan (eds), *The Myth of the Lost Cause and Civil War History* (Bloomington, IN: Indiana University Press, 2000).

Gon, Philip, *The Road to Isandlwana: The Years of an Imperial Battalion* (Johannesburg: Donker, 1979).

Gould, Marty, *Nineteenth Century Theatre and the Imperial Encounter* (Abingdon: Routledge, 2011).

Greaves, Adrian, *Isandlwana* (London: Cassell, 2001).

Greaves, Adrian, *Rorke's Drift* (London: Cassell, 2002).

Greaves, Adrian, *Crossing the Buffalo: The Zulu War of 1879* (London: Weidenfeld & Nicolson, 2005).

Greaves, Adrian, *Fragments and Snippets from the Anglo-Zulu War of 1879* (Tenterden: Debinair Publishing, 2015).

Greaves, Adrian (ed.), *David Rattray's Guidebook to the Anglo-Zulu War Battlefields* (Barnsley: Leo Cooper, 2003).

Greaves, Adrian (ed.), *Redcoats and Zulus: Myths, Legends and Explanations of the Anglo-Zulu War, 1879* (Barnsley: Pen & Sword, 2004).

Greaves, Adrian, and Knight, Ian, *A Review of the South African Campaign of 1879* (Tenterden: Debinair Publishing, 2000).

Greaves, Adrian, and Mkhize, Xolani, *The Tribe That Washed Its Spears: The Zulus at War* (Barnsley: Pen & Sword, 2013).

Greene, Jerome, *Stricken Field: The Little Big Horn Since 1876* (Norman, OK: University of Oklahoma Press, 2008).

Gump, James, *The Dust Rose Like Smoke: The Subjugation of the Zulu and the Sioux* (Lincoln, NE: University of Nebraska Press, 1994).

Guy, Jeff, *The Destruction of the Zulu Kingdom: The Civil War in Zululand* (London: Longmans, 1979).

Haggard, Henry Rider, *Cetywayo and His White Neighbours* (London: Trübner, 1882).

Hall, Sheldon, *Zulu: With Some Guts Behind It—The Making of the Epic Movie* (Sheffield: Tomahawk Press, 2005).

Hamilton, Carolyn, *Terrific Majesty: The Powers of Shaka Zulu and the Limits of Historical Invention* (Cambridge, MA: Harvard University Press, 1998).

Hanson, Victor Davis, *Carnage and Culture: Landmark Battles in the Rise of Western Power* (New York: Anchor Books, 2002).

Hardorff, Richard, *Custer Battle Casualties: Burials, Exhumations and Reinterments* (El Segundo, CA: Upon & Sons, 1990).

Harrington, Peter, *British Artists and War: The Face of Battle in Paintings and Prints, 1700–1914* (London: Greenhill Books, 1993).

Herbert, Christopher, *The War of No Pity: The Indian Mutiny and Victorian Trauma* (Princeton: Princeton University Press, 2008).

Hichberger, J. W. M., *Images of the Army: The Military in British Art, 1815–1914* (Manchester: Manchester University Press, 1988).

Hicks, Jonathan, 'A Solemn Mockery': The Anglo-Zulu War of 1879—The Myth and the Reality* (Barry: Fielding Publishing, 2006).

Holme, Norman, *The Noble 24th: Biographical Records of the 24th Regiment in the Zulu War and the South African Campaigns, 1877–1879* (London: Savannah Publications, 1999).

Hughes, Matthew, and Johnson, Gaynor (eds), *Fanaticism and Conflict in the Modern Age* (London: Frank Cass, 2005).

Hussey, John, *Waterloo: The Campaign of 1815, ii. From Waterloo to the Restoration of Peace in Europe* (Barnsley: Greenhill Books, 2017).

Jackson, F. W. D., *Hill of the Sphinx: The Battle of Isandlwana* (London: Westerners Publications, 2002).

Jonas, R. A., *The Battle of Adwa: African Victory in the Age of Empire* (Cambridge, MA: Belknap Press of Harvard University Press, 2011).

Jones, Huw, *The Boiling Cauldron: Utrecht District and the Anglo-Zulu War, 1879* (Bisley: Shermershill Press, 2006).

Jones, Karen, Macola, Giacomo, and Welch, David (eds), *A Cultural History of Firearms in the Age of Empire* (Aldershot: Ashgate, 2013).

Keegan, Timothy, *Colonial South Africa and the Origins of the Racial Order* (Charlottesville, VA: University of Virginia Press, 1997).

Knight, Ian, *Zulu: Isandlwana and Rorke's Drift, 22–23 January 1879* (London: Windrow & Greene, 1992).

Knight, Ian, *Nothing Remains But to Fight: The Defence of Rorke's Drift, 1879* (London: Greenhill Books, 1993).

Knight, Ian, *The Anatomy of the Zulu Army: From Shaka to Cetshwayo, 1818–1879* (London: Greenhill Books, 1995).

Knight, Ian, *Isandlwana 1879: The Great Zulu Victory* (Oxford: Osprey, 2002).

Knight, Ian, *Zulu Rising: The Epic Story of Isandlwana and Rorke's Drift* (Basingstoke: Macmillan, 2010).

Knight, Ian (ed.), *There Will Be An Awful Row At Home About This* (Shoreham-by-Sea: Zulu Study Group of the Victorian Military Society, 1987).

Knight, Ian, and Castle, Ian, *The Zulu War Then and Now* (London: After the Battle, 1993).

Laband, John, *Fight Us in the Open: The Anglo-Zulu War Through Zulu Eyes* (Pietermaritzburg: Shuter & Shuter and the KwaZulu Monuments Council, 1985).

Laband, John, *The Battle of Ulundi* (Pietermaritzburg: Shooter & Shooter, 1988).

Laband, John, *Companion to the Narrative of Field Operations Connected with the Zulu War of 1879* (Constantia, SA: N & S Press, 1989).

Laband, John, *Kingdom in Crisis: The Zulu Response to the British Invasion of 1879* (Manchester: Manchester University Press, 1992).

Laband, John, *The Rise and Fall of the Zulu Nation* (London: Arms and Armour Press, 1997).

Laband, John, *The Atlas of the Later Zulu Wars, 1883–1888* (Pietermaritzburg: University of Natal Press, 2001).

Laband, John, *Zulu Warriors: The Battle for the South African Frontier* (New Haven: Yale University Press, 2014).

Laband, John, and Knight, Ian, *The War Correspondents: The Anglo-Zulu War* (Stroud: Sutton, 1996).

Laband, John, and Mathews, Jeff, *Isandlwana* (Pietermaritzburg: Centaur Publications and the KwaZulu Monuments Council, 1992).

Laband, John, and Thompson, Paul, *The Buffalo Border, 1879* (Durban: University of Natal, 1983).

Laband, John, and Thompson, Paul, *Kingdom and Colony at War: Sixteen Studies on the Anglo-Zulu War of 1879* (Pietermaritzburg: University of Natal Press, 1990).

Lang, Andrew (ed.), *The True Story Book* (London: Longmans Green, 1893).

Limb, Peter (ed.), *Orb and Sceptre: Studies on British Imperialism and Its Legacies* (Melbourne: Monash University ePress, 2008).

Lindley, Thomas Ricks, *Alamo Traces: New Evidence and New Conclusions* (Lanham, TX: Republic of Texas Press, 2003).

Lloyd, Alan, *The Zulu War* (London: Hart-Davis MacGibbon, 1973).

Lock, Ron, *Blood on the Painted Mountain: Zulu Victory and Defeat—Hlobane and Kambula, 1879* (London: Greenhill Books, 1995).

Lock, Ron, *The Anglo-Zulu War: Isandlwana—The Revelation of a Disaster* (Barnsley: Pen & Sword, 2017).

Lock, Ron, and Quantrill, Peter, *Zulu Victory: The Epic of Isandlwana and the Cover Up* (London: Greenhill, 2002).

Lynn, John, *Battle: A History of Combat and Culture* (Boulder, CO: Westview, 2003).

McCalman, Iain, and Pickering, Paul (eds), *Historical Re-enactment: From Realism to the Affective Turn* (Basingstoke: Palgrave, 2010).

MacDonald, Robert, *The Language of Empire: Myths and Metaphors of Popular Imperialism, 1880–1918* (Manchester: Manchester University Press, 1994).

Mackenzie, John (ed.), *Imperialism and Popular Culture* (Manchester: Manchester University Press, 1986).

Mackenzie, John (ed.), *Popular Imperialism and the Military, 1850–1950* (Manchester: Manchester University Press, 1992).

Mackenzie, John (ed.), *European Empires and the People: Popular Responses to Imperialism in France, Britain, the Netherlands, Belgium, Germany and Italy* (Manchester: Manchester University Press, 2011).

Mackinnon, J. P., and Shadbolt, Sydney, *The South African Campaign, 1879* (London: Sampson Low, Marston, Searle & Rivington, 1882).

MacMunn, George, *The Martial Races of India* (London: Sampson Low, Marston, n.d [1933]).

Marschall, Sabine, *Landscape of Memory: Commemorative Monuments, Memorials and Public Statuary in Post-Apartheid South Africa* (Leiden: Brill, 2009).

Marshall, H. E., *Our Empire Story: Stories of India and the Greater Colonies* (London: Jack, n.d. [1908]).

Mason, Revd Holditch, *The Zulu War: Its Causes, and Its Lessons* (London: William Poole, 1879).

Miller, Stephen (ed.), *Soldiers and Settlers in Africa, 1850–1918* (Leiden: Brill, 2009).

Milton, John, *The Edges of War: A History of the Frontier Wars, 1702–1878* (Cape Town: Juta & Co., 1983).

Moodie, Duncan, *Moodie's Zulu War* (Cape Town: N & S Press, 1988).

Monk, Claire, and Sargeant, Amy (eds), *British Historical Cinema* (Abingdon: Routledge, 2002).

Morrell, Robert, *From Boys to Gentlemen: Settler Masculinity in Colonial Natal, 1880–1920* (Pretoria: UNISA, 2001).

Morris, Donald, *The Washing of the Spears: The Rise and Fall of the Zulu Nation* (London: Jonathan Cape, 1965).

Paris, Michael, *Warrior Nation: Images of War in British Popular Culture, 1850–2000* (London: Reaktion Books, 2000).

Paton, George, Glennie, Farquhar, and Symons, William Penn, *Records of the 24th Regiment: From Its Formation in 1689* (London: Simpson, Marshall, Hamilton, Kent, 1892).

Peck, John, *War, the Army and Victorian Literature* (Basingstoke: Macmillan, 1998).

Perkin, Harold, *The Origins of Modern English Society, 1780–1880* (London: Routledge & Kegan Paul, 1969).

Peterson, Derek, Gavua, Kodzo, and Rassool, Ciraj (eds), *The Politics of Heritage in Africa: Economies, Histories and Infrastructure* (Cambridge: Cambridge University Press, 2015).

Pieterse, Jan, *White on Black: Images of Africa and Blacks in Western Popular Culture* (New Haven: Yale University Press, 1992).

Pimblett, W. Melville, *In Africa With the Union Jack* (London: J. S. Virtue, 1898).

Pollock, John, *Kitchener: The Road to Omdurman* (London: Constable, 1998).

Porter, Andrew (ed.), *The Oxford History of the British Empire: The Nineteenth Century* (Oxford University Press, 1999).

Potter, Simon, *News and the British World: The Emergence of an Imperial System, 1876–1922* (Oxford: Clarendon Press, 2003).

Price, Richard, *Making Empire: Colonial Encounters and the Creation of Imperial Rile in Nineteenth Century Africa* (Cambridge: Cambridge University Press, 2008).

Red Earth: The Royal Engineers and the Zulu War, 1879 (Gillingham: Royal Engineers Museum, 1996).

Richards, Jeffrey, *Visions of Yesterday* (London: Routledge, 1973).

Richards, Jeffrey, *Imperialism and Music: Britain, 1876–1953* (Manchester: Manchester University Press, 2001).

Richards, Jeffrey (ed.), *Imperialism and Juvenile Literature* (Manchester: Manchester University Press, 1989).

Roberts, Randy, and Olson, James, *A Line in the Sand: The Alamo in Blood and Memory* (New York: Free Press, 2001).

Robson, Brian, *The Road to Kabul: The Second Afghan War, 1878–1881* (London: Arms and Armour Press, 1986).

Roy, Kaushik, and Rand, Gavin (eds), *Culture, Conflict and the Military in Colonial South Asia* (Abingdon: Routledge, 2018).

Ruddle, John, *Collectors Guide to Britains Model Soldiers* (Watford: Model and Allied Publications, 1980).

Rundgren, Pat, *What Really Happened at Rorke's Drift* (Dundee, SA: privately published, 2003).

Ryan, Chris (ed.), *Battlefield Tourism: History, Place and Interpretation* (2nd edn, Abingdon: Routledge, 2007).

Scott, Douglas, and Fox, Richard, *Archaeological Insights into the Custer Battle* (Norman, OK: University of Oklahoma Press, 1987).

Sèbe, Berny, *Heroic Imperialists in Africa: The Promotion of British and French Colonial Heroes, 1870–1939* (Manchester: Manchester University Press, 2013).

Skelley, Alan Ramsay, *The Victorian Army at Home: The Recruitment and Terms and Conditions of the British Regular, 1859–1899* (London: Croom Helm, 1977).

Smith, Alison, Blayney Brown, David, and Jacobi, Carol (eds), *Artist and Empire* (London: Tate Publishing, 2015).

Smith, Keith, *Studies in the Anglo-Zulu War* (Doncaster: D. P. & G. Military Publishers, 2008).

Smith, Keith, *The Wedding Feast War: The Final Tragedy of the Xhosa People* (London: Frontline Books, 2012).

Smith, Melvin, *Awarded for Valour: A History of the Victoria Cross and the Evolution of British Heroism* (Basingstoke: Palgrave Macmillan, 2008).

Snook, Mike, *How Can Men Die Better: The Secrets of Isandlwana Revealed* (London: Greenhill Books, 2005).

Snook, Mike, *Like Wolves on the Fold: The Defence of Rorke's Drift* (London: Greenhill Books, 2006).

Spiers, Edward, *The Army and Society, 1815–1914* (London: Longman, 1980).

Spiers, Edward, *The Late Victorian Army, 1868–1902* (Manchester: Manchester University Press, 1992).

Spiers, Edward, *The Victorian Soldier in Africa* (Manchester: Manchester University Press, 2004).

Spiers, Edward, *Engines for Empire: The Victorian Army and Its Use of Railways* (Manchester: Manchester University Press, 2015).

Spiers, Edward (ed.), *Sudan: The Reconquest Reappraised* (London: Frank Cass, 1998).

Stewart, A. T. Q., *The Pagoda War: Lord Dufferin and the Fall of the Kingdom of Ava, 1885–1886* (London: Faber & Faber, 1972).

Storey, William, *Guns, Race, and Power in Colonial South Africa* (Cambridge: Cambridge University Press, 2008).

Stossel, Katie, *A Handful of Heroes: Rorke's Drift—Facts, Myths and Legends* (Barnsley: Pen & Sword, 2015).

Streets, Heather, *Martial Races: The Military, Race and Masculinity in British Imperial Culture, 1857–1914* (Manchester: Manchester University Press, 2004).

Tait, Peta, *Fighting Nature: Travelling Menageries, Animals Acts and War Shows* (Sydney: University of Sydney Press, 2016).

Thompson, Andrew, *Imperial Britain: The Empire in British Politics, c.1880–1932* (Harlow: Pearson Education, 2000).

Thompson, Frank, *Alamo: A Cultural History* (Dallas: Taylor Publishing, 2001).

Thompson, Paul, *Black Soldiers of the Queen: The Natal Native Contingent in the Anglo-Zulu War, 1879* (Tuscaloosa, AL: University of Alabama Press, 2006).

Thornton, Neil, *Rorke's Drift: A New Perspective* (Oxford: Fonthill, 2016).

Truesdale, David, and Young, John, *Victoria's Harvest: The Irish Soldier in the Zulu War of 1879* (Solihull: Helion, 2016).

Trustram, Myna, *Women of the Regiment: Marriage and the Victorian Army* (Cambridge: Cambridge University Press, 1984).

Usherwood, Paul, and Spencer-Smith, Jenny, *Lady Butler: Battle Artist, 1846–1933* (Gloucester: Alan Sutton Publishing for National Army Museum, 1987).

Wagner, Kim, *The Skull of Alum Bheg: The Life and Death of a Rebel of 1857* (London: Hurst, 2017).

Walter, Dierk, *Colonial Violence: European Empires and the Use of Force* (London: Hurst, 2017).

Ward, Stuart (ed.), *British Culture and the End of Empire* (Manchester: Manchester University Press, 2001).

War Office, *Narrative of the Field Operations Connected with the Zulu War of 1879* (London: HMSO, 1881).

Whybra, Julian, *The Roll Call: Men Killed in Action and Survivors of Isandlwana and Rorke's Drift* (Reading: Roberts Medals Publications, 1990).

Whybra, Julian (ed.), *Studies in the Zulu War 1879*, i (Billericay: Gift Ltd, 2012).

Whybra, Julian (ed.), *Studies in the Zulu War 1879*, ii (Billericay: Gift Ltd, 2013).

Whybra, Julian (ed.), *Studies in the Zulu War 1879*, iii (Writtle: One Slice Books, 2016).

Whybra, Julian (ed.), *Studies in the Zulu War 1879*, iv (Writtle: One Slice Books, 2017).

Wilcox, Craig, *Red Coat Dreaming: How Colonial Australia Embraced the British Army* (Port Melbourne, VIC: Cambridge University Press, 2009).

Wilmot, Alexander Wilmot, *History of the Zulu War* (London: Richardson and Best, 1880).

Yorke, Edmund, *Rorke's Drift, 1879: Anatomy of an Epic Zulu War Siege* (Stroud: Tempus, 2001).

Yorke, Edmund, *Isandlwana, 1879* (Stroud: Spellmount, 2011).

Articles

Allison, Helen, 'Private Ashley Goatham: Letters from the Zulu War', *JAZWHS* 8 (2000), 12–17.

Anderson, Catherine, 'A Zulu King in Victorian London: Race, Royalty and Imperialist Aesthetics in Late Nineteenth Century Britain', *Visual Resources* 24 (2008), 299–319.

Anderson, Catherine, 'Red Coats and Black Shields: Race and Masculinity in British Representations of the Anglo-Zulu War', *Critical Survey* 20 (2008), 6–28.

Annis, Mathew, 'Half Devil and Half Child: British Perspectives of Native Opponents in Southern Africa, 1878–1879', *JAZWHS* 23 (2008), 14–24.

Annis, Mathew, '"No Sort of Parallel": American Press Coverage of the Anglo-Zulu War', *JAZWHS* 25 (2009), 4–8.

Arndt, Jochen, 'Treacherous Savages and Merciless Barbarians: Knowledge, Discourse and Violence During the Cape Frontier Wars, 1834–1853', *JMH* 74 (2010), 709–35.

Bailes, Howard, 'Technology and Imperialism: A Case Study of the Victorian Army in Africa', *VS* 24 (1980), 83–104.

Beckett, Ian, 'Victorians at War: War, Technology and Change', *JSAHR* 81 (2003), 330–9.

Bond, Brian, 'The Effect of the Cardwell Reforms in Army Organisation, 1874–1904', *JRUSI* 105 (1960), 515–24.

Bond, Brian, 'Recruiting the Victorian Army, 1870–1892', *VS* 5 (1962), 331–8.

Brown, Kenneth, 'Modelling for War: Toy Soldiers in Late Victorian and Edwardian Britain', *Journal of Social History* 24 (1990), 237–54.

Brown, Michael, 'Cold Steel, Weak Flesh: Mechanism, Masculinity, and the Anxieties of Late Victorian Empire', *Cultural and Social History* 14 (2017), 155–81.

Brown, Ted, 'Casting a Little More Light upon Isandlwana', *SOTQ* 56–7 (1989), 13–15.

Carton, Benedict, and Nauright, John, '"Last Zulu Warrior Standing": Cultural Legacies of Racial Stereotyping and Embodied Ethno-Branding in South Africa', *International Journal of the History of Sport* 32 (2015), 876–98.

Coan, Stephen, 'Sir Henry Rider Haggard and the Anglo-Zulu War in Fact and Fiction', *JAZWHS* 10 (2001), 39–54.

Cobbing, Julian, 'A Tainted Well: The Objectives, Historical Fantasies, and Working Methods of James Stuart, with Counter-Argument', *JNZH* 11 (1988), 115–54.

Coghlan, Mark, 'The Last Casualty of the Anglo-Zulu War: Damage to the Anglo-Zulu War Memorial, Pietermaritzburg', *JAZWHS* 22 (2007), 26–34.

Collins, Bruce, 'Defining Victory in Victorian Warfare, 1860–1882', *JMH* 77 (2013), 895–929.

Cope, A. T., 'The Zulu War in Zulu Perspective', *Theoria* 56 (1981), 41–50.

Cope, Richard, 'Written in Characters of Blood? The Reign of King Cetshwayo kaMpande, 1872–1879', *JAH* 26 (1995), 247–69.

Davison, Patricia, 'Visual Narratives of the Anglo-Zulu War: Cattle Horns Engraved by an Unknown African Artist', *Southern African Humanities* 28 (2016), 81–101.

Diamond, Michael, 'Popular Entertainment and the Zulu War', *JAZWHS* 4 (1998), 41–8.

Diamond, Michael, 'The Victorian Army as Seen from the Music Hall', *SOTQ* 92 (1998), 18–22.

Dodman, Daniel, 'Race, Respect and Revenge: British Attitudes to the Zulu in the Conflict of 1879', *JAZWHS* 23 (2008), 34–46; 24 (2008), 11–38.

Dominy, Graham, '"Frere's War"? A Reconstruction of the Geopolitics of the Anglo-Zulu War of 1879', *Natal Museum Journal of Humanities* 5 (1993), 189–206.

Drooglever, R. W. F., 'Charles Fripp and "The Battle of Isandlwana"', *SOTQ* 70 (1992), 5.

Dunae, Patrick, 'Boys' Literature and the Ideology of Empire, 1870–1914', *VS* 24 (1980), 105–21.

Etherington, Norman, 'Rider Haggard, Imperialism and the Layered Personality', *VS* 22 (1978), 71–87.

Everett, Martin, 'Scenes of Rorke's Drift', *JAZWHS* 18 (2005), 3–4.

Fowler, Simon, '"Pass the Hat for Your Credit's Sake and Pay-Pay-Pay": Philanthropy and Victorian Military Campaigns', *SOTQ* 105 (2001), 2–5.

Fox, David Glynne, 'The Roads to War', *JAZWHS* 5 (1999), 5.

Fox, David, 'Zulu Art or Sailors' Scrimshaw: The Decorated "Zulu" Horns of the Anglo-Zulu War, 1879', [South African] *Military History Journal* 13 (2005), http://samilitaryhistory.org/vol134df.html.

Golan, Daphna, 'Inkatha and Its Use of the Zulu Past', *History in Africa* 18 (1991), 113–26.

Gosling, Chris, 'The Rev. George Smith and Alphonse de Neuville's Painting in Sydney, and an Obituary', *JAZWHS* 22 (2007), 16–18.

Greaves, Adrian, 'Isandlwana: Affairs at Home', *JAZWHS* 3 (1998), 21–7.

Greaves, Adrian, 'Lieutenant Colonel Durnford RE and the Isandlwana Court of Enquiry', *JAZWHS* 4 (1998), 1–8.

Greaves, Adrian, 'Bishop Colenso's Speech', *JAZWHS* 6 (1999), 49–53.

Greaves, Adrian, 'Archaeological Investigations at the Battlefield of Rorke's Drift', *JAZWHS* 8 (2000), 1–6.

Greaves, Andrew, 'Fieldwork Report: Isandlwana, 2000', *JAZWHS* 8 (2000), 7–11.

Greaves, Adrian, 'Lord Chelmsford's Orders to His Column Commanders', *JAZWHS* 13 (2003), 42.

Greaves, Adrian, 'The Rorke's Drift Zulu Village Project', *JAZWHS* 20 (2006), 33–5.

Greaves, Adrian, 'Isandlwana—Decoy and Defeat: How the Zulu Deployed to Attack Isandlwana', *JAZWHS* 29 (2011), 2–10.

Greaves, Adrian, 'Pte. D. Jenkins, G Company, 1st/24th: Was He There—Or Not?', *JAZWHS* 33 (2013), 8–17.

Greaves, Adrian, 'Rorke's Drift: The Enigma and Analysis of the Chard Report', *JAZWHS* 33 (2013), 18–26.

Guy, Jeff, 'A Note on Firearms in the Zulu Kingdom with Special Reference to the Anglo-Zulu War, 1879', *JAH* 12 (1971), 557–70.

Guy, Jeff, 'The British Invasion of Zululand: Some Thoughts for the Centenary', *Reality* 11 (1979), 8–14.

Guy, Jeff, 'Battling with Banalities', *JNZH* 18 (1998), 156–93.

Guy, Jeff, 'Non-Combatants and War: Unexplored Factors in the Conquest of the Zulu Kingdom', *JNZH* 22 (2004), 53–72.

Haggard, Henry Rider, 'The Zulus: The Finest Savage Race in the World', *Pall Mall Gazette* (June 1908), 764–70.

Harness, Arthur, 'The Zulu Campaign from a Military Point of View', *Fraser's Magazine* (Apr. 1880), 477–88.

Harrison, Simon, 'Skulls and Scientific Collecting in the Victorian Military: Keeping the Enemy Dead in British Frontier Warfare', *Comparative Studies in Society and History* 50 (2008), 285–303.

Headrick, Donald, 'The Tools of Imperialism: Technology and the Expansion of European Colonial Empires in the Nineteenth Century', *Journal of Modern History* 51 (1979), 231–63.

Henfrey, Anthony, '"What Doth the Lord Require of Us?" Bishop John William Colenso and the Isandlwana Sermon Preached in the Cathedral Church of St Peter, Pietermaritzburg, March 12th, 1879', *JAZWHS* 5 (1999), 34–43.

Holmes, David, 'Who Wrote the Chard Reports? A Stylometric Analysis', *JAZWHS* 32 (2012), 51–63.

Holmes, David, and Johnson, Elizabeth, 'A Stylometric Foray into the Anglo-Zulu War of 1879', *English Studies* 93 (2012), 310–23.

Jackson, F. W. D., 'Isandhlwana, 1879: The Sources Re-examined' *JSAHR* 43 (1965), 30–43, 113–32, 169–83.

Jackson, F. W. D., 'Zulu War Paintings—Alphonse de Neuville', *JSAHR* 69 (1991), 56–7.

Jackson, F. W. D., and Whybra, Julian, 'Isandhlwana and the Durnford Papers', *SOTQ* 60 (1990), 18–32.

Johnson, Robert, 'General Roberts, the Occupation of Kabul, and the Problems of Transition, 1879–1880', WH 20 (2013), 300–22.

Knight, Ian, 'R. T. Moynan's Painting, "The Last of the 24th Isandlwana"', JSAHR 66 (1988), 155–6.

Knight, Ian, 'Nothing of Value: The British Soldier and Loot in the Anglo-Zulu War of 1879', Natalia 22 (1992), 39–48.

Knight, Ian, '"Kill Me in the Shadows": The Bowden Collection of Anglo-Zulu War Oral History', SOTQ 74 (1993), 9–18.

Knight, Ian, 'Rorke's Drift Re-enacted and Rorke's Drift Remembered', Colonial Conquest 10 (1994), 12–15.

Knight, Ian, 'Ammunition at Isandlwana: A Reply', JSAHR 73 (1995), 237–50.

Knight, Ian, 'Isandlwana Re-enacted', Age of Empires 15 (1999), 24–7.

Knight, Ian, 'The Mysterious Lieutenant Adendorff of Rorke's Drift: Hero or Coward?', JAZWHS 5 (1999), 19–24.

Knight, Ian, 'Wet with Yesterday's Blood: The Disembowelling Controversy', JAZWHS 6 (1999), 7–11.

Knight, Ian, '"The Sun Turned Black": The Isandlwana Eclipse Debate', JAZWHS 7 (2000), 21–2.

Knight, Ian, 'The Myth of the Missing Companies', JAZWHS 9 (2001), 46–50.

Knight, Ian, 'Old Steady Shots: The Martini-Henry Rifle, Rates of Fire and Effectiveness in the Anglo-Zulu War', JAZWHS 11 (2002), 1–5.

Knight, Ian, 'Secrets of the Dead: The Mysteries of Zulu Dawn—A Consideration of Some Questions Raised by the Recent Television Programme', JAZWHS 11 (2002), 34–7.

Knight, Ian, 'Blue Plaque for Zulu King's Visit', SOTQ 127 (2006), 17–19.

Knight, Ian, 'New Zulu Memorial at Rorke's Drift', SOTQ 126 (2006), 24–5.

Knight, Ian, 'The Wrong Rock? An Exploration of the True "Claim to Fame" of an Enduring Feature at Fugitives' Drift', JAZWHS 26 (2009), 35–40.

Knight, Ian, '"Fire in the Sky": The Weather at Isandlwana, 22 January 1879', JAZWHS 29 (2011), 28–30.

Knight, Ian, '"Guided Rather by Accident": The Opening Zulu Movements at Isandlwana', JAZWHS 29 (2011), 11–20.

Knight, Ian, 'Isandlwana, Rorke's Drift and the Limitations of Memory', JAZWHS 33 (2013), 36–43.

Knight, Ian, '"There's a Lot of People Who Say They Were at Rorke's Drift": The Problems Which Beset Those Trying to Compile a Definitive List of Defenders', JAZWHS 33 (2013), 29–35.

Knight, Ian, 'The Battle of Isandlwana Remembered—at Cardiff Castle', JAZWHS 42 (2017), 14–15.

Knight, Ian, '"The Haze Obscures Much!" Where, on the Day of Isandlwana, Did Chelmsford's ADC, Lt. Berkeley Milne Look at the Camp?', JAZWHS 41 (2017), 11–17.

Knight, Ian, 'The Last of the 24th, Isandlwana', JAZWHS 42 (2017), 2–6.

Laband, John, 'Zulu Strategic and Tactical Options in the Face of the British Invasion of January 1879', *Scientia Militaria* 28 (1998), 1–15.

Laband, John, '"War Can't Be Made with Kid Gloves": The Impact of the Anglo-Zulu War of 1879 on the Fabric of Zulu Society', *SAHJ* 43 (2000), 179–96.

Laband, John, 'Anglo-Zulu War Studies: Where To From Here?', *JAZWHS* 12 (2002), 44–7.

Laband, John, '"The Danger of Divided Command": British Civil and Military Disputes over the Conduct of the Zululand Campaigns of 1879 and 1888', *JSAHR* 81 (2003), 339–55.

Laband, John, 'The War Readiness and Military Effectiveness of the Zulu Forces in the 1879 Anglo-Zulu War', *Natalia* 39 (2009), 37–46.

Laband, John, '"Fighting Stick of Thunder": Firearms and the Zulu Kingdom—The Cultural Ambiguities of Transferring Weapons Technology', *W&S* 33 (2014), 229–43.

Lambert, John, 'The Anglo-Zulu War and Its Aftermath', *SAHJ* 45 (2001), 278–90.

Leech, Stephen, 'Rewriting the Zulu Past Beyond *The Washing of the Spears*', *Alternation* 7 (2000), 113–34.

Lieven, Michael, 'Colonel Anthony Durnford: The Imperial Hero and the Contradictions of Liberal Imperialism', *JNZH* 18 (1998), 45–66.

Lieven, Michael, 'Contested Empire: Bertram Mitford and the Imperial Adventure Story', *Paradigm* 1/25 (1998), online, http://faculty.education.illinois.edu/westbury/paradigm/lieven2.html.

Lieven, Michael, 'Heroism, Heroics and the Making of Heroes: The Anglo-Zulu War of 1879', *Albion* 30 (1998), 419–38.

Lieven, Michael, 'A Victorian Genre: Military Memoirs and the Anglo-Zulu War', *JSAHR* 77 (1999), 106–21.

Lieven, Michael, '"Butchering the Brutes All Over the Place": Total War and Massacre in Zululand, 1879', *History* 84 (1999), 614–32.

Lieven, Michael, 'Bias in School History Textbooks: Representations of the British Invasion of Zululand', *Paradigm* 2/1 (2000), online, http://faculty.education.illinois.edu/westbury/paradigm/leiven.html.

Lieven, Michael, 'The British Soldier and the Ideology of Empire: Letters from Zululand', *JSAHR* 80 (2002), 128–43.

Lieven, Michael, '"The Honest Representative of True English…Freedom": The Metropolitan Press and the Anglo-Zulu War of 1879', *JAZWHS* 25 (2009), 9–21.

Lindfors, Bernth, 'Circus Africans', *Journal of American Culture* 6 (1983), 9–14.

Lindfors, Bernth, 'Hottentot, Bushmen, Kaffir: Taxonomic Tendencies in Nineteenth Century Iconography', *Nordic Journal of African Studies* 5 (1996), 1–28.

Lock, Ron, 'Isandlwana: New Clues to the Reason Why', *JAZWHS* 3 (1998), 12–19.

Lock, Ron, and Quantrill, Peter, 'The Encounter with the Zulu Army, 1879', *JSAHR* 83 (2005), 158–64.

Lock, Ron, and Quantrill, Peter, 'The Battle of Isandlwana: The Missing Five Hours', (2010), http://www.rorkesdriftvc.com/isandhlwana/isandlwana-the-missing-five-hours.htm.

McAdam, John, 'Observations on the Film *Zulu*', *JAZWHS* 9 (2001), 51–9.

McAdam, John, '*Zulu Dawn*: A Review', *JAZWHS* 11 (2002), 38–45.

Manning, Stephen, 'Private Snook and Total War', *JAZWHS* 13 (2003), 22–6.

Manning, Stephen, 'British Perception of the Zulu Nation Before and After the War of 1879', *JAZWHS* 17 (2005), 17–22.

Marschall, Sabine, 'Zulu Heritage Between Institutionalised Commemoration and Tourist Attraction', *Visual Anthropology* 21 (2008), 245–65.

Millar, Oliver, 'The Defence of Rorke's Drift by Elizabeth Butler: A Victorian Picture in the Collection of Her Majesty the Queen', *JAZWHS* 15 (2004), 25–6.

Murray, J., 'An African Thermopylae? The Battles of the Anglo-Zulu War, 1879', *Akroterion* 54 (2009), 51–68.

O'Connor, Damian, 'Running for Cover: Parliament and the Anglo-Zulu War, January–March 1879', *JAZWHS* 10 (2001), 30–8.

O'Connor, Damian, 'Imperial Strategy and the Anglo-Zulu War of 1879', *Historian* 68 (2006), 285–304.

Osawa, Hiroaki, 'Wesleyan Methodists, Humanitarianism and the Zulu Question, 1878–1887', *JICH* 43 (2015), 418–37.

Prescot, George, 'Weapons of the Zulu', *The Armourer* (Feb. 2018), 88–9.

Rees, Ruben, 'Historical Interpretation and Representation, 1880–2014', *JAZWHS* 37 (2015), 13–20.

Schalkwyk, Len van, and Taylor, Michael, 'The Excavation and Re-internment of Mortal Remains from Cairn 27, Isandlwana Battlefield, Zululand, South Africa', *JAZWHS* 6 (1999), 12–14.

Seaton, A. V., 'War and Thanatourism: Waterloo, 1815–1914', *Annals of Tourism Research* 26 (1999), 130–58.

Shail, Robert, 'Stanley Baker's "Welsh Western": Masculinity and Cultural Identity in *Zulu*', *Cyfrwng/Media Wales Journal* 1 (2004), 11–25.

Sharrett, Christopher, '*Zulu*, or the Limits of Liberalism', *Cineaste* 25 (2000), 28–33.

Sheeley, Ron, 'My Escape from the Wily Zulu: Captain Tongue, 24th Regiment at Rorke's Drift', *JAZWHS* 14 (2003), 42–4.

Sheeley, Ron, 'The Many Faces of King Cetshwayo', *JAZWHS* 14 (2003), 40–1.

Smith, Keith, 'The Zulu and the Horse', *SOTQ* 118 (2004), 19–24.

Smith, Keith, 'The Annotated Maps of Isandlwana', *SOTQ* 130 (2007), 22–5.

Stopps, Sam, 'Lieutenant Adendorff—Rorke's Drift Defender: Fact or Fiction?', *JAZWHS* 33 (2013), 2–7.

Stossel, Katie, 'Who died defending Coghill and Melvill?', *JAZWHS* 39 (2016), 28–31.

Theron, Bridget, 'King Cetshwayo in Victorian England: A Cameo of Imperial Interaction', *SAHJ* 56 (2006), 60–87.

Thompson, Paul, 'A Fighting Retreat: The Natal Native Mounted Contingent After Isandlwana', *JNZH* 13 (1990–1), 27–32.

Thompson, Paul, 'The Many Battles of Isandlwana: A Transformation in Historiography', *Historia* 52 (2007), 172–217.

Tomaselli, Keyan, 'Shaka Zulu, Visual History and Television', *Southern African Humanities* 15 (2003), 91–107.

Verbeek, Jennifer, 'The Paintings of the Zulu War as Historical Documents', *JNZH* 2 (1979), 49–58.

Verbeek, Jennifer, and Bresler, V., 'The Role of the Ammunition Boxes in the Disaster at Isandhlwana, 22 January 1879', *Journal of the Historical Firearms Society of South Africa* 7 (1977), 22–30.

Verdonck, Joris, '"Those Colours Saved for Better Days": History and Myth in the Poetry of the Battle of Isandlwana, 1879—A New Historicist Reading', *Belgian Journal of English Language and Literature* 4 (2006), 93–108.

Wagner, Erich, 'A Lion Dishevelled: The Response of the British Press to the Battle of Isandlwana', *JAZWHS* 7 (2000), 28–39.

Wall, Brian, and Knight, Ian, 'Secrets of the Dead: Two Views', *SOTQ* 108 (2002), 7–13.

Ward, Andrew, 'Extraordinary But True Stories from Over a Century of Football', *JAZWHS* 19 (2006), 16.

Webb, Colin de, 'A Zulu Boy's Recollections of the Zulu War', *Natalia* 8 (1978), 6–21.

Webb, Denver, 'War, Racism, and the Taking of Heads: Revisiting Military Conflict in the Cape Colony and Western Xhosaland in the Nineteenth Century', *JAH* 56 (2015), 37–55.

Webley, Lita, 'Archaeological Investigations at the Battlefield of Rorke's Drift, Northern Natal', *Southern African Field Archaeology* 2 (1993), 24–34.

Weintraub, Stanley, 'Cetewayo: Shaw's First Hero', *Shaw: The Annual of Bernard Shaw Studies* 19 (1999), 7–22.

West, James, 'What Factors Shaped British Press Coverage of the Reverses, and Successes, Encountered by British Arms during the Anglo-Zulu War of 1879?', *JAZWHS* 35 (2014), 18–23.

Whybra, Julian, 'Contemporary Sources on the Composition of the Main Zulu Impi, January 1879', *SOTQ* 53 (1988), 13–16.

Whybra, Julian, 'The Cochrane Accounts of Isandlwana', *JAZWHS* 13 (2003), 27–30.

Wright, John, 'Making the James Stuart Archive', *History in Africa* 23 (1996), 333–50.

Wylie, Dan, 'A Dangerous Admiration: E. A. Ritter's *Shaka Zulu*', *SAHJ* 28 (1993), 98–118.

Yorke, Edmund, 'Isandlwana, 1879: Reflections on the Ammunition Controversy', *JSAHR* 72 (1994), 205–18.

Dissertations

Bell, Erin, 'Beyond the Exhibit: Zulu Experiences in Britain and the United States, 1879–1884', MA, Carleton, 2011.

Diver, Luke, 'Perceptions Versus Reality? Newspaper Coverage on the Anglo-Zulu War of 1879', MA, NUI Maynooth, 2010.

Leech, Stephen, 'Twentieth Century Images of the "Zulu": Selected Representations in Historical and Political Discourse', MA, UNISA, 1997.

Manning, Stephen, 'Foreign News Gathering and Reporting in the London and Devon Press: The Anglo-Zulu War, 1879—A Case Study', PhD, Exeter, 2005.

Martin, Samuel, 'British Images of the Zulu, c.1820–1879', PhD, Cambridge, 1982.

Masina, Edward, 'Zulu Perceptions and Reactions to the British Occupation of Land in Natal Colony and Zululand, 1850–1887: A Recapitulation Based on Surviving Oral and Written Sources', PhD, Zululand, 2006.

Moeller, Maricki, 'Battlefield Tourism in South Africa with Special Reference to Isandlwana and Rorke's Drift, KwaZulu-Natal', MPhil, Pretoria, 2005.

Orme, Edward, 'Victorian Attitudes Towards "Small Wars": The Anglo-Zulu War (1879), A Case Study', MPhil, York, 1984.

Stearn, Roger, 'War Images and Image Makers in the Victorian Era: Aspects of the British Visual and Written Portrayal of War, c.1866–1906', PhD, London, 1987.

PICTURE ACKNOWLEDGEMENTS

INDEX